Logical Investigative Methods

Critical Thinking and Reasoning
for Successful Investigations

Logical Investigative Methods

Critical Thinking and Reasoning for Successful Investigations

Dr. Robert J. Girod, JD, PhD

Robert J. Girod Consulting, LLC
Fort Wayne, Indiana, USA

CRC Press
Taylor & Francis Group
Boca Raton London New York

CRC Press is an imprint of the
Taylor & Francis Group, an **informa** business

CRC Press
Taylor & Francis Group
6000 Broken Sound Parkway NW, Suite 300
Boca Raton, FL 33487-2742

© 2015 by Taylor & Francis Group, LLC
CRC Press is an imprint of Taylor & Francis Group, an Informa business

No claim to original U.S. Government works

Printed on acid-free paper
Version Date: 20140418

International Standard Book Number-13: 978-1-4822-4313-0 (Hardback)

Library of Congress Cataloging-in-Publication Data

Girod, Robert J.
    Logical investigative methods : critical thinking and reasoning for successful investigations / Robert J. Girod.
        pages cm
    Includes bibliographical references and index.
    ISBN 978-1-4822-4313-0 (hardback)
    1. Criminal investigation. 2. Criminal investigation--Psychological aspects. 3. Forensic sciences. I. Title.

HV8073.G566 2014
363.25--dc23   2014012377

Visit the Taylor & Francis Web site at
http://www.taylorandfrancis.com

and the CRC Press Web site at
http://www.crcpress.com

Dedication

This book is dedicated to my brothers and sisters in law enforcement – the many detectives, investigators, special agents, and attorneys with whom I have had the privilege of working. It is also dedicated to the many instructors and professors who I have studied under and worked with throughout my career. I want to particularly thank my family, always a part of producing each of my books through their many contributions.

My beautiful wife, Laurie, assists me in each and every one of my endeavors and is the "secret of my success," for whatever small contributions that I may make to society. She has devoted herself to her own education, as well as others, and has worked in both law firms and financial institution security and fraud detection. She is the general manager and an investigator for Robert J. Girod Consulting, LLC, a law firm and consulting investigations firm.

Our younger son, Robert J. D. Girod (Bobby), helps with research, technology, and graphics. He created the illustration at the beginning of this book, as well as other art work. He is a "young author" in his own right and anticipates a career in digital forensics. He is an inspiration to me and I am very proud of him and his contributions.

Our older son, Joshua D. Slaughter (Josh), worked in security while he was in college and now serves in the U.S. Navy. He is a loving member of our family, a patriot, and a good "big brother." I am very proud of his accomplishments as well.

Finally, I want to express our appreciation and admiration for our mothers, Carolyn M. Neely and Joann Barton, who are the wonderful matriarchs of our family. Without God I would not have my wonderful family and without them, my small accomplishments would seem inconsequential. And to all of my readers I leave this message and "clue" – Revelations 22:21.

Dr. Robert J. Girod, J.D., PhD.

Contents

About the Author   xvii

1 The Scientific Method: Fact Finding in Investigations   1

Read First: The Most Important Paragraph in This Book   1
What We Hope to Accomplish   1
Convince Yourself First, Then Others   5
Fact Finding and Due Diligence   7
Obviously a Suicide   8
Scientific Method   9
   Steps of the Scientific Method   10
Conclusion   12

2 Cognitive Skills: Perceptions and Thought Processes   13

Introduction   13
What Kind of Learner Are You?   14
Cognitive Psychology and Cognitive Neuroscience   16
Perceptions and Thought Processes   17
Memory: What Detectives and Witnesses Can Recall   18
Eyewitness Testimony: Explicit Versus Implicit Memory   20
Trained Observer: Tachistoscopic Training   21
Cognition and Reasoning: Perception and Logic   23

3 Logic: Deduction and Induction   25

An Introduction to Logic   25
Deductive and Inductive Arguments   26
Formal Logic: The Logical Structure of Science   28
Psychology of Proof: Deductive Reasoning in Human Thinking   28
Deductive Validity   29
Science and Hypothesis: Inductive Logic   30
Inductive Analogy   32
Legal Inferences and the Burdens of Proof   32
Circumstantial Evidence and Inferences: Inductive Evidence   34

4 Critical Thinking: Fact Pattern Analysis   37

Critical Thinking (Reasoning)   37
Axioms   37
Fact Pattern Analysis: What and Why Things Go Wrong   38
   Eyewitness Misidentification   39
   Unreliable or Improper Forensic Science   40
   False Confessions   42
   Government Misconduct   44
   Informants   45
   Bad Lawyering   45
From Critical Thinking to Logical Reasoning   46

5 Logical Reasoning: Legal Inferences   49

Reasoning   49
Convergent and Divergent Thinking   50
Legal Inferences   51
Arguments   52
Argument Analysis or Diagrams: Three Steps   53
Types of Fallacies: Faulty Arguments   53
   Material Fallacies of Relevance   55
   Material Fallacies of Insufficient Evidence 55
   Two Additional Fallacies   56
   Material Fallacies of Relevance   56
   Material Fallacies of Insufficient Evidence 57
   Two Additional Fallacies   58
Recapitulation, Summary, and Conclusion   58

6 Back to Basics: Criminal Investigation Skills   61

Why the "Basics" Are Important or Why *Not* to Skip
This Chapter   61
Thorough and Methodical: Good, Old-Fashioned
Detective Work   61
Sources of Information   62
   Law Enforcement Sources   62
   Government Records   63
   Business Records   63
   Confidential Informants   64
   Undercover Operations   66
   Physical and Technical Surveillance   68
   Interviewing and Interrogation   69

Types of Investigations 69

Crimes against Persons 71

Crimes against Property 76

Fraud and Economic Crimes (Financial and Computer
Crimes) 77

Crimes against Public Morals (Vice and Narcotics) 77

Juvenile and Family Crimes 78

Counterintelligence and Security 78

Summary 78

7   Personality Profiling: The Compass   79

Dimensional Components of Personality Types 79

Personality Type Combinations 82

Compass 83

Characteristics of the Compass Points 85

Communications Types 85

Performance Types 91

Conformist Type 92

Self-Assessment Tests and On-the-Spot Profiling 92

Sixteen Personality Factor Questionnaire (16PF) 93

Minnesota Multiphasic Personality Inventory (MMPI) 94

California Psychological Inventory (CPI) 94

Myers–Briggs Type Indicator (MBTI) 94

Guilford–Zimmerman Temperament Survey 95

Edwards Personality Profile Scale 95

Dynamic Factors Survey (DFS) 95

8   Personality Profiling: The Map   97

How to Communicate with Each Personality Type 97

Map 98

Traits by Associated Types 99

Sixteen Combinations 100

Sergeant Types 101

Salesman Types 102

Accountant Types 103

Artist Types 104

Combination Types 105

Three Levels and Four Rules of Systematic Accuracy 105

Reading Others: Successful Reads 106

**9   Profiling the Criminal Mind: Criminal
      Investigative Analysis**   **109**

Inductive and Deductive Reasoning   109
Crime Classification   110
Crime Scene Analysis   110
Crime Scene Indicators   111
Crime Classification by Type, Style, and Number of Victims   113
    Crime Classification Worksheet   113
Organized and Disorganized Crimes   115
    Organized Nonsocial Typology   117
    Disorganized Asocial Typology   118
Assessment, Staging, and Personation   119
Modus Operandi (M.O.) and Victimology   119
Personation (Signature)   120
Staging   120
Conclusion   121

10   Interviewing and Interrogation   **123**

Introduction to Interrogation   123
"Interrogation" (Interview) of Witnesses and Potential
Informants   124
Deception Detection   124
Interrogation of Suspects   125
Interrogation of Suspects Whose Guilt Is Uncertain   129
Interrogation of Criminal Suspects   130
Written Confessions   131
More Suggestion for Confessions   132
Nine Steps of an Interrogation   133
Formulating Questions   134
Legal Requirements for Interrogations and Confessions   135

11   Kinesic Interviewing and Body Language   **137**

Introduction to Kinesic Interviewing and Interrogation   137
    Proxemics: Personal Zone Distances   137
Body Language   137
Ten Commandments for Observing and Decoding Nonverbal
Communications   139
Kinesic Interview and Interrogation   140
Eight Common Lying Gestures   140
Evaluation, Boredom, Impatience, and Procrastination Gestures   142
Listen and Look for Deception   142

What Deception Sounds Like   143
What Deception Looks Like   145
Reanimation and Acceptance   147
Behavioral Cautions   148
Neurolinguistic Eye Movement: The Three Sensory Channels   148
   Recall: Left   149
   Create (Fabricate): Right   150
Legal Requirements for Interrogations and Confessions   150

12   Deception Detective: Discourse and Content Analysis   151

Introduction   151
Deception Detection: Polygraph and Voice Stress Analysis   151
Scientific Content Analysis (SCAN)   151
Investigative Discourse Analysis and Linguistic Statement
Analysis   153
Parts of Speech and Word Classes   154
Speech Pattern and Discourse Content Analysis: Word Choices   155
Narrative Statement Structure (Form) Analysis   158
Narrative Statement Semantic (Meaning) Analysis   159
   Semantic Indicators   160
   Parts of Speech and Semantic Analysis   161
Amplification of the Narrative   162
Analysis in the Form of Letters (Correspondence)   162
Analysis of Interview and Interrogation Transcripts   162
Conclusion   162

13   Analytical Investigative Methods: Processing Data   165

CPM-PERT Network Diagrams   165
   Network Logic Techniques   166
Network-Based Project Management Methodology   167
Elements of PERT   168
Intelligence Cycle   169
   Planning and Direction   170
   Collection   170
   Processing   170
   Analysis   171
   Dissemination and Feedback   171
Intelligence Analysis   171
Analytical Investigative Methods (AIM)   171

Visual Investigative Analysis (VIA)   173
Financial Information   178
Accounting Cycle   178

14   Communicating Skills: Critical Documentation   179

Investigative Report Writing: "The Job's Not Finished 'til the
Paperwork's Done"   179
Don't Just Record—Investigate   180
  Field Notes and Reports   180
  Narrative   181
  Titles Describing People   182
  Descriptions of Vehicles (CYMBL)   182
  Solvability Factors   182
  Automated Report Templates, Supplemental Reports,
  and the Narrative Summary   182
Elements of a Good Report: Helping Others Know What
You Know   183
Spelling Rules   184
Parts of Speech   185
  Definitions of Terms   186
Punctuation Rules (Made Easy)   187
  Capitalization   187
  Commas   187
  Colons   188
  Semicolons   188
  Dashes   189
  Quotation Marks   189
  Parentheses   189
  Apostrophes   190
  Hyphens   190
  Periods, Question Marks, and Exclamation Points   190
  Quotations   190
A Word on Word Usage   191
  Use the Active Voice, Rather than the Passive Voice 191
  Use First Person: Use of "I" and "Me"   192
  Use of Who and Whom   192
  Focus on the Actor, the Action, and the Object   192
  Run-On Sentences   193
  Incomplete Sentences or Sentence Fragments   193
  Surplus Words and Compound Constructions   193
  Avoid Word-Wasting Idioms   194

Put Conditions and Exceptions Where They Are Clear and
Easy to Read   195
Put Modifying Words Close to What They Modify   195
Avoid Nested Modifiers   195
Clarify the Reach of Modifiers   196
Critique Checklist   196
Revising and Editing   197

15   Logical Presentation Methods: Conveying Information   199

Conveying Information: Telling the Story   199
Prepare to Tell Your Story in Court   199
Storytelling: Theory and Themes   200
Storytelling and Opening Statements   202
Cross-Examination: Discrediting Testimony and Impeachment   202
Logical Presentation Methods   204
Presentation Software: The Power of Microsoft PowerPoint®   204
Graphics and Reconstruction Software: Microsoft Visio
Standard®   208
Digital Imagery and Video Technology and Software   213
Court Testimony and Presentations   213

16   Using Logical Investigative Methods: Recapitulation   215

Recapitulation   215
Scientific Method: Fact Finding in Investigations   215
Steps of the Scientific Method   215
Logic: Deduction and Induction   215
Deductive and Inductive Arguments   216
Legal Inferences and the Burdens of Proof   217
Critical Thinking: Fact Pattern Analysis   217
Logical Reasoning: Legal Inferences   218
Material Fallacies of Relevance   218
Material Fallacies of Insufficient Evidence   219
Two Additional Fallacies   220
Back to Basics: Criminal Investigations Skills   220
Personality Profiling: The Compass   220
Dimensional Components of Personality Types: Four
Dimensional Components   220
Personality Type Combinations   221
Compass   221
Characteristics of the Compass Points   222

Personality Profiling: The Map   225
    How to Communicate with Each Personality Type   225
    Map   226
    Traits by Associated Types   226
    Sixteen Combinations   227
Profiling the Criminal Mind: Criminal Investigative Analysis   228
    Crime Classification   228
    Crime Scene Analysis—Four Steps   228
    Crime Scene Indicators   229
    Crime Classification Worksheet   229
Interviewing and Interrogation   230
    Interrogation of Suspects   230
    Interrogation of Criminal Suspects   231
    Interrogation of Suspects Whose Guilt Is Reasonably
    Certain   231
    Interrogation of Suspects Whose Guilt Is Uncertain   232
    Written Confessions   233
More Suggestion for Confessions   234
    Nine Steps of an Interrogation   235
    Formulating Questions   235
Kinesic Interviewing and Body Language   236
    Ten Commandments for Observing and Decoding
    Nonverbal Communications   236
    Kinesic Interview and Interrogation   236
    Eight Common Lying Gestures   237
    Evaluation, Boredom, Impatience, and Procrastination
    Gestures   237
    Listen and Look for Deception   237
    What Deception Sounds Like   237
    What Deception Looks Like   238
    Reanimation and Acceptance   238
    Behavioral Cautions   238
    Neurolinguistic Eye Movement: The Three Sensory
    Channels   238
Deception Detection: Content and Discourse Analysis   239
    Deception Detection: Polygraph and Voice Stress Analysis   239
    Scientific Content Analysis (SCAN), Investigative
    Discourse Analysis (IDA), and Linguistic Statement
    Analysis (LSAT)   239
    Parts of Speech and Word Classes   239
    Speech Pattern and Discourse Content Analysis: Word
    Choices   240
    Narrative Statement Structure (Form) Analysis   242

Narrative Statement Semantic (Meaning) Analysis 242
Semantic Indicators 242
Amplification of the Narrative 242
Analytical Investigative Methods: Processing Data 242
Intelligence Cycle 242
Accounting Cycle 243
Communicating Skills: Critical Documentation 243
Investigative Report Writing: "The Job's Not Finished 'til
the Paperwork's Done" 243
Don't Just Record, Investigate 243
Logical Presentation Methods: Conveying Information 247
Prepare to Tell Your Story in Court 247
Storytelling: Theory and Themes 248
Storytelling and Opening Statements 249
Cross-Examination: Discrediting Testimony and
Impeachment 249
Logical Presentation Methods 250

Bibliography **251**
Index **253**

About the Author

Robert Girod, JD, PhD earned a double PhD in criminology and public administration from the Union Institute and University, a post-doctoral certificate in leadership from Harvard University, and a JD (Doctor of Jurisprudence) from Thomas M. Cooley Law School. He earned a Master of Science in criminal justice administration from Central Missouri State University, a Bachelor of Arts in sociology from Huntington College, a Bachelor of General Studies in social and behavioral science and an Associate of Science in criminal justice from Indiana University, and a diploma in forensic science from the American Institute of Applied Science.

Dr. Girod is a graduate of the Indiana Law Enforcement Academy, the Fort Wayne Police Academy, the National Police Institute Command & Staff School, and more than 60 advanced police and instructor schools. He is a graduate of more than a dozen military schools, including the U.S. Naval War College, the U.S. Marine Corps Command & Staff College, and the U.S. Air Force Squadron Officer's School.

Dr. Girod is the president and CEO of Robert J. Girod Consulting, LLC, attorneys-at-law and consulting detectives/private investigators, which provides general law practice and investigative services, litigation support, and management services nationwide, including forensic accounting, computer forensics, accident reconstruction, and linguistic interviewing, translation, and interpretation.

Dr. Girod is a command officer with the Haviland and Latty Police Departments in Ohio.

Dr. Girod retired from the Fort Wayne Police Department, after 23 years, as the Robbery-Homicide supervisor and founding member of the FBI Federal Bank Robbery Task Force. He was also a supervisor over Juvenile, Auto Theft, all four detective quadrants, and a patrol supervisor. He has served on the Police Reserve Board, the Police Pension Board, and lectured at the Fort Wayne Police Academy/Regional Public Safety Academy.

Dr. Girod served as a special deputy for the United States Marshal's Service and as a police officer with the Indianapolis Police Department and the Indiana University Police Department. He was a special agent with the Ohio Bureau of Criminal Investigations and an investigator with the Indiana Department of Insurance and the Wells County Prosecutor's Office, where he began his career in 1979. Prior to this, he was a private detective for Zeis Security Systems.

Dr. Girod served for 4 years in the Indiana Guard Reserve and for 18 years in the U.S. Army Reserve, attaining the rank of captain. He held command and staff positions in the military police, basic training (infantry), and Special Forces, but served primarily with the U.S. Army Criminal Investigations Command (USACIDC).

Dr. Girod has been an adjunct professor or associate faculty member at eight universities: Indiana University, Boston University, Huntington University, Concordia University of Wisconsin, Taylor University, Indiana Wesleyan University, Northcentral University, and the Union Institute and University. He has taught more than 30 subjects in management, criminal justice, public administration, political science, history, and sociology at the undergraduate through the doctoral level in traditional, adult education, correspondence, and Internet programs.

Dr. Girod is a member of numerous professional, political, and civic associations and organizations, including the Fraternal Order of Police, the American Bar Association, and the American Legion, and served on the board at the Fort Wayne–Allen County Historical Society (The History Center) and First Church of the Nazarene. In addition to his military awards, Dr. Girod was awarded the Meritorious Service Medal and the Commendation Medal by the Fort Wayne Police Department and a Letter of Commendation by the Director of the Federal Bureau of Investigation. He was listed in the *Who's Who in Law Enforcement* in 1991 and the *International Who's Who in Public Service* in 2000.

Figure 0.1 The butler did it. (Illustration by Robert J. David Girod Jr.)

He is the author of *Profiling the Criminal Mind: Behavioral Science and Criminal Investigative Analysis; Infamous Murders and Mysteries: Cold Case Files and Who-Done-Its*; and *Police Liability and Risk Management: Torts, Civil Rights and Employment Law.* He has also authored numerous articles for various professional periodicals, such as *FBI Law Enforcement Bulletin, Security Management, The Police Marksman,* and *Musubi.*

The Scientific Method
Fact Finding in Investigations

1

Read First: The Most Important Paragraph in This Book

Read this paragraph first. Do not skip it. It is the most important paragraph in this entire book. Why is it the "most important" paragraph? Because it is a proviso or a warning about what *not* to do. If you skip around and only read parts of this book, you will receive little benefit. In fact, that would be typical of exactly what we are trying to eliminate...sloppy, unfinished work. There are few shortcuts to excellence. The shortcut here is that we are outlining a process to reduce mistakes and improve skills. If you plan to read a few pages here and a few sentences there, please do not tell anyone that you "read" this book. If you *really* want to improve your detective skills, commit yourself to excellence. Anything worth having is worth working for. Anything that comes free and easy is worth its price (nothing, i.e., "free").

OK, end of sermon. As Sean Connery said in *The Untouchables*, "Here endeth the lesson!" Now, let's get to the facts. Please read on.

What We Hope to Accomplish

Carl Sagan was a Professor of Astronomy and Space Sciences and Director of the Laboratory for Planetary Studies, at Cornell University. In 1973, Carl Sagan published *The Cosmic Connection*, a daring view of the universe, which rapidly became a classic work of popular science and inspired a generation of scientists and enthusiasts. He wrote of the scientific method, *"The principle conclusion about the scientific method that I draw from this history is this: while theory is useful in the design of experiments, only direct experiments will convince everyone. Based only on my indirect conclusions, there would today still be many people who did not believe in a hot Venus...."* (emphasis added) (Sagan, 2000, pp. 85–86).

In the Army, we trained soldiers by telling them three things: (1) what we were about to tell them, (2) what we were telling them, and (3) what we had just told them. In university research, we call this: (1) Introduction, (2) Body, and (3) Conclusion. Learning any topic is easier if we define our terms and outline the information and steps. After reading this book, I hope this will become second nature to you. You will start with an introduction and tell people what you are about to tell them. You will get to the body of your subject matter and tell people what you want them to understand. Finally, you will summarize with a conclusion, telling people what you just told them, so they will remember (in outline form) what the main points were that you just made.

This book is not intended to make the readers (presumably detectives, investigators, special agents, prosecutors, etc.) philosophers or even experts in the philosophy of logic. However, it is intended to make law enforcement investigations more effective and reliable by using the practical skills of logic, critical thinking, reasoning, and the scientific method. That is, we want to get the right bad guy and make our cases stick because we know the facts and the facts support the theory of our case.

This is what we are going to "discuss" first; that is, I am now going to tell you what I am going to tell you.

Chapter 1, The Scientific Method: Fact Finding in Investigations, is about finding facts, rather than mere assumptions. It is about the method used by scientists and researchers to support or disprove a theory. Detectives are both scientists and researchers. We use science (forensic science, computer science, information science, behavioral science, etc.) and research (fact gathering and analysis) to determine what happened. Not only what, but who, when, where, why, and how. The six steps of the scientific method are as follows: (1) Observation, (2) Question, (3) Hypothesis, (4) Method (Prediction), (5) Result, and (6) Conclusion.

All of this (and more) follows in this chapter, so continue to read on after this brief introduction.

Chapter 2, Cognitive Skills: Perceptions and Thought Processes, is about cognitive psychology. This is the study of mental processes, such as how people perceive, think, remember, and learn. The American Psychological Association (APA) defines cognitive psychology as the study of higher mental processes such as attention, language, memory, perception, problem solving, and thinking. This is important in investigations because it is about how we think about what we see, hear, smell, taste, and feel, how we communicate (or fail to) with others, how we recall facts, perceive data, and solve problems, and the attention we give to or neglect about the facts we call "clues."

Chapter 3, Logic: Deduction and Induction, is about using the philosophy and techniques of "logic" to determine true and false conclusions and probable inferences.

"Nowhere am I so desperately needed as among a shipload of illogical humans." —Mr. Spock in the *Star Trek* episode "I, Mudd."

"Fascinating is a word I use for the unexpected. In this case, I should think 'interesting' would suffice." —Mr. Spock in the *Star Trek* episode "The Squire of Gothos."

Chapter 4, Critical Thinking: Fact Pattern Analysis, is about deciding whether a claim is always true, sometimes true, partly true, or false. While "logic" is about a written set of statements and a system of rules about performing mechanical inferences about those statements, "critical thinking" is about observation, interpretation, analysis, inference, evaluation, and explanation.

Chapter 5, Logical Reasoning: Legal Inferences, is also about deductive and inductive methods for evaluating arguments, but while "logic" is about a set of statements and a system of rules for performing mechanical inferences about those statements, "reasoning" often involves using "intuition" and "common sense." *Intuition* is based upon beliefs that we cannot justify from inferences, but that are based upon our experiences or immediate cognition—a perceptive insight or the act or faculty of knowing or sensing without the use of rational processes. *Common sense* is wisdom acquired through experience or knowledge; it is sound and prudent judgment based on a simple perception of the situation or facts. It is the knowledge and experience that most people already have or it is, more often, used to describe the knowledge and experience the person using the term believes that he or she has or should have. I have found that the people who most often speak of "common sense" possess the least of it or, as Mark Twain said, "Common sense is very uncommon."

Inference is the act or process of deriving logical conclusions from premises known or assumed true. In the law of evidence, an inference is a truth or proposition drawn from another that is supposed or admitted to be true or a process of reasoning by which a fact or proposition sought to be established is *deduced* as a logical consequence from other facts, or a state of facts, already proved or admitted. It is a "logical and reasonable conclusion of a fact" not presented by direct evidence but which, by process of logic and reason, a trier of fact may conclude exists from the established facts. Inferences are deductions or conclusions that, with reason and common sense, lead a jury to infer facts that have been established by the evidence.

Chapter 6, Back to Basics: Criminal Investigations Skills, is a basic review of the skills that detectives and investigators should have. Sometimes it is worthwhile to "recalibrate" ourselves by going back to basics. In some cases, detectives and investigators lack these basic skills because they have never received training in these areas. They have been designated "detectives" or "investigators" through seniority or by being posted to that position. Competence depends upon knowing our basics, so we will make a quick study of these basics.

Chapter 7 (Personality Profiling: The Compass) and Chapter 8 (Personality Profiling: The Map) are about using behavioral science and the "art of profiling" to analyze personality types and behavioral patterns. This type of art and science would give a detective, like the fictitious Sherlock Holmes, an uncanny ability to read people and their actions. This is about analyzing personalities to determine behavior, whereas Chapter 9 is about analyzing artifacts to determine profiles.

Chapter 9, Profiling the Criminal Mind: Criminal Investigative Analysis, is the art and science used by "profilers" (loosely like those portrayed in the movie *Silence of the Lambs*) to read personalities and behaviors from artifacts of a crime scene.

Chapter 10 (Interviewing and Interrogation) and Chapter 11 (Kinesic Interviewing and Body Language) are about using our skills in behavioral science, personality profiling, and criminal investigative analysis to gather information from people with whom we talk. This is the "Sherlockian" skill of gathering facts from not only confessions, but also admissions and omissions. It is the art and science of detecting deception and culling facts from what is said, whether it is true or false. It also includes the use of linguistic skills to analyze statements that may be used for what the intelligence community calls "human intelligence" (HUMINT).

Chapter 12, Deception Detection: Discourse and Content Analysis, is about various methodologies of detecting detection. In particular, we will discuss "scientific content analysis" and "discourse analysis." This involves analyzing language to detect deception.

Chapter 13, Analytical Investigative Methods: Processing Data, is about using analysis skills, data processing, media graphics, etc. to analyze and graphically display organized and understandable information about complex crimes. This can be used in complex serial murder cases, financial fraud cases, espionage cases, or almost any type of case (even civil cases) where complex information must be organized and displayed in a logical and understandable way by those who may not be experts in the subject matter.

Chapter 14, Communicating Skills: Critical Documentation, is about documenting a case. As the old sign hanging in the out-house reads, "The job's not finished until the paperwork is done." In my experience, reviewing the cases of other detectives as both a detective supervisor (managing criminal investigations) and an attorney (supporting litigation) I have found that the weakest link in almost every case is the documentation. I would even concede that it is probably better to hire detectives and investigators with degrees in English composition than in criminal justice. The lack of skills in written communications among law enforcement officers is astonishing. Yet, it is the most important (though boring) thing that we do. If you do not document it, you did not do it! This chapter does not propose to turn officers into grammar professors, but does seek to help detectives and investigators use writing skills to win their cases using simple points.

Chapter 15, Logical Presentation Methods: Conveying Information, is about presenting information to those who need to understand it. Once we have used the scientific method and our cognitive skills, drawn logical deductions and inductions, applied critical thinking processes, made reasonable inferences, used basic investigative techniques, utilized personality and criminal profiling, exploited interviews and interrogations, processed data, and effectively communicated this information in well-documented reports, it is time to convey critical information using presentation skills. Using technology, such as media and presentation software, a lot of information can be displayed and presented in a much shorter time and more understandable way. Remember, a picture is worth a thousand words.

Chapter 16, Using Logical Investigative Methods, is about "putting it all together." Do not skip to the last chapter with the idea that it is a summary of everything that you need to know. Don't be lazy. It won't work this time because this is not merely a "summary chapter," although it is the "Conclusion" we spoke about when we discussed the teaching method of (1) tell them what we are going to tell them, (2) tell them, and (3) tell them what we just told them, or (1) Introduction, (2) Body, and (3) Conclusion. However, we will also see how to apply all of the skills that we have (I hope) just mastered.

Now, on with our show! Let's "discuss" how to convince ourselves of the facts of a case before we try to convince others. (If you have doubts, others will have serious doubts.) Then we must discuss what "fact finding" is (versus throwing a few facts together with a handful of assumptions to make a case "stick") and the "due diligence" required of a moral, ethical, and legal investigation and investigator. While we are there, we need to discuss avoiding the "obvious" (a word that rarely has a place in an investigation). Finally, we will get to using the "scientific method" as a basis for all of this fact finding and due diligence. Here we go.

Convince Yourself First, Then Others

Stephen Hawking, whose work helped to reconfigure models of the universe and to redefine what is in it, is widely considered one of the world's greatest minds. He is a world-renowned theoretical physicist whose scientific career spans over 40 years and his books and public appearances have made him an academic celebrity. In describing how to logically reason through his theories, Hawking wrote:

Now the apparent brightness of a star depends on two factors—luminosity and how far it is from us. For nearby stars we can measure both their apparent brightness and their distance, so we can work out their luminosity. Conversely, if we knew the luminosity of stars in other galaxies, we could work out their distance by measuring their apparent brightness. Hubble argued that there were certain types of stars that always had the same luminosity when they were near enough for us to measure. If, therefore, we found such stars in another galaxy, we could assume that they had the same luminosity. Thus, we could calculate the distance to that galaxy. If we could do this for a number of stars in the same galaxy, and our calculations always gave the same distance, we could be fairly confident of our estimate. In this way, Edwin Hubble worked out the distances to nine different galaxies. (Hawking, 2002, pp. 19–20)

I have been in law enforcement for more than 34 years at the city, county, state, and federal levels. I have been an investigator or detective for nearly 30 of those years and a supervisor for more than half of my career. During that time, I have worked almost every type of case that there is—every type of crime that can be committed and prosecuted. I have lost three cases out of the hundreds of cases that I have worked (probably averaging about 200 cases each year). That is because in each of those cases (including the three that were "lost"), I never sent a case to be prosecuted in which I had not first convinced myself that I had the right perpetrator and could prove that he or she had committed the crime (beyond a reasonable doubt). I first proved to myself that the facts supported my theory of the case. Then, I documented the facts in a manner that could be readily understood by a prosecutor, a judge, and a jury.

When I went to law school, I learned what prosecutors and attorneys needed to present a winnable case. I used this "view from the other side" to improve my cases and those of my detectives. As an attorney and consulting investigator in private practice, I used my skills as an experienced investigator and a licensed attorney to prepare cases for my clients that would support their litigation objectives. I researched what went wrong with some cases to identify problems most often encountered in prosecuting criminal cases. This is called learning from mistakes and is what experience is often based upon. It is when lessons go unlearned that we fail.

I always enjoyed working in Robbery–Homicide, both as a detective and as a supervisor. Homicide has always been, since Cain and Abel, the "top of the hit parade" of crime. When it comes to crime, there is nothing bigger than a murder. As Clint Eastwood said in *Unforgiven*, "You take away all a man has and all he's ever gonna have." When responding to a robbery-in-progress, you are going where most people are trying to get away from—armed felons. As Ernest Hemingway wrote:

... there is no hunting like the hunting of man and those who have hunted armed men long enough and liked it, never really care for anything else thereafter. You will meet them doing various things with resolve, but their interest rarely holds because after the other thing ordinary life is as flat as the taste of wine when the taste buds have been burned off your tongue. (Hemingway, 1936)

Most of us who choose law enforcement as a profession are driven by high adrenalin and high levels of testosterone (gender considerations aside). We want to run with lights and siren to the next "hot run" or get to the "big caper" first. We are not too interested in thinking things through and writing a well-documented report for use in tedious litigation later. But getting there fast and getting "the bad guy" has little value if we do not conduct a thorough, well-reasoned investigation and document it in a manner that will make our case understood by a prosecutor, judge, and jury. What we may "know" may not be readily apparent to others who are not in our heads. Others may not have our knowledge or observations that we take for granted.

Fact Finding and Due Diligence

I once had a detective under my supervision who did fine work in "catching the bad guys." But he was very poor at documenting his cases. He wrote reports as if he was writing to himself and no one else. When I reviewed his reports, I could make scarce sense of what he was trying to convey. He knew what he knew and what he was trying to say, but he assumed others would read his reports from the same perspective and with the same basis of knowledge that he did. I often received complaints from deputy prosecutors who could make no sense of his reports. He knew the "bad guy" was the "guy what done it," but no one else knew the details of the case that the detective knew. Judges and juries could hardly follow his theory of the case because he went from "fact" to "fact" without any *logical* sequence. He would go from a description of a suspect to "the car" without explaining what car or where the car came into the story. He knew what car and how it got involved in the story, so he assumed that it was "obvious" to everyone else. It wasn't.

It is the function of an investigator or a detective to be a "fact finder." The objective is not to "prove" someone committed the crime, but to correctly identify the perpetrator and the facts. That is, it is not "solving" the crime because you can "pin it" on someone. It is only solving a crime if you bring the correct perpetrator to justice. I have made a practice throughout my career of not sending a case for prosecution if I had not first convinced myself (beyond a reasonable doubt) that I had correctly identified the perpetrator of the crime or the culpable party. The legal standard is not "beyond a shadow of a doubt," as you often see in old movies, but "beyond a reasonable doubt." As a law enforcement investigator or detective, you do not want to allow a guilty person to get away and convict an innocent person (or at least one who did not commit *this* crime) merely to close a case (which, in reality, remains unsolved). Anyone who intentionally brings someone to prosecution without a true belief in the person's guilt, merely for a statistical clearance or to appear as if they have solved the crime (when they have not), is worse than the criminal they are allowing to go free. "Due diligence" is a standard for the legal profession and should be the bar for law enforcement. A failure to develop a theory of the case and "prove" it in a logical way is reckless, incompetent, unethical, and immoral.

Obviously a Suicide

I have often heard homicide detectives and crime scene investigators at a death scene say, "Obviously a suicide!" This always bothered me greatly and made me wonder how many murders were committed and went undetected because of this assumption. They thought their work was going to be easy or that it was finished because it was "obvious" that no foul play was involved. They made this assumption because there was a "suicide note" at the scene and a gun near the body. The assumption being made was that someone could not stage a murder to look like a suicide. Has this never happened? Only in movies and on TV? This was flawed logic or a lack thereof. This is a lack of critical thinking and an absence of deductive or inductive reasoning. I have learned from experience and from great detectives who have trained me over my decades as a detective that *all* death investigations should be treated as a murder until proven otherwise.

That bears repeating. This is one of the most important points I want to emphasize in this text. Homicide Investigations Rule 1: Treat *all* death investigations as a murder investigation until proven otherwise. If you begin a suicide, accidental death, or natural death investigation as a murder scene and prove it is not, you have done a thorough investigation with no mistakes. If you treat a murder crime scene and investigation as a suicide, accidental death, or natural death investigation, and later discover it was a murder, you have been incompetent and derelict in your duties. You cannot work your way back at that point.

In the U.S. Army Criminal Investigations Command (USACIDC) we had a saying: Every case we work is practice for the homicides. By the way, please note that all murders are homicides, but not all homicides are murders. A homicide is the killing of one person by a person. I have left out the term "another person" because a suicide is a self-inflicted homicide. So, all murders and suicides (but not accidental or natural deaths) are homicides. Still, even accidental or natural deaths are investigated as murders until it is proven that they are not murders.

Scientific Method

Scientific inquiry is generally intended to be as objective as possible in order to reduce biased interpretations of results. One example of a biased interpretation is making that "obvious" observation; that is, making assumptions based upon what seems apparent without testing the validity of the argument. The *scientific method* is a technique for or a method of investigating phenomena, acquiring new knowledge, or correcting and integrating previous knowledge. To be termed "scientific," a method of inquiry must be based on empirical and measurable evidence subject to specific principles of reasoning. Empirical evidence is a source of knowledge acquired through observation and experimentation.

The scientific method is a method or procedure of systematic observation, measurement, and experiment, and the formulation, testing, and modification of hypotheses. A *hypothesis* (plural *hypotheses*) is a proposed explanation for a phenomenon (why something is so or a fact).

The characteristic that distinguishes the scientific method from other methods of acquiring knowledge is that scientists seek to "let reality speak for itself," supporting a theory when a theory's predictions are confirmed and challenging a theory when its predictions prove false (proving or disproving that "obvious" assumption). Although procedures vary from one field of inquiry to another, identifiable features distinguish scientific inquiry from other methods of obtaining knowledge. Scientific researchers propose a hypothesis or hypotheses as explanations of phenomena, and design experimental studies to test these hypotheses through predictions that can be derived from them. Each step of an experiment must be repeatable (subject to replication) to guard against mistake or confusion in any particular experiment. Theories help form a new hypothesis or hypotheses, or place groups of hypotheses into context.

Another goal of the scientific method is to document, archive, and share all data and methodology so they are available for careful scrutiny by other scientists, giving them the opportunity to verify results by attempting to reproduce them (through replication of the experiment). This practice, called "full disclosure," allows statistical measures of the reliability of data to be established (when data is sampled or compared to chance).

Steps of the Scientific Method

The scientific method is a method used by researchers to support or disprove a theory. It can be used to answer True–False questions. The method involves six common steps:

1. Observation—Observe something using senses or machines.
2. Question—Ask a question about what you observe.
3. Hypothesis—Predict what the answer to the question might be.
4. Method (Prediction)—Figure a way to test whether your hypothesis is correct.
5. Result (Testing)—Experiment with the method you came up with and record the results.
6. Conclusion (Analysis)—State whether your prediction was confirmed and explain your results.

(See Figure 1.1.)

These six steps commonly involve the following process and procedures:

1. **Observation.** Observation involves the act of recognizing or noting an occurrence or phenomenon that is the subject of inquiry.
2. **Formulation of a question.** The question can refer to the explanation of a specific observation, such as "Why did witnesses say they heard four gunshots, but only two bullets were found?" Alternatively, the question can be open-ended, such as, "Does sound travel faster in air

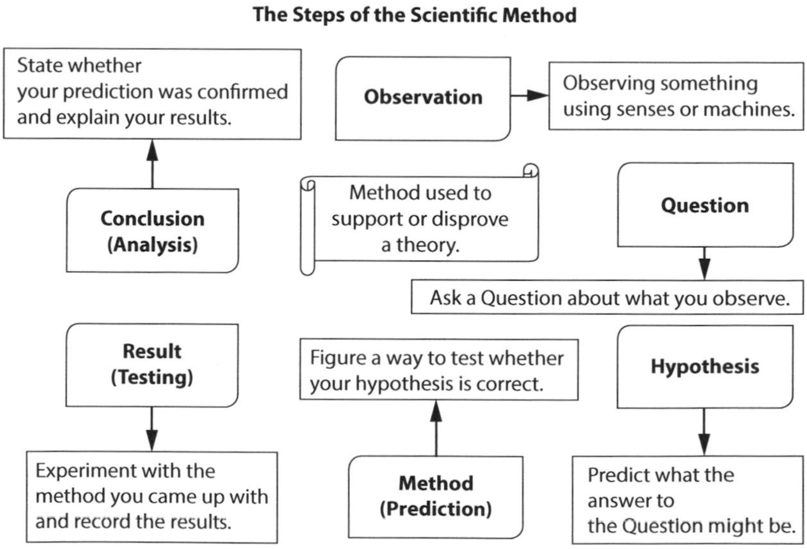

Figure 1.1 Steps of the scientific method.

than in water?" or "Could witnesses have heard echoes of two shots, making it sound like four shots?" This step may involve looking up and evaluating previous evidence from other scientists, including experience. If the answer is already known, a different question that builds on the previous evidence can be posed. When applying the scientific method to scientific research, determining a good question can be very difficult and affects the outcome of the investigation.

3. **Hypothesis.** A hypothesis is a conjecture, based on the knowledge obtained while formulating the question, which may explain the observed behavior or occurrence in question. A *conjecture* is a proposition that is unproven. The hypothesis might be very specific or it might be broad. To be meaningfully tested, a scientific hypothesis must be "falsifiable," meaning that one can identify a possible outcome of an experiment that conflicts with predictions deduced from the hypothesis.

4. **Prediction (Method).** This step involves determining the *logical consequences* of the hypothesis. It involves finding a way to test whether your hypothesis is correct. One or more predictions are then selected for further testing. The less likely that the prediction would be correct simply by coincidence, the stronger the evidence that the prediction is valid. Evidence is also stronger if the answer to the prediction is not already known, due to the effects of hindsight bias. Ideally, the prediction must also distinguish the hypothesis from likely alternatives. If two hypotheses make the same prediction, observing the prediction to be correct is not evidence for either one over the other.

5. **Testing (Result).** This is an investigation of whether the "real world" behaves as predicted by the hypothesis. Scientists (and others) test a hypothesis or hypotheses by conducting experiments to determine whether observations of the "real world" agree with or conflict with the predictions derived from a hypothesis.
   a. If they agree, confidence in the hypothesis increases.
   b. If they do not agree, confidence decreases.
   Agreement does not assure that the hypothesis is true because future experiments may reveal new variables, data, or relevant problems. Large numbers of successful confirmations are also unconvincing if they result from experiments that avoid the risk of refuting the hypothesis.

6. **Analysis (Conclusion).** This involves determining what the results of the experiment show and deciding on the next action to take. The predictions of the hypothesis are compared to those of the "null hypothesis" (statistically inferred general or default position) to determine which is better able to explain the data.

a. If the evidence has "falsified" the hypothesis (shown it to be incorrect), a new hypothesis is required.

b. If the experiment supports the hypothesis, but the evidence is not strong enough for high confidence, other predictions from the hypothesis must be tested.

Once a hypothesis is strongly supported by evidence, a new question can be asked to provide further insight on the same topic. Evidence from other scientists and experience is frequently incorporated at any stage in the process. Many "iterations" may be required to gather sufficient evidence to answer a question with confidence or to build many answers to specific questions in order to answer a single broader question. *Iteration* means the act of repeating a process with the aim of approaching a desired goal, target, or result. Each repetition of the process is also called an "iteration" and the results of one iteration are used as the starting point for the next iteration.

Conclusion

Do not read this Conclusion until you have read the entire chapter. In other words, don't skip through this book or scan the chapters. This will not help you (or anyone else). You must critically analyze data to develop the practical skills of logic, critical thinking, reasoning, and the scientific method to make law enforcement investigations more effective and reliable. I hope that is your goal. Now, read on!

Philosophers have distinguished between two types of reasoning. One is *inductive reasoning*, which involves making a generalized conclusion from premises (statements) referring to particular instances. A key feature of inductive reasoning is that the conclusions of inductively valid arguments are *probably*, but not necessarily, true. The other kind of reasoning is *deductive reasoning*, which allows you to draw conclusions that are definitely valid, if other statements are assumed true (Eysenck and Keane, 2010, p. 533).

While we may prefer to make *deductions* because of the "certainty," most of our everyday reasoning involves *induction* because our world is full of uncertainties. Next, we will learn how our cognitive skills (observation, perception, thought, and decision) prepare us to make logically reasonable deductive and inductive critical thinking decisions about fact patterns and legal inferences.

Cognitive Skills
Perceptions and
Thought Processes

2

Introduction

Cognition is mental activity and involves the acquisition, storage, retrieval, and use of knowledge. The "cognitive approach" to psychology is oriented to theories based upon mental structures and processes; it is based upon the broader field referred to as *cognitive science*, which studies the nature of knowledge, its components, its development, and its use (Matlin, 1994, pp. 2, 9). *Cognitive neuroscience* examines how the structure and function of the brain explain cognitive processes (Matlin, 1994, p. 10).

Why is cognitive psychology useful in the study of logic for detective work? There are at least three reasons: (1) it helps each of us explore what kind of learners we are and how to better learn (and use) this material; (2) learning how thought processes and perception occurs helps us to better understand how we function as "trained observers"; and (3) learning about how the mind operates and how people think helps us to "profile" behavioral patterns.

Logic is the study of reasoning and *reasoning* is an activity that is part social and part solitary, involving the solution of a scientific problem or settling a case at law. Logic is the study of reasoning means and personal and interpersonal activity arguing for one's beliefs. In addition to philosophy, other academic disciplines study reasoning as well. Cognitive psychology and neuroscience, anthropology, sociology of the knowledge, linguistics, computer science (particularly artificial intelligence), ethology, and history of science all study logic or reasoning (Jason, 1994, pp. 1–2).

A *cognitive science* experimentally investigates the nature of knowledge and reasoning. Though *rhetoric* is the study of persuasive communication, it should not be equated as the same as logic because what is logically solid may not be persuasive and what is persuasive may not be logically solid. *Mathematics* is the study of number, form, arrangement, and rules. Symbolic logic and mathematical logic share many distinctions. *Metalogic* is the study of logical systems (Jason, 1994, pp. 2, 11, 13).

What Kind of Learner Are You?

Let's take just a few minutes to discuss learning. This will help us determine what type of learners each of us is so that we can learn this subject more efficiently. It will also help us understand how others learn and think. There are two general categories of learning strategies, into which most people fall: global and analytic. Right-brain learners who like to see the big picture first and then move to specifics are global learners. Global learners capitalize on their tendency to look at the big picture and focus on seeing how everything fits together. They have acute listening skills. Left-brain learners who prefer to start with the specifics before they move on to the big picture are analytic learners. Analytic learners take advantage of their preference for paradigms and lists. They organize material into groups that make sense to them and break information into sub-parts (Davidson et al., 1996, p. x) (see Figure 2.1).

Whether you are a global or an analytical learner, you have your own learning style. Knowing your sensory preferences, the physical channels through which you most efficiently absorb information, will help you develop effective classroom behavior and homework strategies (Davidson et al. 1996, p. xi). There are five basic learning styles: (1) visual, (2) auditory, (3) digital mechanical (note-takers), (4) oral, and (5) kinesthetic (Figure 2.2).

Visual learners learn from visual stimulus and, like most global learners, can identify the big picture from its component parts. Visual learners like to categorize, analyze, and look for patterns. They like to write things down to refer to later. They memorize things by rote (word for word) and review things in written form before hearing it for the first time in class. Visual learners make lists of everything they need to learn in order to stimulate their ability

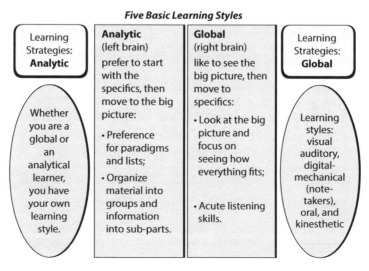

Five Basic Learning Styles

Learning Strategies: **Analytic**	**Analytic** (left brain)	**Global** (right brain)	Learning Strategies: **Global**
Whether you are a global or an analytical learner, you have your own learning style.	prefer to start with the specifics, then move to the big picture: • Preference for paradigms and lists; • Organize material into groups and information into sub-parts.	like to see the big picture, then move to specifics: • Look at the big picture and focus on seeing how everything fits; • Acute listening skills.	Learning styles: visual auditory, digital-mechanical (note-takers), oral, and kinesthetic

Figure 2.1 Analytic (left brain) and global (right brain) learning strategies.

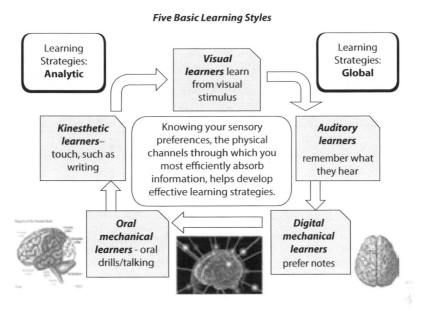

Figure 2.2 Five basic learning styles.

to absorb material through their eyes. They do well on multiple-choice tests because they provide visual options. Reading through transcripts of material as it is heard "teases" the eyes and ears into developing listening skills versus just hearing words (Davidson et al., 1996, pp. xi–xii).

Auditory learners remember what they hear better than what they read. They like to ask questions and can easily put together the big picture from its component parts. Auditory learners learn best through interactive activities, such as role-playing and dialogue (Davidson et al., 1996, p. xii).

Digital mechanical learners generally prefer to take notes. They identify the pieces of the whole picture, summarize a complex point, and explain concepts in writing. They require additional time to record information before absorbing it. They require more effort to participate in interactive activities, such as role-playing, and to work with others on in-class projects (Davidson et al., 1996, p. xii).

Oral mechanical learners prefer oral drills and talking aloud as much as possible. They like dialogues and discussions and should read their assignments aloud. They should try to develop their visual and auditory learning strategies (Davidson et al., 1996, p. xii).

Kinesthetic learners share some of the characteristics of digital mechanical learners, such as writing activity. They prefer to move about and may learn by performing skits and acting out a word meaning by playing charades. Writing things down helps them to remember, and walking around while going over their notes may also be helpful (Davidson et al., 1996, p. xii).

An awareness of one's learning preferences is useful in adapting learning styles to that of the textbook and the instructor (Davidson et al., 1996, p. xii). Knowing learners' strengths and learning preferences allows instructors to manipulate the texts and lectures to match their learning styles. Classroom *communication* is structured in a positive manner. The amount of student participation as the class progresses indicates which direction the communication is flowing. Verbal communication, the best communication device, is enhanced by encouraging students to share their experiences through the discussion of facts, events, examples, analogies, and anecdotes to elicit an association between instructors and students (Greive, 1995, p. 7).

Cognitive Psychology and Cognitive Neuroscience

Cognitive psychology is the scientific study of the mind (the cognitive nature of knowledge and reasoning). Because the operation of the mind cannot be observed directly, its operation must be inferred from what we can measure, such as behavior or physiological responses. Studying both behavioral and physiological aspects together provides a more comprehensive understanding of how the mind operates (Goldstein, 2011, p. 19). *Cognitive neuroscience* is the study of the physiological aspects of cognition (the nature of knowledge and reasoning) (Goldstein, 2011, p. 43).

Signals can be recorded from neurons using *microelectrodes* and demonstrate that "action potentials remain the same size as they travel down an axon and that increasing stimulus intensity increases the rate of nerve firing." Brain imaging measures brain activity by measuring the blood flow in the brain. For example, *functional magnetic resonance imaging* (fMRI) is widely used to analyze brain activity during cognitive functioning and has been used to identify areas of the brain that respond to certain types of stimulation (faces, places, bodies, etc.) (Goldstein, 2011, p. 42).

Similarly, because an active region of the brain requires more "metabolic fuel," researchers, using *regional cerebral blood-flow techniques*, can inject a small amount of radioactive material resembling glucose, the brain's main metabolic fuel, to record the cerebral blood flow to active parts of the brain. Different cognitive tasks increase the regional blood flow in different areas of the brain. It is measured by a technique known as *positron emission tomography* or a *PET scan* (Matlin, 1994, p. 11).

Researchers also use the *evoked potential technique*, placing electrodes on a subject's scalp, to record electrical signals generated from a large number of neurons beneath each respective electrode. While this and the previously described techniques do not identify the response of a single neuron, it can identify electrical changes over very brief periods, identifying responses to different task demands. The *single-cell recording technique* allows for the study of a single neuron, the basic cell of the nervous system, but is not safe for testing humans (Matlin, 1994, p. 11).

The idea of "distributed processing" suggests that specific functions are processed by several different areas of the brain that can be identified. This also suggests that cognitive functions, such as memory, decision making, and problem solving, also occur in different parts of the brain and can be identified. Objects, properties of objectives, and visual stimuli may be able to be measured by patterns of "neural firing" called neural code. Computer programs have been developed that can use data from brain imaging to iden-tify (from a group of objects) the specific object that a person is seeing ("mind reading") (Goldstein, 2011, pp. 41, 44).

Many cognitive psychologists use the computer as a machine metaphor or model for the human mind. *Artificial intelligence* (AI) is a branch of com-puter science that attempts to write programs that emulate the higher mental processes associated with humans, such as language and problem solving. In AI analogies of human intelligence, scientists draw a distinction between "pure AI" and "computer simulation." *Pure AI* seeks to accomplish a task as efficiently as possible, such as winning a chess game, but such strategies show little resemblance to human thought processes. *Computer simulation* takes into account human limitations; for example, most humans do not have the ability to analyze dozens of potential moves simultaneously. Why is any of this useful to detectives and investigators? It helps us more closely under-stand how others and we think and process information. For instance, the *parallel distributed processing (PDP) approach* or *connectionism* suggests that cognitive processes can be viewed as "networks" that "link together neuron-like units" (Matlin, 1994, pp. 12–14).

Perceptions and Thought Processes

Why is understanding "perception" important and how can it be of value to detectives and investigators? First, it is important to understand how our own perceptions occur to help us improve our "powers of observation" or skills as "trained observers" (as we often refer to ourselves in court). Second, it is impor-tant to understand what factors influence the perceptions of witnesses, who we interview during investigations or examine and cross-examine in court. Why do we miss things that we "see, hear, smell, feel, or taste" and why do witnesses, who we do not suspect of lying, "see, hear, smell, feel, or taste" things that con-tradict other witnesses or are (seemingly) impossible to have been factual? Understanding "perception" can help us understand and overcome these issues.

Perception is the process that uses previously acquired knowledge to gather and interpret the stimuli that our senses register (Matlin, 1994, p. 26) and starts with "bottom-up processing," which involves receptors. Signals from receptors cause neurons in the cortex to respond to specific types of stimuli (Goldstein, 2011, p. 77). Perception is determined by three sources of information: (1) information originating from stimulation of the receptors; (2) additional information, such as context, in which an object appears; and (3) knowledge or expectations of the perceiver (Goldstein, 2011, p. 53).

Two aspects of cognitive perception are pattern recognition and attention. *Pattern recognition* involves identifying complex arrangements of sensory stimuli. When you recognize a pattern, sensory processes, transforms, and organizes the raw information provided by sensory receptors and you compare this sensory stimuli with information in other memory storages (Matlin, 1994, pp. 26–27). *Attention* is a concentration of mental activity that can refer to (1) concentration on a mental task at the exclusion of other interfering stimuli (such as examinations) and (2) receiving multiple messages or stimuli at once, but ignoring all but one (e.g., focusing on one conversation at a noisy party) (Matlin, 1994, p. 43).

Selective attention, the ability to focus on one message while ignoring all others, has been demonstrated using "dichotic listening" procedures. One negative, yet well-publicized, example of "selective attention" is driver inattention (distracted driving), which is one of the major causes of automobile accidents. "Inattentional blindness" and "change blindness" experiments provide evidence that without attention (distraction) we fail to perceive things (objects and events) that are clearly visible (or otherwise perceptible) within our field of view (or scope of perception) (Goldstein, 2011, p. 111).

Divided attention is the ability to perform several tasks simultaneously (multitask) in response to several messages or stimuli at once, responding to each as needed. Tasks that are practiced and performed often are easier to perform when required to multitask, indicating that this ability can be learned. Research on practice and divided attention affirms the adage, "Practice makes perfect" (Matlin, 1994, p. 44).

Visual attention can be directed to different places in a scene without eye movements, a process known as "covert attention" (a "top-down" process) (Goldstein, 2011, p. 111).

Consciousness refers to awareness and is closely related to attention, but the processes are not identical. For example, when people drive, they often use automatic processing to put their foot on the brake when they see a red light. They may not even notice that they "saw" the red light and may not be conscious that they performed the "motor action" (putting the brake on) (Matlin, 1994, p. 58).

Memory: What Detectives and Witnesses Can Recall

Memory is important for obvious reasons. First, what detectives and investigators are able to recall is the basis of further investigation, documentation in reports, and testimony in court. What witnesses are able to recall and testify to is the basis of most investigations and litigation of cases. So, understanding how memory works (and fails to work) can help us understand perceptions of essential information for an investigation and subsequent court case.

Memory involves maintaining information over time, from less than a second to a lifetime. For example, we use memory to store the beginning of a word until we have heard the end of the word (such as syllables). We also use memory to remember our names for a lifetime. This is affected by pattern recognition and attention (Matlin, 1994, pp. 66–67). There are at least four "models of memory" (theories): (1) Atkinson-Shiffrin Model, (2) Levels-of-Processing Approach, (3) Tulving's Model: Episodic, Semantic, and Procedural Memory, and (4) Parallel Distributed Processing Approach. However, we need not explore them in depth here. It may make for interesting reading and further research if you want a deeper understanding of memory. Here, it is sufficient to understand something about sensory memory, short-term memory, and long-term memory.

Sensory memory is a large-capacity storage system that records information from the senses, but are fleeting, fragile memories. The *sensory register* or *sensory storage* holds information in a relatively raw, unprocessed form for only a short time after the stimulus is no longer available. Sensory memory is necessary to process the vast amounts of constant, rapidly changing sensory information (sight, sound, touch, smell, taste) and to accurately record sensory stimulation long enough to select the most important stimuli for further processing (Matlin, 1994, pp. 102–103).

Short-term memory assimilates information from sensory memory and retains only the small amount of information that we are actively using. Short-term memory may last for less than a minute and has definite limits. Most short-term memory is forgotten and only a small amount, a mere fraction of all short-term memory, passes to long-term memory (Matlin, 1994, p. 102). There are two types of short-term memory: (1) iconic memory and (2) echoic memory. *Iconic memory* describes visual memory or the "brief persistence of visual impression" that is briefly available for processing even after the stimulus has terminated (Matlin, 1994, p. 104). *Echoic memory* describes auditory memory and the brief impressions that persist after a sound has disappeared (Matlin, 1994, p. 109). The remaining senses also have short-term memory capacities.

Long-term memory is durable. For example, tests have shown that students who learned Spanish in high school or college retained 40% or more of the vocabulary, idioms, and grammar learned as much as 50 years earlier. A number of factors influence the accuracy of long-term memory, such as familiarity of places, mood, whether it involves "expert" knowledge, etc. (Matlin, 1994, pp. 132–133).

But why do some people "recall" things that never actually occurred? Because memory is influenced by our general knowledge about objects and events (schemas), people often mistakenly "recall" events that never actually happened (or did not happen the way they "remember" them). At other times, we cannot remember if we actually performed a task that we intended to or we forget to perform a future action. Research on this has raised issues of concern and validity about "eyewitness" testimony (Matlin, 1994, pp. 132–133).

Eidetic memory is what most people refer to as "photographic memory." Are there not some people who can look at a page and tell you verbatim everything that they have seen? The character Sherlock Holmes was renowned for his ability to see the smallest of details and recall them accurately at a moment's notice. While this is not well documented in real life, there are examples of people who could mentally project an exact image of a picture onto a surface (i.e., paint or draw it), giving the appearance of an exact copy of the original. It is more often found in children (Solso et al., 2008, pp. 216–217). Other examples include people who can remember large amounts of random numbers or the names of dozens of people who they just met moments ago. Still others seem to have the ability to memorize large amounts of information that they have seen only once.

Eyewitness Testimony: Explicit Versus Implicit Memory

An *explicit memory measure* requires participants to remember information, most commonly the ability to "recall" information, such as reproducing information that was learned earlier, or "recognition," which requires identification of items or objects. An *implicit memory measure* requires a participant to perform a task or do something. Matlin illustrates this, using "Schacter's anecdote," as follows:

> A young woman is walking aimlessly down the street, and she is eventually picked up by the police. She seems to be suffering from an extreme form of amnesia, because she has lost all memory of who she is...The police...ask her to begin dialing phone numbers. As it turns out, she dials her mother's number—though she is not aware whose number she is dialing. (Matlin, 1994, p. 138)

In the illustration, the woman was unable to "recall" *explicit memory*, but she was able to perform a task (dialing her mother's phone number) from *implicit memory*. This involves the use of previous experience (dialing her mother's phone number) during ongoing behavior, without consciously making an effort to recall the past. While explicit memory requires conscious recollection of previous experiences, implicit memory tasks do not.

The process of determining the difference between real and imagined events or memories is called *reality monitoring*. Deciding that one really did perform an action that one "remembers" involves evaluating rich "perceptual details" with "little cognitive effort to reconstruct that memory." When one merely imagines having performed a task or action, "memory" lacks perceptual details and reconstruction requires great cognitive effort (Matlin, 1994, pp. 152–153).

Matlin opines that Elizabeth Loftus is one of the best-known researchers on eyewitness testimony. She cites a 1991 article, "Witness for the Defense," by Elizabeth F. Loftus and K. Ketcham, providing an anecdote to illustrate why some psychologists question the reliability of eyewitnesses.

> In 1979, a Catholic priest awaited trial for several armed robberies in Delaware. Seven witnesses had identified him as the "gentleman bandit," referring to the robber's polite manners and elegant clothes. During the trial, many witnesses identified the priest as the one who had committed the robberies. Suddenly, however, the trial was halted; another man had confessed to the robberies.

Matlin goes on to suggest that nearly 80,000 cases each year in the U.S. primarily rely on eyewitness identification and as many as 2000 suspects are wrongfully convicted each year based on eyewitness testimony. While human memory is reasonably accurate and eyewitness testimony, like other memories, is generally accurate, memory and witness reports are not flawless (Matlin, 1994, pp. 154, 171).

Eyewitness testimony can be influenced by pre-existing *schemas* (our general knowledge about an object or an event that has been acquired from experience). It should come as no surprise that "identification accuracy is better when people devote greater time and attention to looking at the face" (Matlin, 1994, pp. 151, 154, 155). People are also less accurate when something distracts them from the face, such as a gun held by a robber. A witness, again not surprisingly, may focus on the gun rather than the details of the robber's face. The length of the "retention interval" also influences facial recognition. Delay intervals as long as weeks, even months, do not automatically reduce recognition accuracy. "However," Matlin says, "If pictures of other faces, such as misleading composite faces, are shown during the delay interval, accuracy is substantially reduced." Errors in eyewitness testimony can arise not only from misleading pictures of faces, but also from misleading information supplied to witnesses after the original incident or event (Matlin, 1994, pp. 151, 154, 155).

Trained Observer: Tachistoscopic Training

Optometrists and ophthalmologists provide health care for our eyes and vision and study factors relevant to what we see and don't see. Another field of study, *tachistoscopic* training, or "flash recognition," is used by many police academies to train law enforcement officers in rapid observations of minute details. Thus, they are "trained observers." In truth, law enforcement officers often do "see" things that others do not. Some call this "profiling," others recognize this as experiential intuition, and still others observe that law enforcement officers are trained, experienced, and in the habit of observing and "seeing" things that others would pay no attention to or dismiss as trivial or meaningless, when it may speak volumes to the trained observer.

Flash Recognition Training (FRT) is a process used to enhance the memory and powers of observation. This involves the use of flash recognition techniques to help improve not only observation, but also memorization of details, such as license plates, faces, and incident scenes. Tachistoscopic training is a perceptual enhancement technique designed to improve the recall of visual information.

A *tachistoscope* is a machine that flashes a series of images very rapidly, as quickly as 1/100th of a second, to create "subliminal imprinting" in the mind. The idea and technology was created by Dr. Samuel Renshaw, an American psychologist (Ohio State University) who trained military personnel during World War II to rapidly recognize aircraft and ships on approach to avoid friendly fire and delays in targeting enemy vessels. The system Dr. Renshaw developed came to be known as the Renshaw Recognition System (RRS) or Flash Recognition Training (FRT), and the concept has been applied to fields of subliminal marketing, advanced mental training, and psychological research. The process has been automated into computer software programs that can flash images on a computer screen that are precisely timed and designed to enhance the ability to recognize certain shapes automatically.

Research subjects using the tachistoscope were able to increase their average reading comprehension rate from around 600 words per minute up to 1416 words per minute with nearly 100% comprehension, though many other subjects had more modest increases in reading speed. The tachistoscope flashes images containing from five- to nine-digit numbers at 1/100th of a second and students are instructed to try to remember the numbers. Typically, 33 half-hour sessions of training are conducted before a reading speed test evaluates if any change has occurred.

Dr. Renshaw's view on how the human eye sees dispels the myth that the eye is similar to an optical device like cameras taking rapid snapshots of individual images in the real world for processing by the brain. Dr. Renshaw theorized that most visual processing occurs subconsciously by memory, and pattern recognition within the brain is unnoticed moment by moment. His tachistoscope merely replicates this form of rapid visual processing and research tests confirm that it is effective.

Cognition and Reasoning: Perception and Logic

Logical reasoning transforms given information in order to reach conclusions (Matlin, 1994, p. 378). *Reasoning* is a cognitive process that starts with information and allows us to come to *conclusions* that go beyond that information, while *deductive reasoning* involves "syllogisms" and usually results in definite conclusions. A syllogism is valid if its conclusion follows logically from its premises. *Inductive reasoning* is based upon evidence and results in conclusions that are "probably" true (probable or more likely than not). In inductive reasoning, conclusions do not follow from logically constructed syllogisms, but from evidence. Conclusions are "suggested" with varying degrees of certainty. That is, the strength of an inductive argument depends on the "representativeness, number, and quality of observations" on which the argument is based (Goldstein, 2011, pp. 386–387).

Logic
Deduction and Induction

3

Science is a way of thinking much more than it is a body of knowledge.

—Carl Sagan

Courses in *logic* have been offered ever since the first universities came into existence 800 to 900 years ago. Logic is the "critical study of reasoning with both theoretical interest and practical utility" (Baker, 1974, p. 1). Mastery of the principles of logical reasoning helps us become more effective in recognizing and avoiding mistakes in reasoning. The objective is clearer and correct thinking processes and results.

The concept of inductive and deductive reasoning became widely recognized in detective fiction through the works of Sir Arthur Conan Doyle in the *Sherlock Holmes* series of novels and short stories. Sherlock Holmes utilized his theory of deductions and inductions to solve mysteries and to profile an individual's personality and background based upon his observations of minute details. The methods portrayed in Sherlock Holmes stories so effectively dramatized the theory of inductive and deductive reasoning that they are taught by the Metropolitan Police Department, Scotland Yard, at their detective school. Scotland Yard first applied these techniques to the investigation of the White Chapel murders, known as the Jack the Ripper case. Though the crime remains unsolved to this day, the London Metropolitan Police and the City of London Police applied the principles to try to solve the case and to identify Jack the Ripper.

An Introduction to Logic

Most people would claim to "be logical." Usually these same people claim to have "common sense." Often they are not "logical" and sense is rather uncommon. What they are really claiming to possess is the ability to "reason" and "wisdom" ("common" sense gained through experiences). Logic is the application of a series of steps in a process to systematically evaluate facts and theories leading to factual conclusions.

Logic is the study of *arguments* and methods of determining whether arguments are correct (*validated*) or incorrect (*flawed*). Statements or a series of statements result in a *premise* or premises. A final statement results in a *conclusion*. Arguments can be stated in terms of correct and incorrect

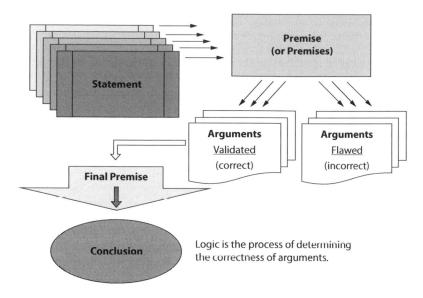

Figure 3.1 Logic: the process of determining the correctness of an argument.

arguments. Logic is the process of determining the correctness of arguments. Every argument contains at least one premise and one conclusion (Carney and Scheer, 1980, pp. 3–4) (Figure 3.1).

Some arguments are not fully stated. When a conclusion, one or more arguments, or neither the arguments nor conclusion are stated, these are referred to as *enthymemes*. A premise (a statement or series of statements) is often omitted because it seems obvious to those who propose the argument. Such *assumptions* make an argument flawed (Carney and Scheer, 1980, p. 8).

Deductive and Inductive Arguments

In an *argument,* a claim is made that the *conclusion* follows from the *premise.* The term "follows" can be distinguished by the types of arguments: (1) deductive arguments and (2) inductive arguments (Carney and Scheer, 1980, p. 10) The difference between deduction and induction is related to the strength of the logical link between the premise and the conclusion. In *deductive* reasoning, one argues that the truth of one's premise is strictly sufficient to establish the truth of one's conclusion. In *inductive* reasoning one is not claiming the link is that strong, but that there is enough of a link (called a "nexus") to support or confirm the conclusion (Baker, 1974, p. 16) (see Figure 3.2).

In a *deductive argument,* the claim that the conclusion follows from the premise essentially asserts that it is impossible for the premise to be true and

Deductive and Inductive Arguments

Deductive argument –	**Inductive argument –**
. The claim that the **conclusion** follows from the premises,	. The claim of the **argument** is that the **conclusion** follows from the **premises**,
. Asserts that it is impossible for the **premises** to be true and the **conclusion** false.	. That it is **improbable** that the conclusion is false because of the truth of each premise.
. If **A** is true, **X** must be the conclusion; **X** cannot be false if **A** is true.	. **A** has never happened, therefore, **X** will not occur; **X** will not occur because **A** has never happened.
In all probability the conclusion is true if the premise is true.	

Figure 3.2 Deductive and Inductive Arguments.

the conclusion false (Carney and Scheer, 1980, p. 10). That is, if A is true, X must be the conclusion; X cannot be false if A is true.

An *inductive argument* is an argument that is not deductive or is non-deductive. Here, the claim of the argument is that the conclusion follows from the premise, in that it is *improbable* that the conclusion is false because of the truth of the premise. The degree of improbability (and, therefore, the probability) will vary from argument to argument (Carney and Scheer, 1980, p. 11). That is, A has never happened, therefore, X will not occur; X will not occur because A has never happened (see Figure 3.2).

In an inductive (non-deductive) argument, the claim is simply that in all probability the conclusion is true if the premise is true. The difference between an *inductive* and *deductive* argument is that an in inductive argument one does *not* suppose that the conclusion *must* be true if the premise is true. One is *not* ruling out the *possibility* that the premise is true and the conclusion is false, only that the premise is evidence to support the *probability* of the conclusion. Whether an inductive argument is correct or incorrect is a matter of how much evidence there is in the premise for the conclusion (Carney and Scheer, 1980, p. 11).

The correctness of a deductive argument is dependent upon the claim being justified. This is called a valid argument (Carney and Scheer, 1980, p. 12). The strength of an inductive argument depends upon the sample upon which generalizations are made. For example:

- Ten Alphas have been observed. All were red. Therefore, all Alphas are red. [Versus]
- Ten million Betas have been observed. All were green. Therefore, all Betas are green.

The second example *appears* to have a stronger *inductive* argument because the sample is larger. However, the strength of an argument also depends upon the *representative* nature of the sample. That is, if there are only 12 Alphas in existence and 200 million Betas, then the first example is more representative and may be the stronger argument.

Formal Logic: The Logical Structure of Science

The objective of *logic* is to provide methods for determining the validity of deductive arguments. A deductive argument is valid if the deductive claim is warranted (Carney and Scheer, 1980, pp. 165). *Deductive reasoning* involves observing a set of characteristics that may be reasoned from a convergence of physical and behavioral actions or patterns within an event or a series of events, such as a crime or series of crimes. *Inductive reasoning* involves observing a set of characteristics based on a premise of broad generalizations and statistical analysis, which leads to the development of a hypothesis.

Valid *deductive* arguments are demonstrative, that is, if the premises are true, the conclusion is necessarily true. An *inductive* argument draws a conclusion "embodying empirical conjectures about the world that go beyond what its premises say..." (Baker, 1974, p. 221). That is, the conclusion is not wholly contained in the premises, therefore the premises cannot *absolutely* ensure the truth of the conclusion and the argument cannot be demonstrative in the way a valid deduction is. If, however, the premises of an inductive argument are true and the reasoning is good, then it is reasonable to believe the conclusion, that is, the conclusion is *probably* true (probability).

Both deductive and inductive arguments require distinguishing between the truth of the conclusion and the logical validity of the reasoning. However, in inductive reasoning we must allow for variations in the *degree of probability* that the premises reach the conclusion (Baker, 1974, p. 222).

Psychology of Proof: Deductive Reasoning in Human Thinking

Reasoning is a psychological process. Deduction is a type of psychological process that involves transforming "mental reorientations." Experimental psychology, however, has traditionally approached deduction as the study of people answering questions about a particular kind of *argument*. An "argument" is a set of sentences (the *premises*) and an additional sentence (the *conclusion*). A deductively correct argument is one in which the conclusion is true when the premises are true (Rips, 1994, p. 3).

The main theme in the theory of mental proof is that when people are confronted with a problem that calls for deduction, they often attempt to solve the problem by generating in "working memory" a set of sentences linking the premises or "givens" to the conclusions (solution). Each link in this network comprises an *inference rule*, which the individual recognizes as intuitively sound. This network of sentences then bridges the gap between the premises and the conclusion by explaining why the conclusion follows. Not everyone is always successful at producing mental proof for every deductively correct argument. They at least claim an attempt at mental proof during their problem-solving process (Rips, 1994, p. 103).

The basic inference system consists of a set of deduction rules that construct mental proofs in the system's working memory. Rips writes, "If we present the system with a group of premises and ask for entailments of those premises, the system will use the rules to generate proofs of possible conclusions." He observes that the model comes up with a proof by first storing input premises and the conclusion (if there is one) in *working memory*. He goes on to say, "The rules then scan these memory contents to determine whether any inferences are possible. If so, the model adds the newly deduced sentences to memory, scans the updated configuration, makes further deductions, and so on, until a proof has been found or no more rules apply." The inference routines "carry out much of the work in the basic system," deciding when deductions are possible, adding propositions to working memory, and continues to move toward a solution (Rips, 1994, pp. 104–105).

Deductive Validity

Deductive reasoning is a method of reasoning that argues from a *general premise* to deduce a more *specific conclusion*. Together with inductive reasoning, they are the two basic forms of valid reasoning. The reasoning builds deductive argument. Deductive reasoning is generally used in argumentative essays and considered the most persuasive and most precise way to support an argument. If you are interested in detective novels, you can find many examples of using the method of deductive reasoning. Deductive arguments may be (1) valid or invalid or (2) sound or unsound. A "valid" deductive argument is one in which the conclusion necessarily follows from the premise. There are three basic stages of deductive reasoning: (1) the premise, (2) the evidence, and (3) the conclusion. We use deductive reasoning quite often in our lives.

The premises are basic facts or factual information used for drawing the conclusions. The premises are the assumptions upon which the argument is built or the reasons for accepting the argument. A premise often begins with words such as assume, since, or because.

The evidence is the information you provide to help you draw the conclusion. It may be some specific information you are analyzing or something you have observed. If we say that the premises are general, then the evidences are some more specific information. We say a deductive argument is sound only if it is valid and the premises are all general facts. First, you need to introduce the factual information as a premise and then bring the evidence that helps you to draw the conclusion.

The conclusion is the final judge of the specific information based on the basic facts and the result you are trying to prove. In many cases, a deduction may have several potential conclusions, but there is only one final conclusion for a particular argument. This conclusion could also be a premise or assumption in any other arguments.

A STUDY IN … DEDUCTIVE REASONING

Taking a well-earned break from their detective work, Sherlock Holmes and Dr. Watson went on a camping trip. After a good meal and a bottle of wine, they settled down for the night and went to sleep.

A few hours later, Holmes awoke and nudged his faithful friend. "Watson, look up and tell me what you see."

"I see millions and millions of stars," Dr. Watson replied.

"What does that tell you?" Holmes asked.

Watson pondered for a moment and then replied, "Astronomically, it tells me that there are millions of galaxies and potentially billions of planets. Astrologically, I observe that Saturn is in Leo. Chronologically, I deduce that the time is approximately a quarter past three. Theologically, I can see that God is all-powerful and that we are small and insignificant. Meteorologically, I see that it is a beautiful night. Why, what does it tell you?"

Holmes was silent for a minute and then replied, "Elementary, Watson. To me, it means someone has stolen our tent."

Science and Hypothesis: Inductive Logic

Inductive reasoning is of great importance because so many of our beliefs about the world cannot be proved by deduction alone. If they are to be proved at all, the reasoning in support of them must include inductive reasoning; it cannot all be deductive (Baker, 1974, p. 222). An *argument* is a set of two or more *statements* and a *claim*. The claim is that one of the statements, the *conclusion*, follows from the other statements, the *premises*. If the claim is that it is impossible for the premises to be true and the conclusion false, the

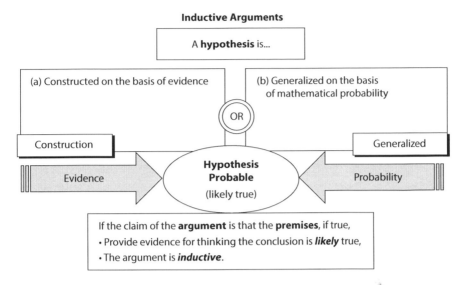

Figure 3.3 Inductive arguments: probability (likely).

argument is *deductive*. If the claim of the argument is that the premises, if true, provide evidence for thinking the conclusion is *likely* true, the argument is *inductive*. Inductive arguments are arguments in which a hypothesis is constructed based on evidence or generalized based on mathematical probability (Carney and Scheer, 1980, p. 345) (see Figure 3.3).

In any inductive argument, the conclusion is not regarded as following by necessity from the premises; rather, the conclusion is regarded as acceptable relative to the premises because the evidence cited in the premises renders the conclusion *probable*. It seems thus that the logic of probability is relevant to any discussion of inductive arguments, and it appears inevitable that any *system* of inductive logic, if such a system is possible, will have to

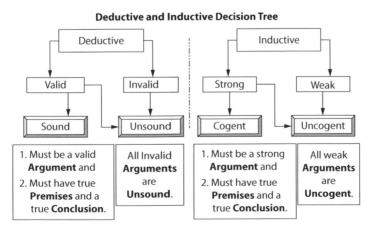

Figure 3.4 Deductive and inductive decision tree.

have as one of its important parts what is called the *calculus of probability*, which consists of rules governing the calculation of probabilities (Carney and Scheer, 1980, p. 436).

An inductive argument is a valid argument if the *degree of probability* claimed for its conclusion is a *reasonable degree of probability* to attribute to the conclusion, relative to the given premises. Yet, even though the reasoning is logically good and starts from true premises, an inductive argument may reach a false conclusion. Therefore, the degree of probability of a conclusion must reach a degree of reasonable probability or *rational credibility* (Baker, 1974, pp. 223–224).

Inductive Analogy

An *analogy* is a parallel or resemblance between two different things. To use words in a *figurative* way is to stretch words beyond the bounds of normal *literal use*. Simile and metaphor are the two most common forms of figurative language. A *simile* is a statement that one thing is *like* something else (similar). A *metaphor* states that one thing *is* something else of a very type or that it does something very different from what it literally does (Baker, 1974, p. 233). An *analogy* is a comparison of two things. There are four basic uses:

1. descriptive
2. definitional
3. argumentative
4. heuristic (an aid in research) (Jason, 1994, pp. 237–238)

Legal Inferences and the Burdens of Proof

Recapping for a moment, *logic* is the study of *arguments* and methods of determining whether arguments are correct (*validated*) or incorrect (*flawed*). In an argument, a claim is made that the *conclusion* follows from the *premises*. "Follows" involves two types of arguments: (1) deductive arguments and (2) inductive arguments. In *inductive* reasoning, there is enough of a link or a "nexus" to support or confirm a conclusion. Here, the claim of the argument is that the conclusion follows from the premises because it is *improbable* that the conclusion is false. The degree of probability will vary. In an inductive (non-deductive) argument, the claim is simply that in all probability the conclusion is true if the premise is true. Inductive reasoning is of great importance because so many of our beliefs about the world cannot be proved by deduction alone. Inductive arguments are arguments in which a hypothesis is either (1) constructed based on evidence or (2) generalized based on mathematical probability.

Even though the reasoning is logically good and starts from true premises, an inductive argument may reach a false conclusion. In any inductive argument, the conclusion is not regarded as following by necessity from the premises, but is accepted because the evidence in the premises renders the conclusion *probable.* An inductive argument is valid if the *degree of probability* for its conclusion is a *reasonable degree of probability* to attribute to the conclusion, relative to the given premises. The degree of probability of a conclusion must reach a degree of reasonable probability or *rational credibility.* In the law, this degree is referred to as the *standard of proof* or the *burden of proof.*

The burden of proof or standard of persuasion required depends upon whether the case is a civil case or a criminal case. In a civil case, the burden of proof required is a *preponderance of evidence* or proof by *clear and convincing evidence.* A preponderance of the evidence simply means that one side has more evidence in its favor than the other, even by the smallest degree. While this is not legally expressed as a percentage, it may be thought of as one side has 51% while the other side has 49%. Clear and convincing evidence establishes the truth of a disputed fact by a high probability. This is also not legally expressed as a percentage, but may be thought of as a "higher percentage" or degree of proof.

Criminal trials employ a higher standard of proof because criminal defendants often face the deprivation of life or liberty if convicted, while civil defendants generally only face an order to pay money damages if the plaintiff prevails. In the movies and on TV, we often hear that a defendant must be found guilty "beyond a shadow of a doubt." This may be true on *Perry Mason,* but is not the actual legal standard. The standard of proof or burden of proof in a criminal case is proof *beyond a reasonable doubt.* So what is "reasonable" doubt?

Federal jury instructions provide that *proof beyond a reasonable doubt* is "proof of such a convincing character that a reasonable person would not hesitate to act upon it in the most important of his own affairs." State judges sometimes describe the standard of reasonable doubt as to the defendant's guilt as, based upon all of the evidence in the case, a jury would be uncomfortable with a guilty verdict or criminal conviction. Remember, "not guilty" does not mean "innocent"; it means there was reasonable doubt as to guilt.

Inference is the process of reasoning from starting points to some conclusion (Jason, 1994, p. 16). It is the act or process of deriving logical conclusions from premises known or assumed to be true. The conclusion drawn is also called an idiomatic. The laws of valid inference are studied in the field of logic. Because *inductive reasoning* relies upon probabilities of the standard of proof, a *preponderance of evidence, clear and convincing evidence,* or *proof beyond a reasonable doubt,* inferences are often relied upon.

Inference is the act or process of deriving logical conclusions from premises known or assumed true. In the law of evidence, an *inference* is a truth or proposition drawn from another that is supposed or admitted to be true or a process of reasoning by which a fact or proposition sought to be established is *deduced* as a logical consequence from other facts, already proved or admitted. It is a "logical and reasonable conclusion of a fact" not presented by direct evidence but which, by process of logic and reason, a trier of fact may conclude exists from the established facts. Inferences are deductions or conclusions that, with reason and common sense, lead a jury to infer facts that have been established by the evidence.

Circumstantial Evidence and Inferences: Inductive Evidence

Evidence may be direct, demonstrative, or circumstantial. Direct evidence tends to prove a fact directly, such as physical evidence of a fact or eyewitness testimony of direct observations of facts. Demonstrative evidence includes any photographs, videos, recordings, charts, diagrams, maps, or other graphics used to establish context among the facts presented in a case. To be admissible, a demonstrative exhibit must represent "fairly and accurately" the real object at the relevant time. Circumstantial evidence is evidence that, when presented with other evidence or facts, tends to establish a reasonable conclusion. This requires some elaboration.

We also see on TV and in movies that "circumstantial evidence" is not admissible. We often hear one of the attorneys exclaim, "Objection, Your Honor! That is circumstantial evidence and, therefore, is inadmissible!" That is *not* correct. While direct evidence supports the truth of an assertion directly, without need for any additional evidence or inference, circumstantial evidence relies on an inference to connect it to a conclusion of fact, for example DNA evidence found at the scene of a crime. It is often used in court and *is* (or at least may be) admissible.

On its own, it is the nature of circumstantial evidence that more than one explanation may still be possible. *Inference* from one piece of *circumstantial evidence* may not guarantee accuracy. Circumstantial evidence usually accumulates into a collection, so that the pieces then become *corroborating evidence*. So we do not rely solely upon premise A (one piece of circumstantial evidence) to prove a case. However, when we add A + B + C + D together, we form a strong inference of "fact" in the absence of a more probable inference. Together, they may more strongly support one particular inference over another. An explanation involving circumstantial evidence becomes more valid as proof of a fact when the alternative explanations have been ruled out.

Testimony can be direct evidence or it can be circumstantial evidence. If a witness claims to have witnessed a crime, this is considered direct evidence.

If a witness claims that he saw the defendant enter a house, heard a gunshot, and saw the defendant leave in a hurry, this is circumstantial evidence. It is the necessity for inference, and not the obviousness of a conclusion, that determines whether evidence is circumstantial.

Critical Thinking
Fact Pattern Analysis

4

Our species needs, and deserves, a citizenry with minds wide awake and a basic understanding of how the world works.

—**Carl Sagan**

Critical Thinking (Reasoning)

Critical thinking is the art of assessing truth claims according to certain general principles or cannons (Dauer, 1989, p. 3). There are two aspects of "truth assessment" in critical thinking: (1) isolating and gathering "facts" that may be accepted without question and (2) reasoning from those accepted "facts" (or likely facts) to determine the truth or falsity of the claims. In this assessment, we look for *maxims* to determine what may be accepted without question and *canons* for identifying what reasons are good reasons (Dauer, 1989, p. 5). Critical thinking is a way of deciding whether a claim is always true, sometimes true, partly true, or false. Critical thinking skills include observation, interpretation, analysis, evaluation, inference, and explanation.

Axioms

The application of logic to mathematics, physics, and other disciplines is often made by means of an axiom system. Logical axioms are usually statements that are taken to be true within the system of logic they define. Certain statements about the subject matter of the discipline are taken as unproved, as fundamental assumptions; these are *axioms*. *Theorems* are generated from these axioms by showing that the theorems validly follow from the axioms, in the same way that a conclusion of an argument validly follows from a set of premises. Historically these have been regarded as "self-evident," but more recently they are considered assumptions that characterize the subject of study. When a discipline is developed by formulating axioms, what validly follows from or is logically implied by the axioms is considered as theorems (Carney and Scheer, 1980, p. 319). An axiom or *postulate*, as it also known, is a premise or starting point of reasoning. An axiom is a premise that is so evident that it is accepted as true without question or controversy.

A theorem is a statement that has been proven by previously established statements, such as other theorems and generally accepted statements, such as axioms. The proof of a mathematical theorem is a logical argument for the theorem statement given in accord with the rules of a deductive system. The proof of a theorem is often interpreted as justification of the truth of the theorem statement.

Fact Pattern Analysis: What and Why Things Go Wrong

The reason we should pursue critical thinking is that we want to get the right "bad guy"—not just pin it on "a bad guy," but solve the case and convict the right "bad guy." Flaws in our thinking process can result in the conviction of the wrong person, which means the right person (the actual perpetrator) goes free. Putting this in perspective, if your grandmother was brutally raped and murdered, would it make you and your family feel better that law enforcement "cleared" the case (statistically), but that the true perpetrator was still a free-roaming predator? Law enforcement and attorneys are required, ethically, morally, and legally, to exercise due diligence in the conduct of criminal investigations and prosecutions or defense.

In 2011, I reviewed and analyzed 43 cases that had been returned to the Detective Bureau by the Prosecutor's Office requesting follow-up information. I wanted to identify what areas were most commonly inadequate in a case. I was able to identify 105 issues, which I was able to categorize in broader terms, as follows:

1. Interview/re-interview (inadequate interviews of witnesses or victims) 25.7%
2. Identify/interview suspect (no identification or interview of suspect) 16.1%
   a. In particular was the question, "Are *suspect* and *perpetrator* the same?" where the same first name but different last names were listed.
3. Report writing (poorly written reports failed to articulate understandable facts) 13.3%
4. Physical evidence and fingerprints (failure to attempt to collect) 10.4%
5. Documents (failure to provide available documents or documentation) 9.5%
6. Photos and videos (failure to provide available photos and videos) 7.6%
7. Identify witnesses (failure to identify witnesses or contact them) 7.6%

8. Property (failure to collect or account for property) 3.8%
9. Photo arrays (none conducted) 2.8%
10. Premises (lack of description or other necessary premises information) 2.8%

I became familiar with the Innocence Project when I was in law school. The Innocence Project is an organization with the objective of exonerating wrongfully convicted persons through the use of DNA evidence. While conducting research for this chapter, I decided to look at the major failures in criminal investigations and prosecutions identified by the Innocence Project to help identify such failures in an objectively constructive critique. Here are six major problems or themes identified by the Innocence Project.

1. Eyewitness misidentification
2. Unreliable or improper forensic science
3. False confessions
4. Government misconduct
5. Informants
6. Bad lawyering

Eyewitness Misidentification

The Innocence Project identified eyewitness misidentification as the single greatest cause of wrongful convictions nationwide, resulting in nearly 75% of convictions overturned through DNA testing. While eyewitness testimony can be persuasive evidence, social science research has found that eyewitness identification is often unreliable. Witness memory, like any other evidence at a crime scene, must be preserved carefully and retrieved methodically to prevent it from being "contaminated." A few anecdotal examples include the following:

- A witness made an identification in a "show-up" procedure from the back of a police car hundreds of feet away from the suspect in a poorly lit parking lot in the middle of the night.
- A witness in a rape case was shown a photo array where only one photo of the person police suspected (the suspect) was marked with an "R."
- Witnesses substantially changed their description of a perpetrator (including key information such as height, weight, and presence of facial hair) after they learned more about a particular suspect.
- Witnesses only made an identification after multiple photo arrays or lineups and then made hesitant identifications (e.g., saying they "thought" the person "might be" the perpetrator), but at trial the jury was told the witnesses did not waver in identifying the suspect. (We will discuss proper photo arrays in Chapter 6.)

Social science researchers identify two primary variables affecting eye-witness identification: *estimator variables* and *system variables*. Estimator variables are those that cannot be controlled by law enforcement, such as the lighting when the crime took place or the distance from which the witness saw the perpetrator. They also include more complex factors, such as race (identifications are often less accurate when witnesses are identifying perpetrators of a different race), the presence of a weapon during a crime, and the degree of stress or trauma a witness experienced while seeing the perpetrator.

System variables are those that law enforcement can and should control, such as the ways that law enforcement agencies retrieve and record witness memory (lineups, photo arrays, and other identification procedures). System variables affecting the accuracy of identifications include the type of lineup used, the selection of "fillers" or members of a lineup or photo array who are not the actual suspect, instructions to witnesses before identification procedures, blind administration (the police officer administering a photo or live lineup is not aware of who the suspect is), administration of lineups or photo arrays (the way they are conducted), and communication with witnesses after they make an identification. (Again, we will discuss proper photo arrays in Chapter 6.)

Case Study: Calvin Willis

In 1982, three young girls were sleeping in a Shreveport, Louisiana, home when a man in cowboy boots came into the house and raped the oldest girl, who was 10 years old. When the police investigated the rape, all three girls remembered the attack differently. One police report said the 10-year-old victim did not see the perpetrator's face. Another report, which was not introduced at trial, said that she had identified Calvin Willis, who lived in the neighborhood. The girl's mother testified at the trial that neighbors had mentioned Willis's name when discussing possible perpetrators. The victim testified that she was shown photos and told to pick the man without a full beard. She testified that she didn't pick anyone, but the police said that she picked Willis. Willis was convicted by a jury and sentenced to life in prison. In 2003, DNA testing proved Willis was innocent and he was released. He had served nearly 22 years in prison for a crime he did not commit.[*]

Unreliable or Improper Forensic Science

Since the late 1980s, DNA analysis has been used to help identify the guilty and exonerate the innocent nationwide. The first DNA exoneration took

---

[*] http://www.innocenceproject.org/understand/Eyewitness-Misidentification.php

place in 1989. Exonerations have taken place in 36 states and since 2000 there have been 243 exonerations. The Innocence Project reports that there have been 301 post-conviction DNA exonerations in the United States. Of the 310 people exonerated through DNA, 18 served time on death row and another 16 were charged with capital crimes, but not sentenced to death. Of these, 193 were African Americans, 93 were Caucasians, 22 were Latinos, and 2 were Asian Americans. The average age of exonerees at the time of their wrongful convictions was 27. The average length of time served by exonerees was 13.6 years. The total number of years served is approximately 4135.*

DNA testing was developed through extensive scientific research at top academic centers. Twenty-nine of the DNA exonerees pled guilty to crimes they did not commit. The true suspects or perpetrators have been identified in 152 of the DNA exoneration cases. In more than 25% of cases in a National Institute of Justice study, suspects were excluded once DNA testing was conducted during the criminal investigation (the study, conducted in 1995, included 10,060 cases where testing was performed by FBI labs).

Meanwhile, forensics techniques that have been properly validated, such as serology blood typing, are sometimes improperly conducted or inaccurately conveyed in trial testimony. In some cases, forensic analysts have allegedly fabricated results or engaged in other misconduct. In many cases, the science, rather than the scientist, has been challenged as inadequate. In other cases, forensic analysts have allegedly made mistakes because of a lack of training, poor support, or inadequate resources.

In still other cases, forensic analysts have been accused of having engaged in misconduct. The Paul Coverdell Forensic Science Improvement Grant Program, a federal grant program, provides funding for state and local crime labs and other forensic facilities on the condition that grant recipients have proper oversight mechanisms in place to handle allegations of serious negligence or misconduct.

Case Study: Alejandro Dominguez

In 1990, Alejandro Dominguez was 16 years old when he was convicted in Illinois of a rape he did not commit. In addition to an eyewitness misidentification, the limited science of a blood type match purportedly led jurors to believe that evidence against Dominguez was stronger than it actually was. One of several errors in the trial was a "reckless omission" by a forensic scientist who testified for the prosecution. The scientist testified that semen was found on the victim's body and that Dominguez's blood type matched the semen sample, indicating that he "could have been" the perpetrator. The scientist did not tell the jury, however, that two-thirds of men in America

* http://www.innocenceproject.org/fix/Eyewitness-Identification.php

would have matched that sample. Dominguez was convicted and sentenced to nine years in prison. He was released after serving four years and initiated DNA testing at his own expense. The tests proved his innocence. His case is reportedly one of many in which limited forensic science or erroneous forensic testimony has led to wrongful convictions.[*]

False Confessions

In approximately 25% of DNA exoneration cases, innocent defendants made incriminating statements, delivered outright confessions, or pled guilty. These cases indicate that confessions are not always a result of "internal knowledge or actual guilt," but are sometimes motivated by "external influences." A variety of factors can contribute to a false confession during a police interrogation. Many cases have included a combination of several of these causes, including:

- coercion
- duress
- diminished capacity
- fear of violence
- the actual infliction of harm
- ignorance of the law
- intoxication
- mental impairment
- the threat of a harsh sentence
- misunderstanding the situation

Some false confessions are explained by the mental state of the confessor. Confessions obtained from juveniles (anyone under the age of 18) are often unreliable because they can be more easily manipulated and are not always fully aware of their situation. Juveniles and adults are both often convinced that that they can "go home" as soon as they admit guilt.[†]

People with mental disabilities also have falsely confessed because they attempt to accommodate and agree with authority figures and many law enforcement interrogators are not given special training on questioning suspects with mental disabilities. An impaired mental state due to mental illness, drugs, or alcohol may also result in false admissions of guilt.[‡]

[*] http://www.innocenceproject.org/understand/Unreliable-Limited-Science.php; http://www.innocenceproject.org/fix/Crime-Lab-Oversight.php
[†] http://www.innocenceproject.org/Content/Eyewitness_Identification_Reform.php
[‡] http://www.innocenceproject.org/Content/Eyewitness_Identification_Reform.php

Mentally capable adults also give false confessions due to a variety of factors like the length of interrogation, exhaustion, or a belief that they can be released after confessing and prove their innocence later.*

The Innocence Project has recommended specific changes in the practice of suspect interrogations in the U.S., including the *mandatory electronic recording of interrogations*, which has been shown to decrease the number of false confessions and increase the reliability of confessions as evidence. Electronic recording of interrogations assists law enforcement by:

- Preventing disputes about how an officer conducted himself or treated a suspect;
- Creating a record of statements made by the suspect, making it difficult for a defendant to change an account of events originally provided to law enforcement;
- Permitting officers to concentrate on the interview, rather than being distracted by copious note-taking during the course of the interrogation;
- Capturing subtle details that may be lost if unrecorded, which helps law enforcement better investigate the crime; and
- Enhancing public confidence in law enforcement, while reducing the number of citizen complaints against the police.†

Case Study: Eddie Joe Lloyd

Eddie Lloyd, who was mentally ill, was convicted of the 1984 murder of a 16-year-old girl in Detroit after he wrote to police with suggestions on how to solve various recent crimes. During several interviews, police fed details of the crime to Lloyd and allegedly convinced him that by confessing he was helping them "smoke out" the real killer. Lloyd eventually signed a confession and gave a tape-recorded statement. The jury deliberated less than an hour before convicting him and the judge said at sentencing that execution, which had been outlawed in Michigan, would have been the "only justifiable sentence" if it were available.‡

In 2002, DNA testing proved that Lloyd was innocent and he was exonerated. In 2006, as mandated in a settlement with Lloyd's family, Detroit Police officials said they would start videotaping all interrogations in crimes that could carry a sentence of life.§

---

* http://www.innocenceproject.org/Content/Eyewitness_Identification_Reform.php
† http://www.innocenceproject.org/Content/False_Confessions_Recording_Of_Custodial
  _Interrogations.php
‡ http://www.innocenceproject.org/understand/False-Confessions.php
§ http://www.innocenceproject.org/fix/False-Confessions.php

Government Misconduct

Some wrongful convictions are a result of honest mistakes. However, in too many cases, the very people who are responsible for ensuring truth and justice—law enforcement officials and prosecutors—lose sight of their duty and focus solely on obtaining convictions. The cases of wrongful convictions uncovered by DNA testing are often indicative of evidence of negligence, fraud, or misconduct by prosecutors or police departments. While most law enforcement officers and prosecutors are honest and trustworthy, the criminal justice system is still made up of humans and the possibility for negligence, misconduct, and corruption exists. If only one officer of every thousand were dishonest, wrongful convictions would continue to occur.

DNA exonerations have exposed official misconduct at every level and stage of a criminal investigation. Misconduct involving law enforcement officials includes:

- Employing suggestion when conducting identification procedures
- Coercing false confessions
- Lying or intentionally misleading jurors about their observations
- Failing to turn over exculpatory evidence to prosecutors
- Providing incentives to secure unreliable evidence from informants

Misconduct involving prosecutors includes:

- Withholding exculpatory evidence from the defense
- Deliberately mishandling, mistreating, or destroying evidence
- Allowing witnesses they know or should know are not truthful to testify
- Pressuring defense witnesses not to testify
- Relying on fraudulent forensic experts
- Making misleading arguments that overstate the probative value of testimony

Case Study: Bruce Godschalk

In some cases, officials can commit fraud long after a person is convicted. Bruce Godschalk was convicted of two rapes in Pennsylvania in 1987. The state's evidence at trial included a false confession Godschalk allegedly gave to police, a misidentification by a victim, and testimony from a jailhouse snitch. When the Innocence Project tried to seek DNA testing on Godschalk's behalf in 2001, a state motion claimed that prosecutors had sent all relevant evidence to a lab without notifying the defendant or the Innocence Project. It falsely claimed that all evidence had been consumed in testing and all tests were inconclusive. A carpet sample with a semen stain was not given to the lab during what the Innocence Project characterized as "secret testing." When this piece of carpet surfaced, testing proved that another man had committed the crime for which Godschalk had been wrongly convicted.*

Informants

In more than 15% of wrongful conviction cases overturned through DNA testing, an informant testified against the defendant. Other sources assert that informants contributed to wrongful convictions in 18% of cases. Often, statements from people with motives to testify are instrumental in convicting innocent persons. This does not mean that all informant testimony is false or improperly motivated or even that improperly motivated testimony is false. However, it should cause us to be aware of informant motives and the prudence of corroborating their testimony.[†]

Case Study: Larry Peterson

Larry Peterson was wrongly convicted in 1989 of murder and sexual assault and sentenced to life in prison. Four people—three of Peterson's co-workers and a jailhouse informant—helped the state convict Peterson with allegedly false testimony. During an investigation of the crime, police interviewed some of Peterson's co-workers several times. After lengthy interrogations, alleged threats of prosecution, and other questionable police tactics, the three men said Peterson had confessed to them during a ride to work. Records have since shown that Peterson did not work on the day these men said the confession occurred. A jailhouse informant with charges pending in three counties also testified that Peterson had admitted guilt to him while in the county jail. DNA finally proved Peterson's innocence in 2005 and he was exonerated in 2006.[‡]

Bad Lawyering

Circumstances and conditions of the justice system often do not favor poor defendants. This is particularly evident when defendants are represented by ineffective, incompetent, or unprepared defense attorneys. The failure of overworked lawyers to investigate, call witnesses, or prepare for trial has led to the conviction of innocent people. When a defense lawyer does not do his or her job, the defendant and justice suffer.

A review of convictions overturned by DNA testing reveals several cases of sleeping, drunk, incompetent, and overburdened defense attorneys, at both the trial level and on appeal. Innocent defendants are convicted or plead

---

* http://www.innocenceproject.org/understand/Government-Misconduct.php
† http://www.innocenceproject.org/Content/DNA_Exonerations_Nationwide.php#
‡ http://www.innocenceproject.org/understand/Snitches-Informants.php

guilty due to less than adequate defense representation. In the some cases, lawyers have:

- slept in the courtroom during trial
- failed to investigate alibis
- failed to call or consult experts on forensic issues
- failed to show up for hearings
- been disbarred shortly after finishing a death penalty case

Case Study: Jimmy Ray Bromgard

Jimmy Ray Bromgard was arrested when he was 18 and spent 15 years in prison in Montana for the brutal rape of an 8-year-old girl, a crime post-conviction DNA testing proved he did not commit. Bromgard's trial attorney performed no investigation, filed no pre-trial motions, gave no opening statement, did not prepare for closing arguments, failed to file an appeal, and provided no expert to refute the allegedly "fraudulent testimony" of the state's hair microscopy expert. Other than the forensic testimony and the tentative identification, there was no evidence against Bromgard.[*]

From Critical Thinking to Logical Reasoning

High-quality reasoning is called *logical reasoning* or *critical thinking*. Logical reasoning is a skill that can be learned and improved. Everyone is capable of reasoning well and everyone is capable of improvement. The opposite of logical reasoning is uncritical thinking, such as "fuzzy" thinking, believing what somebody says simply because he or she says so, or narrowly thinking about a problem without considering the most relevant information. This chapter on critical thinking helps us to look at facts and errors to critically improve the quality of our thinking. We used "fact pattern analysis" here as a conduit to using critical thinking in criminal investigations. In the next chapter, we will explore how logical reasoning can be used to make legal inferences and determine what a "legal" inference is.

Both "critical thinking" and "logical reasoning" (which some would opine are synonymous) help us develop five skills: (1) spotting issues and arguments, (2) detecting inconsistency and lack of clarity in a group of sentences, (3) detecting and avoiding fallacies (reasoning errors), (4) generating and improving arguments and explanations, and (5) writing logically. One principle common to critical thinking and logical reasoning is to ask for reasons before accepting a conclusion, unless you already have good enough

[*] http://www.innocenceproject.org/understand/Bad-Lawyering.php

reasons. If you expect people to accept your own conclusion, then it is your responsibility to give them reasons they can appreciate.

Critical thinking is skeptical without being cynical. Critical thinking can be evaluative without being judgmental and forceful without being opinionated. Before we use this segue, let's look at several suggested, though not formal, suggestions about the principles of logical reasoning:

1. Ask for reasons before accepting a conclusion.
2. Give an argument to support your conclusion.
3. Tailor reasons to your audience.
4. Design your reasons to imply the conclusion.
5. Remember that firmer conclusions require better reasons.
6. Recognize the value of having as much relevant information as possible.
7. Check to see whether explanations fit all the relevant facts.
8. Consider the possible courses of action and weigh the pros and cons.
9. Look at and evaluate the consequences of these various courses of action.
10. Consider the probabilities that those various consequences will actually occur.
11. Use your background knowledge and common sense in drawing conclusions.
12. Defer to the expert.
13. Remember that extraordinary statements require extraordinarily good evidence.
14. Do not draw a conclusion until you have enough evidence.
15. Be consistent in your reasoning and look for inconsistency in the reasoning of yourself and others.
16. You can make opposing explanations less believable by showing that there are alternative explanations that have not been ruled out.

Keep these "principles" or "suggestions" in mind. They can be used not only in detecting crime, but also in detecting truth and deception. Sometimes deception takes the form of outright lying; at other times, it is practiced by telling only part of the truth; and sometimes the whole truth is presented but the problem is in how it is presented. The logical "reasoner's" best defense against the tactic of selective presentation of information is to become well informed. Well-informed persons know what is trivial and what is not and know what is likely to be left out or covered up. All other things being equal, the more you know, the less apt you are to be convinced by bad reasoning.

We will discuss deception and the detection of deception further in other chapters. Now, let's move from "critical thinking" to "logical reasoning" and inferences.

Logical Reasoning
Legal Inferences

5

Reasoning

To defend against our daily exposure to sales pitches, propaganda, political spin, and con games, we should expect and seek good reasons before making decisions or adopting beliefs. Determining a reason is often problem enough, but then we must determine whether an offered reason is good and sufficient reason to make decisions or adopt beliefs. In the previous chapter, we made note of deceptive techniques that rely on lying, exaggerating, and selectively withholding information. We also alluded to a few other techniques of deception: exaggeration, telling only half the truth, and using loaded language. We considered how we could be manipulated even when all the relevant information is available to us; the problem in this case is in how that information is presented. Here we will discuss how we can use "reason" (logical reasoning) to make inferences and use these inferences to make decisions and adopt new beliefs. We will also examine how fallacies are errors in reasoning that can be used to deceive or distort logical inferences and conclusions.

Reason is the capacity for consciously making sense of things, applying logic, establishing and verifying facts, and changing or justifying practices, institutions, and beliefs based on new or existing information. Reason or *"reasoning"* is associated with thinking, cognition, and intellect.

The terms "logic" or "logical" are sometimes used synonymously with the term "reason" or with the concept of being "rational." Sometimes logic is defined incorrectly as a form of reason. However, reason and logic can be thought of as distinct and independent, though related, concepts, although logic is one important aspect of reason. Logic is done inside a system while reason is done outside the system. Reason is a type of thought, while logic involves the attempt to describe rules or processes by which reasoning operates. Logical reasoning is sometimes described as the process of using a rational, systematic series of steps based upon sound procedures and given statements to arrive at a conclusion.

Strategies in *reasoning* involve clearly expressed mental processes with the purpose of achieving a specific objective. Reasoning strategies are consciously controlled and vary based upon instructions, preferences, or experience of individuals. The three commonly associated paradigms—(1) transitive inference reasoning, (2) syllogistic reasoning, and (3) propositional reason-ing—are theories that have no apparent strategic component. Yet, Dr. Walter Schaeken and his fellow professors say, "People can be motivated to make more or less effort at *deduction* by instructions and other factors" (emphasis added) (Schaeken et al., 2000, p. 18).

Dr. Schaeken and his associates may help clarify the relationship between reasoning and deductive and inductive thinking. They write, "The natural mode of hypothetical is *inductive*. That is, we tend to consider just open state of affairs . . . at a time . . . " They go on to say, "This leads to generally effective, *rational*, decision making in most situations . . . To avoid biases and achieve *deductive* accuracy—in short, to be *rational*—on such problems requires explicit, strategic thinking—a conscious effort at *deduction*" (emphasis added) (Schaeken et al., 2000, p. 19).

A "reasoning strategy" is a set of cognitive processes (operations that affect mental contents or the process of thinking) that are used for solving *deductive reasoning* tasks, but which have insufficient evidence to assert that such processes themselves constitute the entirety or even part of the "funda-mental reasoning mechanism" (Schaeken et al., 2000, p. 24).

One of the most remarkable characteristics of the human mind is its capacity to draw valid *inferences* from verbally expressed statements. This *deductive* component of human thought is illustrated by the competent behavior demonstrated by those who apply the analysis of *formal reason-ing* as the science of logic (Schaeken et al., 2000, p. 49). Let us consider next, and more specifically, the use of "inferences" in the legal context or "legal inferences."

Convergent and Divergent Thinking

Convergent thinking reasons from very broad to very detailed; it identifies logical connectors and narrows the topic. *Divergent thinking* reasons from very detailed to very broad; it starts with facts and creates an explanation. Reasoning statements are often created by drawing *inferences* from the facts. Good reasoning statements explain cause and effect (why), bad reasoning statements simply repeat unsupported opinions. It is important to state where a conclusion comes from (using "marker words" such as "because," "it cannot be . . . ," etc.). Convergent and divergent thinking help draw inferences from fact patterns.

Permissible inferences are used to point at one or more specific facts in the fact pattern and explain why that fact (or facts) creates a belief (i.e., makes one think something or "infer" it). This is accomplished by looking at clues in the facts and determining what those facts prove.

Impermissible inferences are those where you cannot point to specific facts that caused you to think or believe something. Instead, you have made something up that is not justified by the fact pattern. Legal inferences are often drawn from deductive reasoning, inductive reasoning, and reasoning by analogy.

Legal Inferences

As stated earlier, an inference is the process of reasoning from starting points to some final conclusion (Jason, 1994, p. 16). It is the act or process of deriving logical conclusions from premises known or assumed to be true. Because *inductive reasoning* relies upon probabilities of the standard of proof, either a *preponderance of evidence, clear and convincing evidence*, or *proof beyond a reasonable doubt*, inferences are often relied upon. In the law of evidence, an *inference* is a truth or proposition drawn from another that is supposed or admitted to be true or a process of reasoning by which a fact or proposition sought to be established is *deduced* as a logical consequence from other facts, already proved or admitted. It is a "logical and reasonable conclusion of a fact" not presented by direct evidence but which, by process of logic and reason, a trier of fact may conclude exists from the established facts.

Therefore, the next thing to do is determine how to make these "legal inferences" from the fact patterns with which we are presented. A "fact pattern" is what law students learn and lawyers use to apply rules to the facts at hand. In other words, the rule states the law and the attorney must try to apply the law to the facts of a new case. Lawyers do this by determining how their case is the same or how it is different from the one being cited.

For example, in *Miranda v. Arizona*, the U.S. Supreme Court decided (held) that when a suspect is in custody and subjected to interrogation, he or she must be advised of his or her Constitutional rights (at least those outlined in the *Miranda* case). In a new case, a lawyer may analyze a fact pattern in which a client was stopped on the street, questioned by the police, and released with no implied arrest indicated. Here the analysis would be different. In the *Miranda* case, two prongs were established: (1) custody and (2) interrogation. In the new fact pattern, there was questioning (the second prong), but no custody (the first prong). Therefore, the rule in the *Miranda* case does not apply to the new fact pattern. This is not an example of an "inference," but is an example of "fact pattern" analysis.

Law students brief cases to learn the legal principles behind them by preparing written "briefs" which include some variation of the IRAC acronym: Issue, Rule, Analysis, and Conclusion. This is also often stated as Facts, Issue, Rule (law), Reasoning (analysis), and Holding (Conclusion). Each variation of this analysis results in the same thing: analysis of fact patterns to determine what is the same and what is different about cases in order to decide if a rule (law) applies in a new fact pattern.

Inferences are deductions or conclusions that, with reason and common sense, lead a jury to infer facts that have been established by the evidence. Arguments are stated as a means to drawing conclusions, so it is important to understand exactly what deductive and inductive arguments are.

Arguments

An *argument* consists of a set of statements, one of which is the *conclusion* and the remainders are *premises*. The main objective of logic is to evaluate arguments. That is, to figure out which are good (and why) and which are bad (and why) (Jason, 1994, pp. 69–70). Since logic is the study of the evidential relationships between premises and conclusions of arguments and since there are exactly two such relations (validity and strength), then we have two branches of logic: *deductive logic* and *inductive logic*.

Deductive reasoning is one type of reasoning for which systematic rules have been developed (Dauer, 1989, p. 90). Deductive logic is the study (including analysis and assessment) of arguments from the point of view of validity. The deductive logician is concerned with figuring out what validity is and how to detect it. An argument is *deductively valid* if it is impossible for the premises to be true and the conclusion false (Jason, 1994, p. 71).

The theory of deductive reasoning has the following characteristics:

1. It is goal-directed reasoning that begins with a definite starting point known as a set of *premises.*
2. *Deductive inferences* have *conclusions* that necessarily "follow" from the premises (based upon the principles of logic).
3. Consequently, a *valid deduction* yields a *conclusion* that must be "true" given that the *premises* are "true."

There are many other forms of reasoning as well, such as *inductive reasoning* (induction), *reasoning by analogy, calculation, creation*, and so forth (Schaeken et al., 2000, p. 301).

Inductive logic is the study (again including analysis and assessment) of arguments from the point of view of inductive strength. The inductive logician is concerned with the notion of probability, what it is, and how to measure it. An argument is *inductively strong* if it is not impossible, but unlikely, that the conclusion would be false given that the premises are true (Jason, 1994, p. 71).

Argument Analysis or Diagrams: Three Steps

The first step of an argument analysis or argument diagram is to determine (1) which statements are premises and (2) which statement is the conclusion. The second step is to determine whether the argument claim is justified. In a *deductive* argument, one asks if it is true that if the premises are supposed true, then it is impossible that the conclusion is false. In an *inductive* argument, one asks if it is true that if the premises are supposed true, then it is improbable that the conclusion is false. The third step is to determine whether the premises are (in fact) true. If the premises are true and the argument is correct, then the argument is sound and there are rational grounds for affirming the conclusion. However, it is imperative at this step to remember that to determine the correctness of an argument it is essential first to state the argument clearly (Carney and Scheer, 1980, p. 18) (see Figure 5.1).

Types of Fallacies: Faulty Arguments

A *fallacy* is an argument that is incorrect, but may appear, in some contexts, to be a correct statement. Illogical reasoning occurs when people construct arguments that are fallacious without realizing it. A *formal fallacy* is an invalid deductive argument that resembles a valid deductive pattern that persons can be misled into perceiving as valid. An *informal fallacy* is an incorrect argument, but its incorrectness is not a function of having an invalid form; rather it is a consequence of the ambiguity of language or inattention to the subject matter of the argument (Carney and Scheer, 1980, pp. 29–30) (see Figure 5.2).

Argument Analysis or Diagrams

Step 1: Determine *(Correctness of an argument = state the argument clearly.)*   (a) Which **statements** are **premises** and   (b) Which **statements** is the **conclusion**.
Step 2: Determine whether the argument claim is justified; ASK is it true that, if the premises are supported true...   • **Deductive** argument - then it is **impossible** that the conclusion is false.   • **Inductive** argument - then it is **improbable** that the conclusion is false.
Step 3: Determine whether the **premises** are (in fact) **true**.   • If true and the argument is correct,   • the argument is sound and   • there are rational grounds for affirming the conclusion.

Figure 5.1 Argument analysis or diagrams.

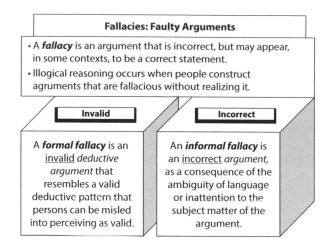

Fallacies: Faulty Arguments

• A **fallacy** is an argument that is incorrect, but may appear, in some contexts, to be a correct statement.

• Illogical reasoning occurs when people construct agruments that are fallacious without realizing it.

Invalid

A **formal fallacy** is an invalid *deductive argument* that resembles a valid deductive pattern that persons can be misled into perceiving as valid.

Incorrect

An **informal fallacy** is an incorrect *argument*, as a consequence of the ambiguity of language or inattention to the subject matter of the argument.

Figure 5.2 Fallacies: faulty arguments.

Fallacies of ambiguity are generally deductive arguments that appear to be valid, but are not, due to a shift in meaning of a word, phrase, or sentence. *Material fallacies*, on the other hand, are incorrect for reasons other than ambiguity of language. There are two types of material fallacies: (1) *fallacies of relevance* (arguments that have premises that are irrelevant to the conclusion) and (2) *fallacies of insufficient evidence* (incorrect inductive arguments). That is, the premises contain information that may appear relevant but which, in fact, is not relevant in establishing that the conclusion is true (Carney and Scheer, 1980, p. 30) (see Figure 5.3). There are two additional

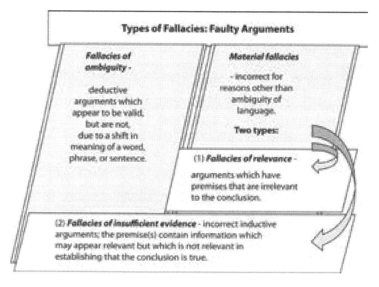

Types of Fallacies: Faulty Arguments

Fallacies of ambiguity -

deductive arguments which appear to be valid, but are not, due to a shift in meaning of a word, phrase, or sentence.

Material fallacies

- incorrect for reasons other than ambiguity of language.

Two types:

(1) **Fallacies of relevance** - arguments which have premises that are irrelevant to the conclusion.

(2) **Fallacies of insufficient evidence** - incorrect inductive arguments; the premise(s) contain information which may appear relevant but which is not relevant in establishing that the conclusion is true.

Figure 5.3 Types of fallacies: faulty arguments.

Material Fallacies	
Material Fallacies of Relevance	**Material Fallacies of Insufficient Evidence**
1. Ad Hominem Fallacy	1. False-Cause Fallacy
2. Tu Quoque Fallacy	2. Fallacy of Special pleading
3. Ad Populum Fallacy	3. Fallacies of Ambiguity
4. Ad Verecundiam Fallacy	4. Fallacy of Equivocation
5. Ad Ignorantium Fallacy	5. Fallacy of Syntactical Ambiguity
6. Petitio Principii Fallacy	6. Division and Composition Fallacies
7. Fallacy of Inconsistency	7. Fallacy of Accent
8. Complex Questions	**Two Additional Fallacies**
9. Genetic Fallacy	1. Fallacy of Weak Analogy
10. Straw Man Fallacy	2. Fallacy of False Dilemma

Figure 5.4 Material fallacies.

fallacies, which do not fall into either of these categories. They are listed and explained next (see Figure 5.4).

Material Fallacies of Relevance

1. The Ad Hominem Fallacy
2. The Tu Quoque Fallacy
3. The Ad Populum Fallacy
4. The Ad Verecundiam Fallacy
5. The Ad Ignorantium Fallacy
6. The Petitio Principii Fallacy
7. The Fallacy of Inconsistency
8. Complex Questions
9. Genetic Fallacy
10. The Straw Man Fallacy

Material Fallacies of Insufficient Evidence

1. False-Cause Fallacy
2. The Fallacy of Special Pleading
3. The Fallacies of Ambiguity
4. The Fallacy of Equivocation
5. The Fallacy of Syntactical Ambiguity
6. The Division and Composition Fallacies
7. The Fallacy of Accent

Two Additional Fallacies

1. The Fallacy of Weak Analogy
2. The Fallacy of False Dilemma

Now that we have named, categorized, and listed the two types of material fallacies (material fallacies of relevance and material fallacies of insufficient evidence), and the two additional fallacies (weak analogy and false dilemma), we can identify and briefly explain each of these.

Material Fallacies of Relevance

The *ad hominem fallacy* is an argument directed at the person, rather than his or her views. Rather than presenting relevant reasons against a person's views, someone may try to cause a rejection of the person's views by rejecting the person through remarks directed at the person holding the view. Therefore, *ad hominem* fallacies are known as *abusive ad hominems* and *circumstantial ad hominems* (Carney and Scheer, 1980, p. 31).

The *tu quoque fallacy* is a fallacy committed when one tries to respond to a charge made by an opponent by making the same or similar charge against him or her (Carney and Scheer, 1980, p. 35).

The *ad populum fallacy* is an argument in which one bypasses relevant reasons and appeals to popular opinion, sentiment, pity, fear, or emotions to gain acceptance or rejection of a conclusion (Carney and Scheer, 1980, p. 36).

The *ad verecundiam fallacy* is an attempt to support a conclusion by citing another who asserts the same conclusion. This may or may not be a reliable authority to cite (Carney and Scheer, 1980, p. 41).

The *ad ignorantium fallacy* is an argument that asserts that because there is no proof that A is false, A is true or because there is no proof that B is true, B is false (Carney and Scheer, 1980, p. 43).

The *petitio principii fallacy* involves circular arguments. For example, A is true, therefore A is true, or A is true because B is true; B is true because C is true and C is true because A is true. In both of these examples, the conclusion merely repeats the premise or reason (Carney and Scheer, 1980, p. 45).

The *fallacy of inconsistency* is an argument of contradictory premises. It is a formally valid argument, but one that is faulty because it is necessarily unsound and necessarily an argument where the premises do not provide relevant reasons for affirming the conclusion (Carney and Scheer, 1980, p. 47).

Complex questions presuppose "facts" or make assumptions (that may not be true) (Carney and Scheer, 1980, p. 50).

Genetic fallacy occurs when the manner in which one acquires a view or source of a view is criticized with the purpose of casting doubt on the view itself (Carney and Scheer, 1980, pp. 50–51).

The *straw man fallacy* is committed when a claim is misinterpreted (deliberately or accidentally) in an attempt to refute the misinterpreted claim. The argument is presented as a refutation of the original claim (Carney and Scheer, 1980, p. 52).

Material Fallacies of Insufficient Evidence

A fallacy in an inductive argument is an error of thinking that true premises (which in fact lend little or no support to a conclusion) lend it significant support (Carney and Scheer, 1980, p. 59).

False-cause fallacy occurs when in an argument one mistakes what is not the cause of a given effect for its real cause (Carney and Scheer, 1980, p. 59).

The *fallacy of special pleading* involves a failure to mention evidence that is unfavorable to a claim where all evidence is presumably mentioned. To avoid such fallacious arguing, one should consider both sides of the issue and try to demonstrate that a stronger case can be made for the side one favors. (Carney and Scheer, 1980, p. 61) The legal ramifications of failing to reveal known evidence that is unfavorable can be severe. The Brady Rule, which was created by the U.S. Supreme Court in *Brady v. Maryland*, 373 U.S. 83 (1963), held that "the suppression by the prosecution of evidence favorable to an accused . . . violates due process where the evidence is material either to guilt or to punishment, irrespective of the good faith or bad faith of the prosecution."

The *fallacies of ambiguity* present "reasons" that are irrelevant to the truth or falsity of the conclusion (Carney and Scheer, 1980, p. 69).

The *fallacy of equivocation* is the use of a word or words with different meanings than is appropriate in the present context. When a word or expression with two different meanings is used (incorrectly) and the correctness of the argument depends upon the word or expression, maintaining the meaning throughout the argument results in a fallacy of equivocation (Carney and Scheer, 1980, p. 69).

The *fallacy of syntactical ambiguity* occurs where a sentence can have different meanings (1) because of its syntactical structure or (2) because it has a word or expression that can be understood in at least two ways (Carney and Scheer, 1980, p. 72).

The division and composition fallacies are similarly related. The *fallacy of division* occurs when one argues that something, which is true only of the whole, is true of its parts taken separately. The *fallacy of composition* occurs when one argues that what is true only of the parts of some whole is also true of the whole (Carney and Scheer, 1980, p. 74).

The *fallacy of accent* occurs when one changes the meaning of a sentence by accenting some word or phrase (Carney and Scheer, 1980, p. 75).

Two Additional Fallacies

The *fallacy of weak analogy* is a material fallacy of insufficient evidence. In an *argument by analogy*, one argues that because two things are similar in some respects they are similar in other respects (Carney and Scheer, 1980, pp. 94–95).

The *fallacy of false dilemma* occurs when a dilemma is unrealistic because (1) the disjunctive premise is false or (2) one or both of the conditional premises are false (Carney and Scheer, 1980, pp. 103–104).

Recapitulation, Summary, and Conclusion

Traditionally, the field of reasoning strategies (thinking strategies) in problem-solving and decision-making has focused on the analysis of a "single person" making a decision, where the "normatively right" solution can be determined without taking into account the behavior of others (individuals or groups). In such cases, specifically designed tasks are presented to participants and strategies of thinking are singled out through the sequence of answers of participants. The experimental situations relate to scenarios of "everyday life" problems. However, such strategies and scenarios do not take into account the actions of others interacting with us in such problems (Schaeken et al., 2000, p. 287).

In such "interactive" problems, one analytical tool used for modeling in problem-solving and decision-making is "game theory." The game theory of "interaction decision making" (1) makes the behavioral assumption that individuals are "rational" and have well defined preferences, which they maximize, and (2) specifies the "normative thinking procedures" individuals should follow to find the "solution" of the game (Schaeken et al., 2000, p. 287).

To reach *legal inferences*, deductions, or conclusions that, with reason and common sense, lead a jury to infer facts that have been established by the evidence, we employ the act or process of deriving logical conclusions from premises known or assumed to be true. Because illogical reasoning occurs when people construct arguments that are fallacious, we must guard against fallacies in our reasoning. A *fallacy* is an argument that is incorrect, but may appear, in some contexts, to be a correct statement. We do this by recognizing the two types of fallacies.

Fallacies of ambiguity are arguments that appear to be valid, but are not, due to a shift in meaning of a word, phrase, or sentence. *Material fallacies* are either (1) *fallacies of relevance* (ten arguments which have premises that are irrelevant to the conclusion) or (2) *fallacies of insufficient evidence* (seven incorrect inductive arguments with premises that contain information that may appear relevant but is not relevant in establishing that the conclusion is true). There are two types of material fallacies: (1) material fallacies of relevance and (2) material fallacies of insufficient evidence. There are two "additional" fallacies worth mentioning: (1) the fallacy of weak analogy and (2) the fallacy of false dilemma.

We use reasoning to make valid inferences upon which to base our conclusions. We do this by "using" *argument analysis* or *argument diagrams*. There are three steps to this process: (1) determine (a) which statements are premises and (b) which statement is the conclusion; (2) determine whether the argument claim is justified; and (3) determine whether the premises are, in fact, true. If the premises are true and the argument is correct, then the argument is sound and there are rational grounds for affirming the conclusion. Remember, it is essential to state the argument clearly.

Back to Basics Criminal Investigation Skills

6

Why the "Basics" Are Important or Why *Not* to Skip This Chapter

Why is it important to discuss "basics" in a text on "advanced" techniques? My experience has been that many detectives and investigators never master the basics for one reason or another. One reason is that they are never properly trained. Many agencies do not select detectives or investigators based upon merit, but on seniority, that is, if they put in enough time on the job, they are selected. Most detectives chosen in this manner argue that they are selected because of their experience. However, often a claim of 20 years of experience is nothing more than one year of experience 20 times.

Another reason for a lack of training in basic investigative skills is that law enforcement managers and administrators often lack any understanding of the investigative process themselves. They assume that detectives will learn or "figure out" how to do their jobs because they are filling a "detective" position. They often assume that "on-the-job" training (OJT) is sufficient. However, when inexperienced investigators are trained by other investigators who also lack basic skills, a generational problem develops within the institution as a whole. This results in supervisors and managers who lack the skills necessary to manage the investigative function.

If you are reading this text, you probably possess a level of professionalism that extends beyond this problematic situation. For you, let's say it is reason enough to go "back to basics" because we all need to refresh our basic skills from time to time. While we are on the subject, allow me to opine that I believe it is essential for all police detectives to maintain their skills as basic police officers. However, for the purposes of our topic at hand, we are concerned with the fundamental skills of criminal investigations.

Thorough and Methodical: Good, Old-Fashioned Detective Work

First, "good, old-fashioned detective work" is based upon being thorough in our methodology and methodical in our techniques. In other words, use your experience and common sense to pay attention to details. Observe what is out of place. Look for what stands out or what doesn't fit the puzzle. Use checklists and protocols to do things the same way each time. This ensures that you do not miss something by skipping steps. Your experience tells you what is out of place and what does not fit. Thoroughness ensures that you pay attention to minute details that lesser experienced investigators might miss. Being methodical involves using tried and tested methods (based upon the experience, mistakes, and successes of others who have developed training, procedures, checklists, and protocols) to ensure that even the smallest details are not neglected because things are done the same way every time.

The U.S. Army Criminal Investigations Command (USACIDC) always had an unofficial policy—"Everything we do is practice for the homicides." In other words, there were no "big" and no "small" investigations. Everything was investigated with the same meticulous attention to detail. It was not considered a "waste of time," but preparation for the "big" ones (homicides). The lesson to be learned from this is do not get in a hurry because the task does not seem to be important; do everything well every time you do it.

Sources of Information

Sources of information are the records, databases, and documentary sources of information that provide pieces for the puzzle. For example, if you have a vehicle description, but no plate or VIN information, and the vehicle parks at a certain address, a check of county treasurer records or the county recorder's office can reveal who owns and pays taxes on that address. This can give a name, which may in turn provide information to check for the ownership of the vehicle (and others) through the state bureau of motor vehicles. It is a piece to the puzzle. This is only one example of thousands. Get to know the plethora of ever-changing and evolving sources of information. A few basic, fundamental, essential sources are included here.

Law Enforcement Sources

Law enforcement sources include police reports, accident reports, tow and inventory reports, arrest records, traffic tickets, intelligence files, field interview cards, pawnshop records, jail records, criminal history records, fingerprint and AFIS files, DNA and CODIS databases, firearms databases, etc.

Government Records

City, township, county, state, and federal records are full of information. Universities, school districts, special fire districts, and other special taxing or governmental entities are all sources of information.

City agencies have records on licenses (business, vendor, transient merchant, dog, building, and other licenses and permits), utility records, property records, etc. Townships often have records on public assistance. Become familiar with city agencies and services in your area of operation.

Counties keep birth, death, and marriage licenses, property and tax records, lien holder and deed records on properties, public health and social services records, probation and court records, voter registration and election board records, etc. Become familiar with county and township agencies and services in your area of operation.

States keep records on vital statistics, such as birth, death, and marriage records. Most regulated businesses and professions obtain licenses from state licensing agencies, insurance and financial instructions departments, etc., and the secretary of state in each state usually maintains records on corporations organized in their state. Become familiar with state agencies and services in your area of operation.

The federal government keeps volumes of records, including (but by no means limited to) those maintained by the IRS, SEC, FTC, FBI, CIA, NSA, DIA, and dozens of other "alphabet" agencies. The DoD and VA also keep military records, as does the National Archives. Become familiar with federal government agencies and services. There are several agencies within each of the several cabinet departments. Know them and understand what they do and the information that they collect.

Business Records

Business records include data and files from banks and credit unions, insurance agencies and companies, real estate brokers, securities brokers (stocks, bonds, and commodities), etc. Businesses also keep records on sales and purchases, clients and customers, employees and personnel records, taxes, etc. Many have video of events that occur in or around their premises.

Utility companies have records on customers and premises that use the services of the telephone company, cellular phones, cable and satellite television, the Internet (including routers or Wi-Fi), water, sewer, trash collection, etc. (Do not forget the value of trash when dumpster diving, which is legal for "abandoned" property or trash; seek local legal counsel on this issue.)

Confidential Informants

People are sources of information too. In the intelligence community, we call this "human intelligence" (HUMINT). In law enforcement, they are victims, witnesses, informants, etc. Confidential informants are a unique resource and challenge, warranting extra attention and requiring that you "handle with care." An *informant* is anyone who provides information of an investigative nature to law enforcement (e.g., citizens, criminals, prisoners, and other sources).

Confidential informants don't just happen. They must be sought out, recruited, and cultivated. Many detectives think they are only used for drug investigations. This is an unfortunate misconception, usually a result of a lack of training and supervision. On rare occasions, informants will come to you. You must determine their credibility, reliability, and motives. Most confidential informants are paid. They are exploited for the information they possess and observations they have made, as spies who can and will provide otherwise unavailable intelligence, and to make buys of contraband or introductions of undercover investigators to do so.

Informants are developed through other law enforcement personnel (referrals by patrol, vice and narcotics, other detectives, other agencies, etc.), arrested persons, supervisor leads, personal contacts, etc. Select informants based upon their reliability and verify their information.

The motive of a confidential informant is also important to ascertain. Motives may include fear, hate, revenge, greed (mercenary or paid informants), competition or personal advantage, ego or vanity ("cop buffs" or "wannabees"), etc. Not all motives are bad, but all should be ascertained and considered. Information from informants should also be corroborated whenever possible.

The first step in using informants is to document them (see Figures 6.1 through 6.3). While the identity of an informant should remain confidential, their use should be made known to a supervisor and their identity documented. This ensures accountability of informant funds (paid to informants for their services) and the credibility of the source (the confidential informant). They should be assigned a "confidential informant" or CI number. A CI documentation form should be used to record their name, date of birth, social security number, race, gender, height, weight, address, phone numbers, and place of employment.

Informants used to buy contraband (drugs, weapons, stolen property, secrets, and other prohibited chattels) should be subjected to a pre-buy search and a post-buy search. Allowing them to make a buy of contraband without ensuring that they did not possess the contraband beforehand may raise a reasonable doubt about whether they bought it from the target or already possessed it to "frame" the target of the investigation (the suspect). A post-buy search is necessary to ensure that they turn over all of the purchased

CONFIDENTIAL INFORMANT APPLICATION

CI#:_____NAME:_____PD#:_____PD#:_____
AKA:_____
AGE:_____DOB:____SEX:____RACE:____SSN:____HEIGHT:_____WEIGHT:___
BUILD:_____MARKS/SCARS/TATTOOS:_____
PHONE NUMBER_____CELL PHONE_____
ADDRESS:_____HOW LONG:_____
DO YOU OWN:_____RENT:_____LEASE:____AMOUNT PER MONTH:_____
PREVIOUS ADDRESS:_____HOW LONG:_____
EMPLOYED AT:_____
ADDRESS:_____HOW LONG:_____
WORK PHONE:_____
VEHICLE MAKE/MODEL:_____

SPOUSE INFORMATION

MARRIED:_____DIVORCED:_____SINGLE:_____SEPARATED:_____
SPOUSE'S NAME:_____AGE:_____DOB:_____
ALIAS(AKA):_____HEIGHT:_____WEIGHT:_____
ADDRESS:_____TX:_____CELL:_____
EMPLOYED AT:_____

CI QUESTIONNAIRE
ARRESTS

Have you ever been arrested?_____Where?_____
Charge(s):_____
Disposition:_____
Have you ever used any drug or narcotic?_____What?_____
Are you using any drug or narcotic now?_____What?_____
Are you addicted to any drug or narcotic now?_____What?_____

Have you ever been treated for any mental illness?_____
Disposition:_____
Are you under any doctor's care at this time?_____
List type of care:_____
HAVE YOU EVER WORKED WITH A POLICE AGENCY BEFORE:_____WHERE:___
LIST THE NAMES OF OFFICERS YOU HAVE WORKED WITH:_____
ARE YOU WILLING TO TESTIFY IN COURT OR A GRAND JURY:_____
ARE YOU WILLING TO TAKE A POLYGRAPH OR VOICE STRESS:_____
ARE YOU WILLING TO BE SEARCHED:_____
WHAT TYPE OF COMPENSATION DO YOU EXPECT TO RECEIVE:_____
HAVE YOU EVER TESTIFIED IN COURT:_____WHEN:_____
DISPOSITION:_____
DETECTIVE ASSIGNED TO CI:_____PHOTO TAKEN:_____
AUTHORIZED BY:_____ PROSECUTORS OFFICE. DATE:_____

Figure 6.1 Confidential Informant (CI) Application.

contraband and that continuity of evidence is ensured by the accountable investigator. Accountability of evidence is essential.

The informant must understand immediately that the investigator, not the informant, controls the investigation. Do not make promises that you cannot keep and maintain frequent contact to maintain control.

STATEMENT OF UNDERSTANDING

I UNDERSTAND I WILL BE COOPERATING WITH THE_____POLICE DEPARTMENT
_____BUREAU BY OBTAINING INFORMATION AND EVIDENCE OF VIOLATIONS OF
_____LAWS OF THE STATE OF_____AND/OR THE UNITED STATES OF
AMERICA IN COOPERATING WITH AGENTS OF THE_____POLICE DEPARTMENT IN
OBTAINING SUCH INFORMATION OR EVIDENCE, I UNDERSTAND THE FOLLOWING:

1. I AM NOT AN AGENT OR EMPLOYEE OF THE CITY OF_____OR OF THE
    _____POLICE DEPARTMENT.
2. I CANNOT AND WILL NOT COMMIT ANY CRIME WHATSOEVER.
3. IF I DO VIOLATE ANY CRIMINAL LAW, I CAN AND WILL BE PROSECUTED.
4. I WILL NOT RECEIVE OR POSSESS ANY DRUGS WITHOUT THE EXPRESS OR PRIOR
    APPROAVAL OF AN AGENT OF THE_____POLICE DEPARTMENT_____
    BUREAU.
5. I WILL NOT SELL OR DELIVER ANY CONTROLLED SUBSTANCE, OR ANY SUBSTANCE
    PURPORTED TO BE SAME, TO ANYONE.
6. I WILL NOT SELL OR DELIVER OR CAUSE TO BE SOLD OR DELIVERED ANY
    CONTROLLED SUBSTANCE OR ANY SUBSTANCE PURPORTED TO BE CONTROLLED
    SUBSTANCE TO ANY PERSON WHO WOULD THEN SELL OR DELIVER SUCH
    CONTROLLED SUBSTANCE OR ANY SUBSTANCE PURPORTED TO BE SUCH, TO
    ANY MEMBER OF THE_____POLICE DEPARTMENT_____BUREAU OR ANY
    OTHER PERSON.
7. I WILL NOT USE MY SEX, SEXUALITY, OR SEXUAL ACTIVITY TO PERSUADE OR INDUCE
    ANY PERSON TO SELL OR DELIVER ANY CONTROLLED SUBSTANCE OR SUBSTANCE
    PURPORTED TO BE SUCH TO ANY MEMBER OF THE_____POLICE
    DEPARTMENT_____BUREAU,
    NOR WILL I OFFER MONETARY, TANGIBLE, OR INTANGIBLE INDUCEMENT.
8. I UNDERSTAND I MAY NEVER SEARCH A SUSPECT, DWELLING, PAPERS OR PERSONAL
    EFFECTS OF SUSPECT.
9. I WILL NOT BECOME INVOLVED IN ANY ACTIVITIES THAT WOULD CONSTITUTE
    ENTRAPMENT.
10. I WILL NOT ATTEND MEETINGS WITH ANY PERSON OR SUSPECT WHEN HIS
    ATTORNEY IS PRESENT UNLESS SUCH ATTENDANCE CANNOT BE AVOIDED.
    IF ATTENDANCE CANNOT BE AVOIDED,
    I SHALL REPORT NOTHING I MAY OVERHEAR WHILE PRESENT AT SUCH MEETING
    UNLESS I OBSERVED THE COMMISSION OF A CRIME.
11. ANY MONIES PAID TO ME BY THE_____POLICE DEPARTMENT _____
    BUREAU ARE SUBJECT TO THE PAYMENT OF INCOME TAXES.

Figure 6.2 Confidential Informant (CI) Statement of Understanding.

Undercover Operations

Undercover operations involve the adoption of a clandestine pseudo-identity to become a part of an organization or associate with persons to gain information or intelligence, conduct investigations, or document assets and

12. I WILL MAINTAIN CONTACT WITH DESIGNATED AGENTS OF THE_____POLICE DEPARTMENT_____BUREAU, ACCORDING TO THEIR REQUESTS AND WILL CONTINUE TO CONTACT THEM THROUGHOUT ANY INVESTIGATIONS IN WHICH I AM INVOLVED. I WILL IMMEDIATELY ADVISE SUCH AGENTS IN THE EVENT OF ANY CHANGE OF RESIDENCE, TELEPHONE NUMBER, AND OR PLACE OF EMPOLOYMENT OR MARITAL STATUS.

13. I WILL NOT DIVULGE THE EXISTENCE OR NATURE OF MY COOPERATION WITH AGENTS OF THE _____POLICE DEPARTMENT_____BUREAU, NOR WILL I PROVIDE DETAILS OF ANY INVESTIGATION OF WHICH I AM INVOLVED TO ANY PERSON OR PERSONS WITH THE EXCEPTION OF THE PERSONS AUTHORIZED OR APPROVED BY THE_____POLICE DEPARTMENT_____BUREAU.

14. I AM AGREEING TO COOPERATE WITH THE_____POLICE DEPARTMENT _____BUREAU OF MY OWN FREE WILL AND ACCORD, AND NOT AS A RESULT OF INTIMIDATION OR THREATS.

15. IN AGREEING TO WORK FOR THE_____POLICE DEPARTMENT_____ BUREAU, I UNDERSTAND THAT NO AGENT MAY MAKE ANY PROMISES OR PREDICTIONS, EXPLICIT OR IMPLICIT, REGARDING THE DISPOSITION OF ANY CRIMINAL CHARGES THAT ARE PENDING AGAINST ME, BUT THAT SUCH AGENTS WILL EXERT MAXIMUM EFFORT TO BRING MY COOPERATION TO THE FULL ATTENTION OF THE _____PROSECUTOR'S OFFICE AND OR THE UNITED STATES ATTORNEY'S OFFICE.

16. I UNDERSTAND THAT THE INFORMATION AND ASSISTANCE I PROVIDE MAY BE USED IN A CRIMINAL PROCEEDING AND WHILE THE_____POLICE DEPARTMENT_____BUREAU WILL USE ALL LAWFUL MEANS TO MAINTAIN CONFIDENTIALITY OF MY COOPERATION. I ALSO UNDERSTAND THAT I MAY BE REQUIRED TO TESTIFY ABOUT ANY INFORMATION OR EVIDENCE THAT I OBTAINED OR ASSISTED IN OBTAINING.

17. I FURTHER REALIZE THAT I AM LEGALLY OBLIGATED TO APPEAR WHEN SUBPOENED FOR TRIALS, DEPOSITIONS AND OTHER CRIMINAL PROCEEDINGS. I REALIZE THAT REFUSAL OR FAILURE TO APPEAR ON THE DATE AND TIME SPECIFIED WILL RESULT IN THE PROSECUTION OF MYSELF TO THE FULLEST EXTENT OF THE LAW PROVIDED BY THE_____CRIMINAL CODE AND/OR THE APPLICABLE FEDERAL LAW.

COOPERATING INDIVIUAL_____ DATE_____
WITNESS_____ DATE_____
WITNESS_____ DATE_____

Figure 6.3 Confidential Informant (CI) Statement of Understanding (continued).

contraband for seizure and arrests. The objective of an undercover assignment is to gain the confidence of the target of an investigation (suspect) or to infiltrate a criminal organization or group to obtain information, intelligence, or evidence.

Undercover operatives must carefully construct a cover or back story and a covert undercover identity. Depending upon the level of the undercover investigation, this may require the creation of an identity, using false identification (driver's license, birth certificate, social security number, etc.), a cover address, phone, and place of employment.

Physical and Technical Surveillance

Surveillance is the covert observation of places, persons, or vehicles with the goal of obtaining information about the identities or activities of the subject of the surveillance. The surveillant may also identify leads or locate evidence for use in the investigation.

Surveillance may be stationary or fixed or moving (foot or mobile). The nature of the surveillance will require a balancing of the priorities between not losing the subject of the surveillance and not being detected. There are times when the priority is not to be detected, while at other times the priority is not to lose the subject, even at the risk of detection. These two priorities are usually in competition and both can only be achieved when sufficient resources are deployed (see Figure 6.4 and Figure 6.5).

Technical surveillance includes the use of video and still cameras, imagery enhancing optics (IR heat sensing, night vision, and other imagery), GPS and other tracking devices, audio and computer surveillance devices, etc.

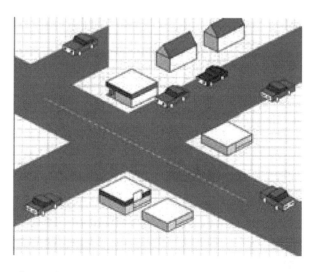

Figure 6.4 Stakeout box for pickup and follow.

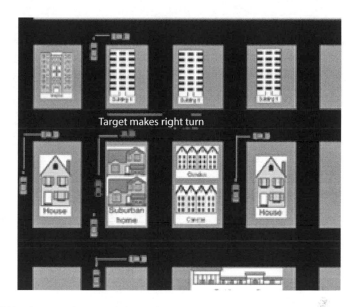

Figure 6.5 Floating box mobile stakeout.

Interviewing and Interrogation

Interviewing and interrogation will be discussed more in Chapter 10 and Chapter 11. This skill set is used so often by all investigators that it requires special attention. Some topics that should be added to this are studies of:

- Truth detection
- Polygraph
- Voice stress analysis
- Forensic hypnosis
- Linguistic analysis

Types of Investigations

Once you have mastered the fundamental techniques of conducting investigations (sources of information, confidential informants, undercover operations, surveillance, and interviews and interrogation), there are methods that are unique to specific types of investigations. First, it is essential to learn the elements of the crime (the legal elements that must be met for the Probable Cause Affidavit) and the "lesser included offenses" (those elements that are sufficient for a lesser crime). Criminal offenses generally fall into one of the following categories:

- Crimes against Persons
  - Homicide (murder, suicide, feticide, voluntary manslaughter, involuntary manslaughter, reckless homicide)
  - Sex crimes (rape, child molesting, criminal deviate conduct, sexual battery, etc.)
  - Robbery (bank robbery, armed robbery, strong arm robbery, carjacking, home invasion, etc.)
- Crimes against Property
  - Arson
  - Burglary (residential burglary, residential entry, business burglary, criminal trespass, etc.)
  - Auto theft (vehicle theft, conversion, receiving stolen auto parts, etc.)
  - Larceny (theft and criminal conversion)
- Fraud and Economic Crimes (Financial and Computer Crimes)
  - Carnival cons and scams
  - Confidence games and Bunco frauds
  - Consumer fraud
  - Tax fraud
  - Financial and corporate economic crimes
  - Computer fraud and thefts
- Crimes against Public Morals (Vice and Narcotics)
  - Drugs and narcotics (interdiction, diversion, distribution, manufacture, etc.)
  - Prostitution
  - Gambling and illegal gaming
  - Pornography
  - Alcohol and tobacco violations
- Juvenile and Family Crimes
  - Crimes by juveniles
  - Crimes against juveniles
  - Crimes against the elderly
  - Crimes against the family
  - Juvenile gang activity
- Counterintelligence and Security
  - Physical security measures
  - Protective operations
  - Counterespionage
  - Counterterrorism
  - Treason
  - War crimes

Crimes against Persons

Death Investigations

Death investigations should always be worked as a murder case until proven otherwise; that is, murder, feticide, voluntary manslaughter, involuntary manslaughter, and reckless homicide should be investigated as such until there is evidence to prove that the death was a suicide, an accidental death, a natural death, or a justifiable homicide such as self-defense. Too many investigators find a note and a gun beside a body and opine that it is "obviously a suicide; no need to go any further." On the other hand, they assume that a death is "natural" because the victim was elderly, in poor health, or on medication. How easy it would be to commit a murder in venues where these "investigators" work! Make no assumptions and base opinions on facts and evidence. Law enforcement investigators owe this duty to the victims for whom they now speak.

The first officer on the scene should secure the scene, ensure that inner (evidentiary) and outer (working) crime scene areas are "taped off" with crime scene tape, and start a crime scene entry log to document everyone who has been in the crime scene, including witnesses, medics, firefighters, police officers, coroners, prosecutors, mortuary personnel (if they have entered before the scene is released), etc. Anything that has been moved, altered, or disturbed should be brought to the attention of the crime scene technician, who will then make the coroner and detective aware of this. First responders should document this in their reports, even if they believe they did something wrong (two wrongs don't make a right). It is better to document changes that were made in the crime scene in the heat of the response than fail to reveal this vital information.

Keep those entering to a minimum; this is not a show. The only personnel who should enter are the first responders (medics, firefighters, police officers), the crime scene technicians who are processing the scene (usually 2 to 3), and the coroner and the lead detective after the crime scene has been processed. The coroner and the lead detective should be walked through the scene by crime scene technicians after evidence has been collected, but before the scene is disturbed further. The "walk-through" with the crime scene technician helps the coroner and the lead detective better understand the scene, what happened, and what evidence was collected. Evaluate the forensic evidence. Determine what the evidence may indicate happened.

Detectives should canvass the area and interview witnesses. They should determine whether any security cameras are nearby that may have information or if any witnesses videoed anything. Detectives should make notes and a debriefing should be conducted following the investigations at the scene. The debriefing allows first responders, detectives, crime scene technicians, and others at the scene to brief the lead detective, the coroner, and the prosecutor on what details each participant has collected. This gives all the pieces of the puzzle to one lead detective to assemble and present to the coroner and the prosecutor after a supervisor has reviewed the case content.

The lead detective should collect reports from everyone at the scene to incorporate in the case file. The lead detective also collects a copy of all supporting reports, such as crime scene logs, evidence continuity forms, inventory forms, etc. In addition, the lead detective should attend the postmortem autopsy to brief the pathologist on what is known, to answer any questions the pathologist has, and to ask the pathologist for what he or she can tell the detective about what happened.

Determine the cause of death, time of death, artifacts of the crime, suspects, witnesses, motives, elements of the crime, etc. The detective should be familiar with gunshot and stab wounds (contact, near contact, and distant), entrance and exit wounds (which are not always as "obvious" as many detectives think), ligature marks, bruises, etc.

Robbery Investigations

Bank robbery investigations should be conducted in the same manner as homicide investigations in that the crime scene should be taped off (inner and outer perimeter), a crime scene entry log should be established, a lead detective should be assigned to coordinate all investigative activities (not the detective's supervisor), a debriefing should be conducted by the supervisor for the lead detective (so he or she knows what everyone else did), etc. (Figure 6.6 and Figure 6.7).

If the crime scene warrants it, other armed robberies (where a weapon is used), strong-arm robberies (where no weapon is indicated), home invasion robberies, car-jackings, etc. should be worked in the same manner. If there is little evidence, as in the case of a street robbery with no "scene," little physical evidence, and no witnesses (other than the victim), such measures may not be warranted.

Sex Crimes

Sex crimes investigations (rape, child molestation, criminal deviate conduct, sexual battery, etc.) will also be worked similarly, but often have characteristics unique to this type of crime, such as physical evidence that may need to be collected at a sexual assault treatment center or hospital. Child protective services may be required. Crime scene technicians may assist forensic nurses in the collection of a "rape kit" (also known as a "Sirchie Kit") and documentation, such as photographs and collection of evidence with proper continuity forms. A protocol should be in place to guide first responders, investigators, medical personnel, and prosecutors in the conduct of such investigations, which will vary from one community to another.

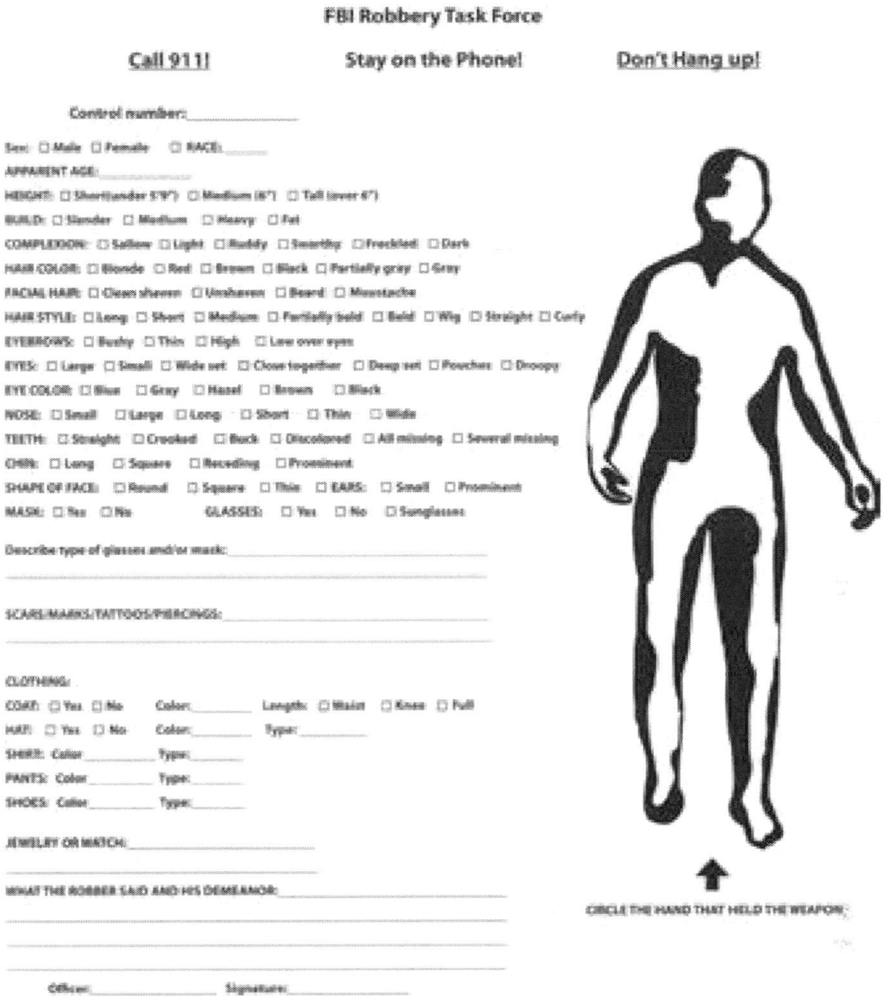

FBI Robbery Task Force

Call 911! Stay on the Phone! Don't Hang up!

Control number:______

Sex: ☐ Male ☐ Female ☐ RACE:______

APPARENT AGE:______

HEIGHT: ☐ Short (under 5'8") ☐ Medium (6") ☐ Tall (over 6")

BUILD: ☐ Slender ☐ Medium ☐ Heavy ☐ Fat

COMPLEXION: ☐ Sallow ☐ Light ☐ Ruddy ☐ Swarthy ☐ Freckled ☐ Dark

HAIR COLOR: ☐ Blonde ☐ Red ☐ Brown ☐ Black ☐ Partially gray ☐ Gray

FACIAL HAIR: ☐ Clean shaven ☐ Unshaven ☐ Beard ☐ Moustache

HAIR STYLE: ☐ Long ☐ Short ☐ Medium ☐ Partially bald ☐ Bald ☐ Wig ☐ Straight ☐ Curly

EYEBROWS: ☐ Bushy ☐ Thin ☐ High ☐ Low over eyes

EYES: ☐ Large ☐ Small ☐ Wide set ☐ Close together ☐ Deep set ☐ Pouches ☐ Droopy

EYE COLOR: ☐ Blue ☐ Gray ☐ Hazel ☐ Brown ☐ Black

NOSE: ☐ Small ☐ Large ☐ Long ☐ Short ☐ Thin ☐ Wide

TEETH: ☐ Straight ☐ Crooked ☐ Buck ☐ Discolored ☐ All missing ☐ Several missing

CHIN: ☐ Long ☐ Square ☐ Receding ☐ Prominent

SHAPE OF FACE: ☐ Round ☐ Square ☐ Thin ☐ EARS: ☐ Small ☐ Prominent

MASK: ☐ Yes ☐ No GLASSES: ☐ Yes ☐ No ☐ Sunglasses

Describe type of glasses and/or mask:______

SCARS/MARKS/TATTOOS/PIERCINGS:______

CLOTHING:

COAT: ☐ Yes ☐ No Color:______ Length: ☐ Waist ☐ Knee ☐ Full

HAT: ☐ Yes ☐ No Color:______ Type:______

SHIRT: Color______ Type:______

PANTS: Color______ Type:______

SHOES: Color______ Type:______

JEWELRY OR WATCH:______

WHAT THE ROBBER SAID AND HIS DEMEANOR:______

Officer:______ Signature:______

CIRCLE THE HAND THAT HELD THE WEAPON.

Figure 6.6 FBI Bank Robbery Task Force Identification Form (front).

In most crimes against persons, the victim is a witness and may have seen the perpetrator. (Remember that a "suspect" is someone who may have committed the crime and a "perpetrator" is the one who did commit it.) Line-ups are not used as often as they once were. When they are used, they should be conducted in a manner similar to show-ups and photo arrays. A show-up may be conducted if there are reasonable grounds to believe that a "suspect" may be the "perpetrator," that is, he or she was near the crime scene, matches the description, and is otherwise suspicious to the police. Detectives should consult with competent legal counsel (prosecutors) from their area to determine the current state of the law in their venue. However, here are my recommendations on show-ups and photo arrays.

VEHICLE IDENTIFICATION

APPROXIMATE YEAR_____   MAKE_____   MODEL_____
NUMBER OF DOORS_____   MISCELLANEOUS_____

WEAPON IDENTIFICATION

SEMI-AUTOMATICS

REVOLVERS

SHOTGUNS

RIFLES

ASSAULT TYPES

KNIFE

APPROXIMATE KNIFE LENGTH_____   TYPE_____
COLOR OF WEAPON
BLUED or BLACK_____   STAINLESS STEEL_____
CHROME_____   OTHER_____

Figure 6.7 FBI Bank Robbery Task Force Identification Form (back).

If a suspect is stopped within a reasonable time, near the crime scene, and could match the description of the perpetrator, if he or she is under arrest for any other charge (warrants, resisting law enforcement, etc.), then take the suspect to the scene. If the suspect is not under arrest, ask the suspect if he or she will voluntarily accompany you back to the scene. If the suspect will not, bring the witness to the suspect. Advise the witness that the suspect may or may not be the perpetrator and to identify the suspect only if the witness can and not because the suspect was brought there by the police.

Similarly, a photo array should be conducted after selecting six to eight photos of the same demographics and general appearance. Do not pick five bald men and one with long hair, five black men and one Hispanic man, five fat men with beards and one skinny man with no facial hair. They do not need to be twins, but should be of similar physical characteristics.

Make copies of the array, with the original documenting the photo numbers of all photos used. Before showing the photos to the witnesses, advise them of the following:

1. I am about to show you a photo array containing six (or eight) photos.
2. The perpetrator may or may not be one of the persons in the array.
3. If the perpetrator is in one of the photos, his or her appearance may or may not have changed (he or she may be older, may have lost or gained weight, changed hair style, added or shaved facial hair, or otherwise changed appearance).
4. Look at all of the photos before you say anything.
5. Once you have looked at all of the photos, if you see the perpetrator and can positively identify him or her, say so. However if it just looks like the perpetrator, specify that (in other words, articulate or tell me whether you are identifying the perpetrator or merely saying that it "looks like" him or her).

This last suggestion helps prevent detectives from taking a non-decisive "identification" and making it a positive identification. You do not want to have a witness state in court, "I just said it looked like him, but I wasn't sure."

Finally, show the witnesses the photo array. Once they have articulated their certainty (in their own words), have them circle the photo on one of the copies, sign, and date the identification. Do the same with other witnesses. The original photo array and the signed copies are evidence and should be "bagged and tagged" with a continuity slip and stored in the property room as evidence.

Crimes against Property

Property crimes are sometimes witnessed, too. The procedures for photo arrays just discussed should be used for all photo array identifications.

Arson

Arson is often committed to conceal other crimes, for insurance fraud or other profit, because of mental illness, or for vandalism, revenge, spite, or anger. Arson investigators attempt to determine the "cause and origin" of the fire, that is, what caused the fire (e.g., accelerants, incendiaries, etc.) and what was the point of origin or where the fire started. Who had motives and alibis?

Burglary

Some state statutes refer to burglary, while others refer to breaking and entering (B&E), and still others have both, defining them by different elements. Lesser and included offenses (offenses which share some, but do not require all of the elements and usually carry lesser penalties) include residential entry, criminal trespass, criminal mischief (vandalism), etc.

Residential burglary and business burglary usually include the elements of (1) breaking, (2) entering, (3) a building or structure (in some states a residence and in some states and at common law "at night"), (4) with intent to commit a felony therein (an important element that differentiates burglary from residential entry or another lesser and included offense). The intent to commit a "felony therein" means that it can be shown that there was intent to commit a theft, arson, rape, robbery, murder, or other "felony therein."

Business burglaries commonly occur at night, on weekends, during holidays, and at other times when the business is not commonly open. Residential burglaries often occur during the day when the perpetrator assumes that the resident is at work or otherwise away from home. Sometimes they occur when the resident is outside doing lawn work or is otherwise at home but occupied outside. This is not always the case and such "burglaries" can often turn into a home invasion robbery.

A "fence" is someone who knowingly sells or otherwise disposes of stolen property. The fence may or may not be the burglar and, when he or she is not, is still committing the offense of "receiving stolen property," "possession of stolen property," or some similar crime. Burglary investigations should routinely include checking "pawn file" records, online sites for buying and selling items, and classified ads in newspapers or free ad papers. Serial numbers should be entered in NCIC and local databases as stolen so they can be "run" when officers locate the items, possibly hundreds of miles away and years later.

A modus operandi (method of operation) can often be identified in serial burglaries using crime analysis methods to determine common days, dates, times, locations, types of property, methods of entry, etc. Fingerprints, DNA evidence, video, and witness evidence may be available.

Auto Theft

Auto theft includes vehicle theft, conversion, receiving stolen auto parts, theft of aircraft, boats, and other vehicles, usually classified by a vehicle identification number (VIN). Other offenses can include the alteration or counterfeiting of vehicles and VINs. Stolen vehicles are often evidenced by license plates hanging by one screw or in the back window, broken side windows, punched columns, etc.

Larceny

Larceny, as it is known in some states, or theft and criminal conversion are also property crimes that are investigated in a similar manner as burglaries are. They do not have the element of requiring a breaking or entering into a building or structure of another, only the possession or control of the property of another with intent to deprive them of the use or value of the property. Obviously, to have such "intent" requires that the perpetrator knowingly or intentionally deprives the owner of such use or value. Photo arrays and pawnshop checks are often used for such investigations as well.

Fraud and Economic Crimes (Financial and Computer Crimes)

Financial crimes that are witnessed, such as forgeries, may also require a photo array. Follow the previously mentioned procedures for all photo arrays. Fraud usually includes any scheme or device used to deprive a victim of property, money, or anything of value. Con games range from simple carnival cons to sophisticated Bunco confidence games. Financial crimes include counterfeiting, forgery, check deception, credit card fraud, and similar financial crimes involving currency, negotiable instruments, or financial transactions. Economic crimes include corporate and consumer fraud, securities fraud, bank fraud, real estate fraud, insurance fraud, tax fraud, mail fraud, embezzlement, etc. Computer fraud is both a financial crime and a technical crime. Because it often affects commerce or finance, I have mentioned it here. Such frauds and economic crimes are so complex that they require entire books on each topic alone.

Crimes against Public Morals (Vice and Narcotics)

Drug and narcotics investigations include interdiction (stopping drug smuggling), diversion (detecting the diversion of drugs from legitimate supplies, such as medical sources), distribution, manufacture, etc. Again, these topics can and do fill entire books alone.

Vice investigations include the investigation of what was once called "public morals" violations. This includes the investigation of prostitution, illegal gambling and gaming, pornography, illegal alcohol and tobacco violations, etc.

Often both vice and narcotics violations involve organized crime and racketeer influenced corrupt organizations (RICO violations). The use of informants, undercover investigators, intelligence, etc. is essential and extensive.

Juvenile and Family Crimes

Juvenile crimes are crimes committed by juveniles and gang activity. Family crimes often involve crimes committed against juveniles, the elderly, the endangered (mentally and physically handicapped), or the family. They often include "status offenses" or offenses committed by virtue of the offender's minority (not having reached majority of age), such as alcohol, tobacco, or curfew violations. Often these status offenses lead to more serious crimes, such as burglary, robbery, drug offenses, etc.

Counterintelligence and Security

Counterintelligence and security investigations are usually concerned with physical security measures, protective operations, counterespionage, counterterrorism, treason, war crimes, etc.

Summary

While many investigations require specific techniques, most share common elements and skills. Mastering the basics of investigative skills is essential before one can master the advanced techniques we are discussing. If the reader is not thoroughly familiar with the basics outlined here, he or she should acquire such skills and continually add to them.

Personality Profiling
The Compass

7

Profiling is the art and science of assessing a comprehensive amount of information about a person's personality. It is used in law enforcement, in business, by reporters, and in other fields. A personal "comprehensive profile" identifies how a person prefers to communicate, perform, and make decisions. Profiling may involve personality profiling, geographical profiling (of crime patterns), and criminal investigative analysis (of crime scenes and crime artifacts).

The Korem Profiling System is used, not only in law enforcement, but also in many professions and environments. The reader should add Dan Korem's book to his or her library and acquire training in this area by attending one of his seminars. This system helps identify: (1) how a person communicates, performs, and makes decisions, and (2) how to operate with each specific profile. The Korem Profiling System provides two "tools" referred to as a "compass" and a "map."

Dimensional Components of Personality Types

There are four dimensional components that comprise personality types (Figure 7.1):

1. How people are energized (motivated) (Tieger and Barran-Tieger, 1998, p. 68) (Figure 7.2)
   a. *Extroverted*—"outer world"
   b. *Introverted*—"inner world" (Tieger and Barran-Tieger, 1998, p. 39)
2. What kind of information people notice and remember (learning type) (Tieger and Barran-Tieger, 1998, p. 73) (Figure 7.3)
   a. *Sensing*—being in the moment and seeing things realistically
   b. *Intuition*—seeing possibilities and implications (Tieger and Barran-Tieger, 1998, p. 39)
3. How people make decisions (decision-making) (Tieger and Barran-Tieger, 1998, p. 78) (Figure 7.4)
   a. *Feeling*—understanding and relating to people
   b. *Thinking*—making logical, objective decisions (Tieger and Barran-Tieger, 1998, p. 39)

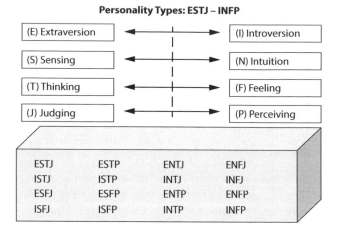

Figure 7.1 Personality types.

Extraverts – Introverts

Extraverts	Introverts
• Enthusiastic demeanor	• Calm, measured demeanor
• Talk more	• Talk less
• Talk faster and louder	• Talk slower and more quietly
• More animated	• More reserved
• Think out loud	• Think, then talk
• Easily distracted	• Able to focus attention
• Change subjects quickly	• Stay on one subject at a time
• Like to be around people	• Spend time alone
• Often seek center stage	• Avoid limelight
• Act first and think later	• More cautions and hesitant
• Interrupt and finish sentences	• Start conversations without preference

Figure 7.2 Extraverts and Introverts.

4. How people prefer to organize the world around them (organizational) (Tieger and Barran-Tieger, 1998, p. 85) (Figure 7.5)
   a. *Judging*—planning
   b. *Perceiving*—winging it or adapting (Tieger and Barran-Tieger, 1998, p. 39)

(Tieger and Barran-Tieger, 1998, p. 11)

Sensing – Intuition

Sensing	Intuition
• Clear, straightforward speech pattern	• Complex speech patterns and compound sentences
• Sequential thoughts	
• Literal; use facts and real examples	• Roundabout thoughts (one to next)
• Language as a tool	• Figurative; analogies and metaphors
• More aware of their bodies	• Language to express self
• Attracted to jobs requiring practicality	• More "in their heads"
• Less likely to have graduate degrees	• Attracted to jobs requiring more creativity
• Prefer non-fiction reading	• More likely to have graduate degrees
• Direct and to the point	• Prefer fiction reading
• Facts and details	• Repeat, rephrase and recap
• Remember past accurately	• Global issues or "big picture"
• Listen until others complete thoughts	• Envision the future
• About 65% of Americans	• Finish other's sentences
	• About 35% of Americans

Figure 7.3 Sensing and Intuition.

Thinking – Feeling

Thinking	Feeling
• Act cooler, more distant to others	• Act warmer, friendlier toward others
• May seem insensitive	• Sensitive to other's feelings
• May be blunt and tactless	• Gentle and diplomatic
• Often appear business like	• Engages in social niceties
• May engage in argument or debate for fun	• Avoid arguments, conflict and confrontation
• More "thick-skinned"	• Feelings hurt more easily
• Get to the point	• Engage in small talk first
• Seldom asks if timing is inconvenient	• Ask if timing is inconvenient
• Appear low-keyed and matter-of-fact	• May appear excited or emotional
• Give praise sparingly	• Generous with praise
• Usually very assertive	• May lack assertiveness
• Impersonal language	• Use people's names often
• Use people's names sparingly	• Often in helping jobs
• Often in jobs of strategy	• 65% females
• 65% male	

Figure 7.4 Thinking and Feeling.

Judging – Perceiving

Judging	Perceiving
• More formal and conventional	• More casual and unconventional
• More serious	• More playful
• Like to take charge and be in control	• Good at adapting
• Like to make decisions; decide quickly	• May procrastinate and put off decisions
• Definitive and express strong opinions	• May be more tentative and more "wishy-washy"
• Often in a hurry; like rapid pace	• Prefer more leisurely pace
• A "finished," neat appearance	• Often " unfinished" look (unkempt)
• Dress more for appearance	• Dress more for comfort
• Neat car interior	• Messy car interior
• Like to set and reach goals	• Likely to change goals
• Driven to finish projects	• Prefer to start projects
• Like rules, systems, and structure	• Find rules, systems, and structure confining and limiting
• Usually well *organized*	• Often *disorganized*
• Make lists and check off completed items	• May make lists but seldom completes all items
• Neat and tidy work space	• Usually messy, cluttered workspace
• Walk faster with deliberate movements	• May walk slower
• May have straighter posture	• May slouch more
• Seek jobs that give control	• Seek jobs that are fun

Figure 7.5 Judging and Perceiving.

Personality Type Combinations

Personality Types have been classified as combinations of Extroverted or Introverted, Sensing or Intuition, Thinking or Feeling, and Judging or Perceiving. Each type is a combination of four of the eight characteristics or four opposing pairs. The percentages represent the percentage of individuals believed to fall within each type-combination.

- **ESTJ**—Extroverted, Sensing, Thinking, Judging (12–15%)
- **ISTJ**—Introverted, Sensing, Thinking, Judging (7–10%)
- **ESFJ**—Extroverted, Sensing, Feeling, Judging (11–14%)
- **ISFJ**—Introverted, Sensing, Feeling, Judging (7–10%)
- **ESTP**—Extroverted, Sensing, Thinking, Perceiving (6–8%)
- **ISTP**—Introverted, Sensing, Thinking, Perceiving (4–7%)
- **ESFP**—Extroverted, Sensing, Feeling, Perceiving (8–10%)
- **ISFP**—Introverted, Sensing, Feeling, Perceiving (5–7%)

- **ENTJ**—Extroverted, Intuition, Thinking, Judging (3–5%)
- **INTJ**—Introverted, Intuition, Thinking, Judging (2–3%)
- **ENTP**—Extroverted, Intuition, Thinking, Perceiving (4–6%)
- **INTP**—Introverted, Intuition, Thinking, Perceiving (3–4%)
- **ENFJ**—Extroverted, Intuition, Judging, Feeling (3–5%)
- **INFJ**—Introverted, Intuition, Feeling, Judging (2–3%)
- **ENFP**—Extroverted, Intuition, Feeling, Perceiving (6–7%)
- **INFP**—Introverted, Intuition, Feeling, Perceiving (3–4%)

(Tieger and Barran-Tieger, 1998, p. 39)

Compass

The Korem Profiling System compares the "talk" and the "walk" by breaking profiles into two parts: (1) *talk* refers to how a person prefers to communicate and (2) *walk* refers to how a person performs and makes decisions (Korem, 1997, p. 11) (see Figure 7.6 and Figure 7.7).

Similar to psychologist William Marston's DISC assessment theory, such theories accurately assess behavioral profiles based upon personality traits. In the DISC theory, Marston also identified four measureable traits: (1) dominance, (2) inducement, (3) submission, and (4) compliance. (This is somewhat similar to Korem's control, express, ask, and tell.) This theory was then developed into a personality assessment tool (personality profile test) by industrial psychologist Walter Vernon Clarke. The version used today was developed from the original assessment by John Geier, who

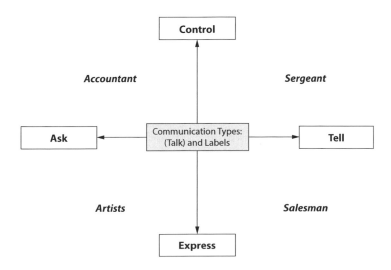

Figure 7.6 Communications types and labels.

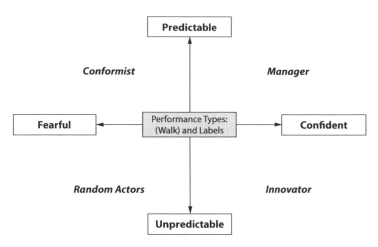

Figure 7.7 Performance types and labels.

simplified the test for better, more concise results.* The Korem "compass" provides four points:

Communications Types (Talk):

1. CONTROL–EXPRESS: Does this person CONTROL or EXPRESS his or her emotions when he or she communicates? (Controlled or expressive emotions; e.g., quiet or outgoing)
   - **Control**—controlled, quiet, private, introverted, suspicious, intro-spective, indifferent, detailed, thoughtful, pensive (deep thought)
   - **Express**—outgoing, dramatic, emotional, explosive, expressive, extro-verted, fiery, passionate, sensitive, short-fused (Korem, 1997, p. 9)[†]
2. ASK–TELL: Does this person prefer to TELL others what he or she thinks or does this person prefer to be more indirect and ASK others what they think? The ASK–TELL gauge or question identifies whether someone prefers to dominate a dialogue when he or she communi-cates. Does this person prefer to be directive or assertive and lead a conversation or prefer to be more indirect and ask others what they think first? This gauge does not try to identify whether a person asks questions, but how the person asks questions, makes statements, or carries on conversations (Korem, 1997, p. 29).[‡]
   - Ask
   - Tell

Performance Types (Walk) (How a person makes decisions and per-forms on the job):

---

* https://www.discprofile.com/what-is-disc/history-of-disc/
† (Korem, pp. 9, 29 and 105)
‡ (Korem, pp. 9, 43 and 105)

3. CONFIDENT–FEARFUL: Is this person CONFIDENT or FEARFUL when he or she makes decisions? This is the only one of the four gauges with an inherently negative plot point; the others are neither positive nor negative (Korem, 1997, p. 105).* At one end of the scale are people who act confidently because they believe they can control or influence events and circumstances (job, work environment, family, social environment, etc.). At the other end of the scale are people who do *not* feel in control of their lives and are fearful (Korem, 1997, p. 90). Evaluation questions include the following:

   Do I or does this person . . .
   a)   prefer to initiate actions? (Confident)
   b)   prefer to let others take the lead? (Fearful)
   c)   prefer to act to take control of circumstances? (Confident)
   d)   believe that most things just happen as a result of events that are outside of my or their control? (Fearful)
   e)   make decisions confidently? (Confident)
   f)   usually hesitate or become somewhat fearful when making decisions or taking action? (Korem, 1997, p. 95)

4. PREDICTABLE–UNPREDICTABLE: Are this person's actions typically PREDICTABLE (conventional) or UNPREDICTABLE (unconventional)? (Korem, 1997, pp. 9 and 97–105)†

Characteristics of the Compass Points

Communications Types

Control–Express
Positive Control
- *Extreme:* control their emotions during a volatile crisis and provide stability to a group.
- *Non-Extreme:* usually quiet, take it all in, and full of wisdom.

Negative Control
- *Extreme:* cold, suspicious, recluse who refuses to help others for fear of having to express feelings.
- *Non-Extreme:* reserved and, at times, indifferent to feelings of others.

Positive Express
- *Extreme:* expressive, like a coach firing up the team before a game.
- *Non-Extreme:* warm and makes people feel at home.

---

* (Korem, pp. 9, 90–96 and 105)
† (Korem, pp. 9 and 97–105)

Negative Express

- *Extreme:* short temper and explodes at inappropriate times.
- *Non-Extreme:* philanthropic, but occasionally allows emotions to reject wise counsel (Korem, 1997, pp. 39–40).

Ask–Tell

Ask: inquisitive, curious, appears naïve or uninformed, agreeable, non-assertive, altruistic, weak, indirect, laid-back, etc.

Tell: strong, confident, overbearing, assertive, outgoing, unsympathetic, egotistical, directive, and fearful (Korem, 1997, p. 46).

Positive Ask

- *Extreme:* an example is a physician who always asks patients how they feel.
- *Non-Extreme:* truth-seeker who asks questions but does not inject his or her own opinion into the story.

Negative Ask

- *Extreme:* extremely weak, naïve, and uninformed (the office "brown nose" who obsessively asks about everything to "score points").
- *Non-Extreme:* subordinate who occasionally hesitates before offering an opinion when candor is needed.

Positive Tell

- *Extreme:* a leader; for example, a military leader.
- *Non-Extreme:* an example is a salesperson who delivers a presentation that successfully matches his or her product or service with the client's needs and desires.

Negative Tell

- *Extreme:* an example is a cult leader or dictator who tells and directs others with evil intent.
- *Non-Extreme:* an example is the CEO who has occasional lapses of sensitivity when giving directions (Korem, 1997, p. 48).

Labels are useful to describe communication types and actions. These include:

- Sergeant: Control–Tell (Figure 7.8)
- Salesman: Express–Tell (Figure 7.9)
- Accountant: Control–Ask (Figure 7.10)
- Artists: Express–Ask (Figure 7.11) (Korem, 1997, pp. 63–64)

Sergeant: Control – Tell

Positive Actions	Negative Actions	Other Tendencies
• Action-oriented	• Egotistical	• Forceful
• Assertive	• Hot tempered	• Willing to use force
• Determined	• Impatient	• Self-sufficient
• Directive	• Insensitive	• Strong-willed
• Influential	• Machiavellian	• Stubborn
• Persistent	• Myopic	• Unsympathetic
• Pragmatic	• Overbearing	
• Self-confident	• Relentless	
• Take charge	• Won't accept direction	

Figure 7.8 Label: Sergeant. Communications types and actions: Control–Tell

Salesman: Express – Tell

Positive Actions	Negative Actions	Other Tendencies
• A "joiner"	• Egotistical	• Desire to please
• Excitable	• Easily discouraged	• Dramatic
• Friendly	• Gullible	• Dreamer
• Happy-go-lucky	• Idealistic	• Emotional
• Optimistic	• Impulsive	• Open
• Outgoing	• Manipulative	• Plays favorites
• Passionate	• Overly ambitious	• Reactive
• Politically attuned	• Undisciplined	• Talkative
• Trusting	• Unfocused	

Figure 7.9 Label: Salesman. Communications types and actions: Express–Tell

Labels are also useful to describe performance types and actions. These include:

- Manager: Confident–Predictable (Figure 7.12)
- Innovator: Confident–Unpredictable (Figure 7.13)
- Conformist: Fearful–Predictable (Figure 7.14)
- Random Actor: Fearful–Unpredictable (Figure 7.15) (Korem, 1997, pp. 111–112)

Accountant: Control – Ask

Positive Actions	Negative Actions	Other Tendencies
• Analytical	• Compulsive	• Aloof
• Clam and cool	• Critical	• Debater
• Dependable	• Pessimistic	• Focuses on history
• Detail-oriented	• Resist interaction	• Introspective
• Easy-going	• Slow	• Introverted
• Efficient	• Suspicious	• Perfectionist
• Moralistic	• Unexcitable	• Picky
• Objective	• Uninvolved	• Proper
• Orderly	• Weak	• Stubborn
• Poised		• Stuffy
• Thoughtful		• Tranquil

Figure 7.10 Label: Accountant. Communications types and actions: Control–Ask

Artist: Express – Ask

Positive Actions	Negative Actions	Other Tendencies
• Creative	• Argumentative	• Enduring
• Sympathetic	• Critical	• Focus on how they feel
• Agreeable	• Emotionally rash	• Idiosyncratic
• Avoids	• Low self-esteem	• Respectful
• Conflict	• Moody	• Retiring
• Supportive	• "Spineless"	• Tolerant
• Sensitive	• Unsure	
• Deep-feeling		
• Self-sacrificing		
• Loyal		
• Amiable		
• Compassionate		
• Self-effacing		

Figure 7.11 Label: Artist. Communications types and actions: Express–Ask

Manager: Confident – Predictable

Positive Actions	Negative Actions	Other Tendencies
• Assumes responsibility • Conventional • Decisive • Dependable • Efficient • Goal-oriented • Logical • Organized • Persistent • Practical/pragmatic • Precise • Thrifty	• Bureaucratic • Compulsive • Entrenched • "Nit-picker" • No risk tolerance • "Pesty" • Staid (sober; serious minded) • Unyielding • Will unnecessarily defend status quo	• Adapts to system • Can operate independently • Challenges with predictable outcome • Initiates within boundaries • Logic-oriented • Operates within boundaries • Predictable • "Square" • Resists change or disruption of scedules • Relies upon experience rather than creativity

Figure 7.12 Label: Manager. Communications types and actions: Confident–Predictable.

Innovator: Confident – Unpredictable

Positive Actions	Negative Actions	Other Tendencies
• Creative • Decisive • Free-thinking • Initiates action • Innovative • Not afraid of changes • Risk-taker • Self-assured • Seeks challenges • Problem-solver	• Aimless • Anarchist • Antisocial • Disorganized • Egocentric • Frivolous • Irresponsible • Rebellious • Reckless	• Non-conformist • Unconventional • Idea drive • Negligent • Needs freedom • Uninhibited • Motivated by change • Spontaneous • Operates without structure • Relies upon creativity v. experience

Figure 7.13 Label: Innovator. Communications types and actions: Confident–Unpredictable.

Conformist: Fearful – Predictable

Positive Actions	Negative Actions	Other Tendencies
• Cautious	• Fear of failure	• Avoids risks or ownership of problems
• Compulsive	• Gullible	
• Dutiful	• Indecisive	• Analytical
• Manageable	• Insecure	• Compliant
• Loyal	• *Neurotic*	• Doesn't require challenge
• Precise	• Subservient	• Guarded
• Reliable	• Uncreative	• Follower
• Supportive	• Uninteresting	• Obedient
	• Unquestioning	• Repetitive actions
	• Unwilling to assume blame	• Rule-oriented

Figure 7.14 Label: Conformist. Communications types and actions: Fearful–Predictable.

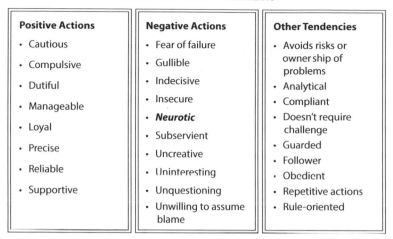

Random Actor: Fearful – Unpredictable

Positive Actions	Negative Actions	Other Tendencies
• None	• Anxious	• Despondent
	• Dangerous	
* More likely if person has ASK trait.	• Deceptive	• Hard to read
** More likely if person has Control trait.	• Distrusting	• Impulsive
	• Hot-tempered	• Rigid/unbending**
	• Indecisive	
	• Insecure	• Seeks protection through control
• **Blindly loyal***	• Irresponsible	
	• Moody	
• Lack of Conscience	• Secretive	
	• Self-absorbed	• *Antisocial*
• Manipulative	• Vacillating	
• Unwilling to accept responsibility	• Volatile	• *Egocentric*

Figure 7.15 Label: Random Actor. Communications types and actions: Fearful–Unpredictable.

Performance Types

Confident–Fearful
Positive Confident
- *Extreme:* hard-charging, for example, a coach.
- *Non-extreme:* a leader who demonstrates quiet confidence.

Negative Confident
- *Extreme:* arrogance, for example, a tycoon.
- *Non-extreme:* a "cocky" athlete (Korem, 1997, p. 96).

Application Tip: When a person is Confident and...

- You need to be directive, use a person who is higher on the Confident gauge.
- You are providing choices, you can provide more choices (Korem, 1997, p. 102).

Positive Fearful
- *Extreme:* none (no positive attributes are associated with extreme "fearful").
- *Non-extreme:* operating with caution when caution is due because of the nature of the activity, for example, the operator of a fail-safe system for a nuclear warhead or a barge operator who navigates channels cautiously.

Negative Fearful
- *Extreme:* unjustified paranoia, for example, a manager who is unjustifiably paranoid of those around him or her.
- *Non-extreme:* avoiding confrontation when it is necessary (Korem, 1997, p. 96).

Application Tip: When a person is Fearful and...

- You need to be directive, use a person who is lower on the Fearful gauge.
- You are providing choices, it is helpful to provide fewer choices (Korem, 1997, p. 102).

Predictable–Unpredictable
Predictable (Conventional) refers to persons who are usually characterized by regularity and conformity in their actions. They are described as consistent, conventional, dependable, formal, industrious, logical, orderly, organized,

persistent, precise, punctual, rigid, reliable, self-disciplined, staid, and stuffy. (They may not be described by all of these adjectives.)

Unpredictable (Unconventional) refers to persons whose are infrequent, random, surprising, or unconventional and range from unconventionally creative to rebellious and reckless. They are described as unconventional, aimless, frivolous, forgetful, freewheeling, inconsistent, intemperate, irreverent, negligent, nonconforming, rebellious, reckless, and spontaneous. (They may not be described by all of these adjectives.)

Positive Predictable
- *Extreme:* a staunch defender.
- *Non-extreme:* dependable support personnel.

Negative Predictable
- *Extreme:* resists even admitted positive change.
- *Non-extreme:* sometimes stuffy or staid (Korem, 1997, pp. 97, 101).

Application Tip: When a person is Predictable and you are suggesting change, be prepared for more resistance (Korem, 1997, p. 102).

Positive Unpredictable
- *Extreme:* unconventional inventor.
- *Non-extreme:* adapts well to changing trends and forecasts.

Negative Unpredictable
- *Extreme:* reckless leaders and cult figures.
- *Non-extreme:* absentminded or mind constantly wanders (Korem, 1997, pp. 97, 101).

Application Tip: When a person is Unpredictable and you are suggesting change, he or she will be more likely to be receptive (Korem, 1997, p. 102).

Conformist Type

There is one additional, exceptional type of which to take note. A *predictable* trait may sometimes override a *fearful* trait, causing decision-making to be more predictable. This is referred to as a Conformist type (Korem, 1997, p. 103).

Self-Assessment Tests and On-the-Spot Profiling

There are seven commonly used "self-assessment" tests that are worth discussing and may be useful for "on-the-spot profiling." A brief description of each follows.

- 16PF
- MMPI
- California Psychological Inventory
- Myers–Briggs Type Indicator
- Guilford–Zimmerman Temperament Scale
- Edwards Personality Profile Scale
- DFS

Sixteen Personality Factor Questionnaire (16PF)

The Sixteen Personality Factor Questionnaire (16PF) is a multiple-choice personality questionnaire that was developed over several decades of research by Raymond B. Cattell, Maurice Tatsuoka, and Herbert Eber. In the 1940s, Cattell used the techniques of factor analysis to try to discover and measure the source traits of human personality. The questionnaire measures the "16 primary traits" and the "Big Five secondary traits."

The traits evaluated are as follows:

1. Warmth, which is considered to indicate friendliness toward others and willingness to participate.
2. Reasoning, which is thought to be indicative of cognitive ability and intellect.
3. Emotional stability, which refers to the candidate's ability to adapt while under stress and whether they are easily upset.
4. Dominance, which ascertains levels of aggression, assertiveness, and cooperation.
5. Liveliness, which tends to indicate whether the candidate is likely to be cheerful or expressive as opposed to introverted or serious.
6. Rule-consciousness, which generally conveys attitudes toward authority and likelihood of obedience.
7. Social boldness, which refers to whether an individual is likely to be timid or shy as opposed to being uninhibited or outgoing.
8. Sensitivity, which considers whether the candidate is compassionate and sympathetic to others or if he or she tends to be more objective.
9. Vigilance, which specifies how trusting, accepting, or suspicious the individual may be around others.
10. Abstractedness, which can refer to being imaginative or solution-oriented but at the higher level can also suggest being impractical.
11. Privateness, which can indicate how forthright or non-disclosing an individual might be.
12. Apprehension, which is descriptive of whether someone may be more self-assured or insecure.

13. Openness to change, which is regarded as flexibility and a liberal attitude as opposed to being attached to the familiar.

14. Self-reliance, which identifies how self-sufficient or group-oriented an individual might be.

15. Perfectionism, which refers to self-discipline and precision as opposed to impulsiveness.

16. Tension, which conveys the likelihood of being time-driven or impatient instead of being relaxed and patient.

Minnesota Multiphasic Personality Inventory (MMPI)

The Minnesota Multiphasic Personality Inventory (MMPI) is one of the most widely used, objective personality tests. The most recent version of the test, the MMPI-2 Restructured Form (MMPI-2-RF), was developed by Dr. Yossef Ben-Porath, of Kent State University, and Dr. Auke Tellegen, of the University of Minnesota. The test is used to assist in identifying personality structure and psychopathology. It is best known as the personality test that is used in conjunction with Secret and Top Secret security clearances within federal agencies, such as the Department of Defense, Central Intelligence Agency, and Federal Aviation Administration.

California Psychological Inventory (CPI)

The California Psychological Inventory (CPI) is a self-reporting inventory developed by Harrison Gough and currently published by Consulting Psychologists Press. The test was first published in 1956 and the most recent revision was published in 1987. It was created in a similar manner to the MMPI, with which it shares 194 items. Unlike the MMPI, which focuses on maladjustment or clinical diagnosis, the CPI was created to assess the "everyday folk" concepts that ordinary people use to describe the behavior of the people around them.

Myers–Briggs Type Indicator (MBTI)

The Myers–Briggs Type Indicator (MBTI) assessment is a psychometric questionnaire designed to measure psychological preferences in how people perceive the world and make decisions. These preferences were extrapolated from the typology theories of Carl Jung. Jung theorized that there are four principal psychological functions by which we experience the world—sensation, intuition, feeling, and thinking—and that one of these four functions is dominant most of the time.

Guilford–Zimmerman Temperament Survey

The Guilford–Zimmerman Temperament Survey provides a nonclinical description of an individual's personality characteristics for use in career planning, counseling, and research.

Edwards Personality Profile Scale

Developed by psychologist and University of Washington professor, Allen L. Edwards, the Edwards Personality Profile Scale or Edwards Personal Preference Schedule (EPPS) is a forced choice, objective, non-projective personality inventory. The EPPS was designed to illustrate the relative importance to individuals of several significant needs and motives.

Dynamic Factors Survey (DFS)

The Dynamic Factors Survey (DFS) is a comprehensive factor-analytic investigation of interest that was developed by J. P. Guilford, Paul R. Christensen, and Nicholas A. Bond, Jr. in the 1950s to address the need for a more extensive, rational coverage of the many variables that should be included in an adequate assessment of personality. Interests were defined as dimensions of motivation. In addition to the vocational-interest inventories, they identified factors that are considered broader and more basic motivational variables.

Personality Profiling
The Map

8

How to Communicate with Each Personality Type

Once you have determined a person's personality, using the four dimensional components described at the beginning of Chapter 7 and the descriptive illustrations in the figures at the end of this chapter, you can use this information to better communicate with each type. Here are a few tips on how to communicate with each type.

Extraverts: Communicate verbally, allowing them to talk and think aloud. Include a variety of topics, but keep the conversation moving. Expect immediate action (Tieger and Barran-Tieger, 1998, p. 143).

Introverts: Communicate in writing, when possible, or ask them to listen carefully when talking to them. Talk about one thing at a time and give them enough time to reflect. Do not finish their sentences for them (Tieger and Barran-Tieger, 1998, p. 143).

Sensors: State the topic clearly. Be prepared with facts and examples and present information in a step-by-step fashion. Draw upon past, real experiences, emphasizing practical applications. Finish your own sentences (Tieger and Barran-Tieger, 1998, p. 143).

Intuitives: Talk about the "big picture" and its implications, as well as about "possibilities." Brainstorm options and use analogies and metaphors, while engaging their imaginations. However, do not overwhelm them with details (Tieger and Barran-Tieger, 1998, p. 143).

Thinkers: Be organized and logical, taking into consideration cause and effect and focusing on the consequences. Appeal to their sense of fairness. Do not ask them how they "feel," but rather what they "think." Do not repeat yourself (Tieger and Barran-Tieger, 1998, p. 143).

Feelers: Mention first the points of agreement that you share and show appreciation for their efforts and contributions. Recognize the legitimacy of "feelings" and talk about "people" concerns. Be friendly and considerate, smiling and maintaining good eye contact (Tieger and Barran-Tieger, 1998, p. 143).

Judgers: Be on time, prepared, organized, and efficient. Do not waste their time. Come to conclusions and do not leave issues unresolved.

Be decisive and definitive, while still allowing them to make decisions. Stick with plans that have been made (Tieger and Barran-Tieger, 1998, p. 143).

Perceivers: Expect several questions. Give them choices and don't force them to decide prematurely. Provide them with opportunities to discuss options and change plans. Focus on the process, not the product. Be open to new information (Tieger and Barran-Tieger, 1998, p. 143).

Map

Research suggests that the personality of a criminal offender is not fundamentally different from that of the non-criminal. In fact, the only difference seems to be in the criminal's thinking patterns or reasoning. Data also seem to suggest that the extremely violent have an inability to withstand frustration, which in turn serves as a catalyst for action (Holmes, 1989, p. 28).

The profiling "map" of the Korem System is the "comprehensive profile" (Figure 8.1). There are 16 different profiles (Figure 8.2), each having strengths, weaknesses (shortcomings), and interaction suggestions (Korem, 1997, p. 10). Once you have plotted people on the four gauges of the compass and identified their communication type and performance types, you can combine them into a Comprehensive Profile. The comprehensive profile provides a map that shows how a person's communication type interacts with his or her performance type (Korem, 1997, p. 149). Some performance types may share the same or similar actions because *types* that share a common *trait* may share some similar *tendencies* (Korem, 1997, p. 113).

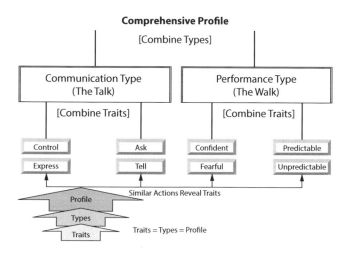

Figure 8.1 Comprehensive profile.

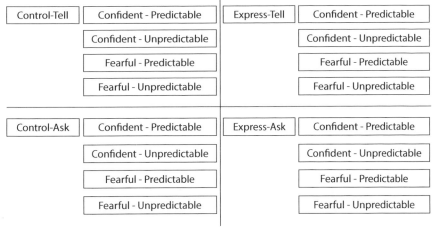

Figure 8.2 Sixteen combinations.

Traits by Associated Types

Dr. David Lieberman developed what he calls "blueprints to the mind" to "go beyond reading basic thoughts and feelings" to learn how "people think so you can profile anyone, predict behavior, and understand a person better than he does himself" (Lieberman, 2007, p. 108). Lieberman observes, "We find that unchanging, universal, and overriding forces of human nature *direct* one's personality" and the "components of these forces" gives us an "accurate, predictable read of a person almost every time, in every unique situation" (Lieberman, 2007, p. 111).

Dan Korem also developed a similar "blueprint" for profiling, predicting, and understanding behavior. The Korem system identifies these "components" by the following trait types:

Manager–Confident/Predictable: described as an organizer or decision-maker who prefers to make decisions in methodical and standardized ways; most comfortable in steady, calm, and predictable environments (Korem, 1997, p. 108).

Innovator–Confident/Unpredictable: described as an idea-generator who will "try anything once," is motivated by change and variety, is sufficiently self-confident to challenge situations and take risks (Korem, 1997, pp. 108–109).

Conformists–Fearful/Predictable: typically compliant, dutiful, reliable, and obedient, that is, a supporter or sustainer. Insecurity and fear, when making decisions, causes them to have an aversion to tak-

ing risks. They are often nervous and uninteresting (Korem, 1997,
pp. 108–109).

Random Actor–Fearful/Unpredictable: described as typically deceptive,
manipulative, scheming, and volatile. They act out of a strong perception of a need for self-defense and self-protection. They are often loyal
to anyone who is able to control their fate or allay their fears. They are
described as manipulators or public menaces. This is the least common but potentially the most dangerous and volatile of the performance types. Some of those who are plotted high (5 points) on the
gauge for this type may be psychotic (Korem, 1997, pp. 107–110).

Dr. Ronald Holmes and Dr. Stephen Holmes write, "Among the various types of mass killers, there is probably no more mysterious one than the
psychotic type. This type of killer has a severe psychotic condition, including
a severe break with reality, and may hear voices or have visions." They go on
to observe, "This person is not simply neurotic, that is, he has a condition
that impairs his interaction with society on a daily or near-daily basis." They
point out the important distinction that this type is *not* psychopathic and
does not have the character disorder associated with a psychopath (Holmes
and Holmes, 2001, p. 105).

Dr. Robert Hare wrote, "Psychopathy is a personality disorder defined by
a distinctive cluster of behaviors and inferred personality traits...Like any
psychiatric disorder, diagnosis is based on the accumulation of evidence that
an individual satisfies at least the minimal criteria for the disorder" (Hare,
1993, p. ix). Therefore, (1) psychotics and psychopaths are not the same and
(2) leave diagnosis to those qualified to do so, while understanding their
behavioral profiles.

Not all Random Actors pose a threat. The lower the *Fearful* and
Unpredictable traits, the less likely he or she will be severely volatile, manipulative, etc. The higher the *Fearful* trait, the more likely that negative actions
may be manifested, driven by paranoia, self-centered decision-making, etc.
(Korem, 1997, p. 113).

Sixteen Combinations

How such profiling systems work is based more upon how a person makes
conclusions, rather than what they are specifically thinking. Dr. David
Lieberman writes, "You can tell what someone is thinking because, in reality
he's not thinking. Outside of real creative thought, human beings are actually
forced into conclusions about how and what they see. What often passes for
thought is really a response based on *emotionally* preprogrammed choices"
(Lieberman, 2007, p. 114).

Dr. Lieberman makes a useful analogy, saying, "From the three primary colors—red, blue, and yellow—you can create millions of distinct and discernible colors. For instance, mixing blue and red makes purple, yellow and red makes orange, and yellow and blue makes green." Using the Lieberman "Primary Colors" example helps us understand the components of character traits or the various combinations of personality. He notes, "Similarly, when you understand the primary colors of the mind, all you need to know is how much of each 'color' is present to tell the 'shade' of the person's thoughts within a situation." As in a painting, the temperature, color saturation, brush types, etc. alter the paint formula in subtle ways, so too do "secondary factors" alter or affect people's thinking (Lieberman, 2007, pp. 118–119).

The "sixteen combinations" identified by the Korem system include the following.

Sergeant Types

Sergeant/Manager–Control/Tell/Predictable/Confident

Interaction Tips: Be direct and concrete in language. Focus on the bottom line and, when possible, help them to adapt to ambiguity and the fact that they cannot control all situations. Don't expect good "coaching" from them. Keep presentations short and to the point. Showing some emotion is okay, but refrain from replacing facts with emotions. When confronted, they will turn to their TELL trait in response. Be prepared with facts and hard, concrete language (Korem, 1997, p. 156).

Sergeant/Innovator–Control/Tell/Unpredictable/Confident

Interaction Tips: Do not be misled by open problem-solving behavior; they will still try to dominate the relationship. Anticipate a "high drive" work style resulting from their desire to control implementation of several ideas. Present a range of ideas before presenting specific recommendations. Watch for confidence indicators, which will reveal the strength of their desire to control. Stay a few steps ahead of anticipated questions, which will show your creative ability to keep up with their UNPREDICTABLE trait and avoid losing control of the situation. Don't let creative dialogue interfere with closing the sale or acceptance of ideas. When confronted, they may turn to their TELL trait (Korem, 1997, pp. 157–158).

Sergeant/Conformist–Control/Tell/Predictable/Fearful

Interaction Tips: Be sure to deliver on all promises and commitments. Expect rigid interpretations of rules and don't ask for compromises or exceptions. Allow time to gain approval of leaders. Remove ambiguity from both the presentation and in the expected outcome. Do not ask them to take risks.

They are not problem-solvers and will lay the blame at the feet of anyone else. When confronted, they will first turn to their TELL trait, and then become defensive. When backed into a corner, they will be driven by their FEAR trait when making decisions (Korem, 1997, pp. 159–160).

Sergeant/Random Actor–Control/Tell/Unpredictable/Fearful

Interaction Tips: Avoid implied threats or criticisms. Focus on building their self-confidence and providing structure to offset unpredictability. Avoid sudden changes in direction or plans. Do not give them a lot of freedom when making decisions, as this will increase the possibility that they will rely upon guile to defend or conceal their position. Avoid making presentations when risk is involved or FEAR is high, especially in long-term interactions. Keep presentations direct and language clear and unambiguous. When confronted, they will try to dominate; use a higher TELL trait when seeking closure. Do not drag it out; be swift and appeal to some positive goal toward which they can direct their attention. Their threats will be overt and not subtle (Korem, 1997, p. 162).

Salesman Types

Salesman/Manager–Express/Tell/Predictable/Confident

Interaction Tips: Encourage them to consider alternative ideas and new solutions before making a decision. Provide clear, unambiguous directives. Be direct and open. Expect decisiveness, rather than extensive discussion. Sell new ideas based upon previous successes and build upon experience. Firmly sell the bottom line, referring to past successes and how they predictably will lead to future successes. When confronted, use a stronger TELL trait, but adopt an open communication style. Appeal to their EXPRESS trait to encourage empathy, but be careful not to increase the explosiveness when there is tension. When there is resistance, detail the predictable results that will occur if cooperation is not provided. Focus on concrete issues, potential loss of stature, and their experiences rather than abstract ideas and concepts (Korem, 1997, pp. 163–164).

Salesman/Innovator–Express/Tell/Unpredictable/Confident

Interaction Tips: Avoid assigning them long-term roles involving routine performance. Focus on their tendency toward the need for change and personal recognition. Give them leadership roles in problem solving, but not in solution implementation. Sell the benefit of ideas and innovations, rather than the bottom line. In presentations, use low ASK traits as long as verbal skill and ideas are good, although TELL is preferable. Confront them with a stronger TELL, as well as either EXPRESS or CONTROL traits. Focus on creative options that will increase their personal stature or how their stature, ideas, or creative input may depreciate (Korem, 1997, p. 165).

Salesman/Conformist–Express/Tell/Predictable/Fearful

Interaction Tips: Don't expect big results quickly. They tend to be socially open, but slow-paced. Give them detailed instructions on how to interact. Avoid quick changes. Encourage them to recognize their tendency to be loyal and consider the integrity of those they serve. Avoid presentations that force them to make decisions out of confidence. Appeal to the fact that your idea seems to fit in with the norm. During confrontation, establish rapport and use EXPRESS traits to make a connection with their sociable SALESMAN style. Obtain concessions in small bites. If retaliation occurs, it will probably be spontaneous. When tension increases, appeal to their positive CONFORMISTS actions to reduce explosiveness (Korem, 1997, p. 167).

Salesman/Random Actor–Express/Tell/Unpredictable/Fearful

Interaction Tips: Get everything in writing. Don't tell them anything that is confidential. To maintain consistent performance, maintain control of their rewards and penalties. Do not expect the entire truth, such as the negative side of their story. Appeal to positive actions found in their COMMUNICATION type. Do not ask them to perform anything requiring reliability. Do not confront them in front of their peers or followers. Bring closure quickly and be prepared to protect yourself from direct and loud "in your face" retaliation (Korem, 1997, p. 169).

Accountant Types

Accountant/Manager–Control/Ask/Predictable/Confident

Interaction Tips: Allow time for detailed analysis and discussion of issues. Avoid placing them in roles requiring strong interpersonal control and exchange. Back up recommendations with details and keep things in a neat, orderly manner. Do not underestimate their ability to deliver. Presentations should be clear and concise, but detailed. Don't misconstrue a lack of verbal participation as a lack of interest. Listen carefully to input and do not interrupt when you have asked a question. They do not like confrontation, so have details down and well organized (Korem, 1997, p. 171).

Accountant/Innovator–Control/Ask/Unpredictable/Confident

Interaction Tips: Give them autonomy and the freedom to work on their own. Reward them with professional recognition more than money or positions of power. When questioning or seeking input, use nondirective, open-ended questions. Wait for answers, even after answered, as they may offer more while continuing to process the question. They are likely to defend personal territory and ideas indirectly and may ramble under pressure. They may play "devil's advocate" as a means of deflection. Keep them focused on the issues and give them time to think them through (Korem, 1997, pp. 172–173).

Accountant/Conformist–Control/Ask/Predictable/Fearful

Interaction Tips: Refrain from asking them to make presentations or speak in public. Find ways to reduce their fear if you want them to speak about an issue. Avoid issues that force them to reveal emotions and avoid references to your own power, position, or confidence. They should be placed in moderately challenging situations and given encouragement. Presentations should be laid back, non-urgent, and require little or no feedback. Confrontations should be more ASK style (Korem, 1997, pp. 174–175).

Accountant/Random Actor–Control/Ask/Unpredictable/Fearful

Interaction Tips: Be aware of buried emotions and pent-up feelings. Help them to talk about issues and focus on resolving fears and concerns. Watch for passive-aggressive responses as indicators of concerns that may cause them to "erupt." Do not ask them to buy into situations that require their personal interaction with others, but only behind-the-scenes, carefully controlled environments. Bring closure quickly to avoid their backing out on a commitment. Do not give them advance notice of confrontation and close quickly (Korem, 1997, pp. 176–177).

Artist Types

Artist/Manager–Express/Ask/Predictable/Confident

Interaction Tips: Be open and expressive in initial interactions and allow extra time to for them to "warm up" to others. Once a project is started, they are likely to be more demanding taskmasters. Encouraging them to explain why their profile may be confusing (and beneficial) may help promote team welfare. Presentations should be laid back with predictable results. Expressing emotions may sometimes be helpful. Avoid using excessive EXPRESS traits in confrontations (Korem, 1997, p. 179).

Artist/Innovator–Express/Ask/Unpredictable/Confident

Interaction Tips: They are usually easy to read and are the most likely source of great creative genius. Expect them to make challenges and criticisms. They will likely not provide details or precision. Provide realistic balance to their idealism. Do not require them to display strong control-oriented leadership. Ask for a response and wait for it. Use low CONTROL traits when confronting them and reach out to their EXPRESS traits to get them to open up. Appeal to the opportunity for understanding and feelings that will be settled or restored and new creative venues to be explored (Korem, 1997, p. 181).

Artist/Conformist–Express/Ask/Predictable/Fearful

Interaction Tips: Do not force them into quick decisions or reactions. Do not ask them to give others negative or critical feedback. After an agreement is reached, allow time for it to "settle in" before assuming it is a "done deal." Encourage them (as with all CONFORMIST profiles) to recognize their tendency toward loyalty and to carefully consider the integrity of those they serve so their trusting nature is not abused. Seek backup support from their colleagues to bolster their lack of decision-making initiative. Fear and sensitivity will cause them to retreat into themselves when confronted (Korem, 1997, p. 183).

Artist/Random Actor–Express/Ask/Unpredictable/Fearful

Interaction Tips: Be prepared for spontaneous and open displays of positive and negative emotion. Focus on minimizing fear-producing events or discussions. Do not place them in "sensitive" or politically complex situations or relationships. Avoid presentations that require important decision-making. Focus on ideas, rather than bottom-line issues, using slow, deliberate ASK traits, while preparing for fear-provoking issues. When confronting them, reduce fear with reassurances that keep their EXPRESS and FEARFUL traits in check. Appeal to their desire to be amiable and respectful, that is, positive actions. When they try to harm you, they will try to get in close, playing off your "feelings" of intimacy, and use anything that you give away about yourself personally (Korem, 1997, p. 185).

Combination Types

A person is a *combination type* when one of his or her plot points is near the middle of the gauge. He or she shares actions from both sides of the gauge (Korem, 1997, p. 65).

Three Levels and Four Rules of Systematic Accuracy

The Korem Profiling System provides three levels of information that can be accessed through profiling:

1. Snapshot Read—a short two-line description, which is useful in short-term, non-critical interactions.
2. Fine-tuned Read—identification of specific positive and negative actions, which is useful in longer-term, more critical interactions.

3. Comprehensive Profile—a full sheet of data, which includes general strengths, weaknesses, tendencies, and suggestions for interaction (Korem, 1997, p. 11).

Dan Korem writes, "Each time we make an observation that answers one of these questions, we have made a *read*. When we compile several *reads* together, we identify a *profile*, which provides a more complex picture of a person" (Korem, 1997, p. 19).

1. People typically act in consistent, similar ways, called *traits*. When two or more *traits* are combined together, they are called *types*. When two or more *types* are combined, you have a *profile*.
2. Always measure different people with the same "gauges" or questions.
   a. Consistent *traits* are *types*.
   b. Overgeneralizations are *stereotypes*.
3. Anything worth measuring is worth measuring at least twice. (Making quick assessments and then looking for information to confirm their initial hunches is one of the biggest mistakes made by interviewers.)
4. The best "gauges" or questions focus on actions that are related to what you are trying to predict. In this case, how does someone prefer to:
   a. communicate (perform),
   b. perform (walk),
   c. make decisions, and
   d. is this person creative?

(Korem, 1997, pp. 20, 26)

Reading Others: Successful Reads

It may seem to be paradoxical thinking to include this here, but I do not think so. I think it is an appropriate segue to quote Dr. Stanton Samenow, noted criminal psychologist, who wrote, "Criminals cause crime—not bad neighborhoods, inadequate parents, television, schools, drugs, or unemployment. Crime resides within the minds of human beings and is not caused by social conditions" (Samenow, 1984, p. 6). Having said that, it is important to understand the "the minds of human beings" and successful reads will help achieve that objective. There are seven tips on how to successfully make reads. These are:

1. Read the overall persona while looking for "leakage." We all have different ways of expressing the same trait. The "overall persona" does

not look for one specific action over another, but the combined effect of a person's action, speech, attire, etc. "Leakage" refers to breaks in consistency (Korem, 1997, p. 73).

2. Test Your reads. Create positive and negative assumptions that will test your read (Korem, 1997, p. 77).

3. Past behavior is the best predictor of future behavior. Most of us are creatures of habit. Most people do not jump from one extreme to another unless they are confronted by a life-changing experience. Be sure that the data you receive about a person's past behavior is accurate, and then test this by taking additional, real-time reads (Korem, 1997, p. 78).

4. Under pressure, one's traits are typically revealed. People typically act in consistent, similar ways called *traits*. Under pressure, our true traits and associated actions are usually revealed (Korem, 1997, pp. 78–79).

5. First reads can be productive. Use first impressions to create as many hunches as possible (Korem, 1997, p. 80).

6. People can learn actions outside their actual trait or type.

7. Unobtrusive reads are the most effective. Making "reads" indirectly or from the background is best (Korem, 1997, p. 83).

8. Do environment and time affect actions? People operate within a range and not at a specific plot on a gauge. It is best to observe a person in a full range of action (environment and time) (Korem, 1997, p. 85).

9. Learn to read your opposite traits and types. Most people have difficulty reading people who are the opposite of their trait or type because we do not live in "the other person's shoes" (Korem, 1997, p. 86).

Dr. Samenow noted, "It is critical that all of us know who the criminal is, that we realize that he thinks and acts differently from the rest of us. Only then will realistic and compassionate decisions, effective programs, rational policies, and sound legislation be forthcoming" (Samenow, 1984, p. 257).

Profiling the Criminal Mind
Criminal Investigative Analysis

9

Inductive and Deductive Reasoning

Inductive criminal profiling generalizes an individual criminal from behavioral and demographic characteristics shared by other criminals who have been studied in the past. It is considered by some to be an inaccurate short cut for proper investigative techniques.

Deductive reasoning is the process of reasoning the specific out of the general.

Deductive criminal profiling is the process of interpreting forensic evidence (crime scene photos, autopsy reports and photos, physical evidence, etc.) and a thorough study of offender victimology to accurately recreate crime scene behavior patterns. From these patterns, the profiler construes offender characteristics, demographics, emotions, and motivations.

Criminal profiling, as it is commonly known, or criminal investigative analysis (CIA), as it is more formally known, involves the application of social and behavioral science with forensic science to draw conclusions about the criminal perpetrator.

Most murders are solved because they involve intimates and the list of suspects usually starts with the victim's family, friends, associates, and acquaintances. Where the perpetrator is a stranger, however, and no victim–perpetrator relationship exists, investigators must assemble a list of suspects through a process referred to as "framing" or establishing the "circle of the investigation." This often involves searching for suspects with relevant criminal or psychiatric histories, collection of intelligence, or the receipt of tips from the public. This can lead to information overload and thousands of potential suspects. Profiling or behavioral analysis can help reduce this list to a more manageable and likely list. It can also help investigators connect crimes that are related. The inability to recognize such connections has been described as "linkage blindness." However, profiling and crime analysis can help to overcome this and lead to identifying perpetrators.

Dr. Ronald Holmes has written, "When a particular bizarre and sadistic crime has been discovered, an immediate question comes to mind: 'What kind of person would commit such an act?' Most crimes of this nature defy understanding and leave us with a sense of bewilderment and astonishment." He makes an excellent observation, writing, "The real question is, 'What makes someone do something like this?' ... To address such a question, profiling reconstructs a personality sketch for evaluation." A personality, he notes, is nothing more than the sum total of what a person is. It is that person's total set of values and attitudes or, as Dr. Holmes has observed, it is "the way he views motherhood and fatherhood, law and order, Democrats and Republicans, and all the other social, cultural, religious, and personal experiences that have been a part of his life" (Holmes, 1989, p. 34).

Crime Classification

To classify a crime, an investigator must ask questions about the victim, the crime scene, and the nature of the victim–offender exchange. Victimology is one of the most useful tools in classifying violent crimes. Crime analysis attempts to evaluate why (motive) a particular victim was targeted for a violent crime (Douglas et al., 1992, pp. 6–7). The *Crime Classification Manual* (CCM) is to the criminal profiler as the DSM-IV is to the mental health community. The CCM classifications include (1) homicide, (2) arson, and (3) rape and sexual assault. Important questions to be asked by investigators when classifying crimes include:

1. Was the victim known to the offender?
2. What were the victim's chances of becoming a target for violent crime?
3. What risk did the offender take in perpetrating this crime?

(Douglas et al., 1992, p. 7)

Crime Scene Analysis

The crime scene reflects the personality of the perpetrator. The traits of his or her personality will be reflected in the perpetration of the crime, as it is with the obsessive-compulsive. People may change certain aspects of their personality, but the "central core" is "set" and only minor changes occur due to time, circumstance, pressure, etc. (Holmes, 1989, p. 37).

There are four steps of crime scene analysis in criminal profiling or criminal investigative analysis:

1. The detection of *staging* and *personation* at the crime scene.
2. The *modus operandi* (method of operation) and *signature* aspects of violent crime.

3. Crime scene photography (documentation and evaluation of the scene).
4. Prescriptive interviewing; interfacing the interview/interrogation with crime classification witness typologies.

Crime Scene Indicators

Indicators help analyze the type of crime that has been committed. Indicators include:

1. How many crime scenes are involved? (Douglas et al., 1992, p. 8)
2. Environment/Place/Time refers to the conditions or circumstances in which the offense occurred, for example,
   a. *Environment*: busy streets or deserted country road
   b. *Place*: indoors or outdoors
   c. *Time*: daylight or the middle of the night
      – How long did the perpetrator stay at the scene?
      – Usually the amount of *time* is proportional to the degree of comfort the perpetrator feels committing the offense at the particular *location*.
      – This may indicate that a lingering perpetrator lives or works near the crime scene, knows the neighborhood, etc. (Douglas et al., 1992, pp. 8–9)
3. How many perpetrators were involved? This helps determine whether the offense should be categorized as (a) criminal enterprise or (b) group cause (Douglas et al., 1992, p. 9).
4. Organized or Disorganized/Physical Evidence:
   a. Does the scene reflect that this is a *group excitement killing* that is *spontaneous* and *disarrayed*, with a great deal of physical evidence?
   b. Does the scene reflect that a *methodical, well-organized* perpetrator is involved, who did not leave prints or physical evidence?
   c. The amount of *organization* or *disorganization* at the crime scene will be suggestive of the perpetrator's *level of criminal sophistication*, demonstrate how well he or she was able to *control the victim*, and suggest how much *premeditation* was involved.
   d. The crime scene will rarely be completely organized or disorganized, but will likely be at some point on a continuum between neat/orderly and sloppy/disarranged. (Douglas et al., 1992, p. 9)

5. Weapon:
   a. Was the weapon used a "weapon of choice," brought to the scene by the perpetrator?
   b. Was the weapon used a "weapon of opportunity," acquired at the scene by the perpetrator?
   c. Was the weapon left behind or taken from the scene?
   d. Is there evidence that multiple weapons or ammunition were used? (*Note*: This does not always indicate multiple perpetrators.)
   e. In the case of arson, did the fire start from accelerants brought to the scene?
   f. In the case of arson, did the fire start from materials on hand at the scene? (Douglas et al., 1992, p. 9)

6. Body Disposition:
   a. Was the body openly displayed or otherwise placed in a deliberate manner to ensure discovery?
   b. Was the body concealed or buried to prevent discovery?
   c. Did the perpetrator seem to have no concern as to whether the body would be discovered? (Douglas et al., 1992, p. 9)

7. Missing or Left Items:
   a. The presence of additional, unusual artifacts, drawings, graffiti, or other items are often associated with extremist murders or gang murders.
   b. Perpetrator communications, such as ransom demands or extortion notes, may be involved.
   c. Items taken from the scene are often associated with felony murder, burglary, arson for concealment, sexual assault, etc.
   d. Personal items taken, which have little or no monetary value, may be taken by perpetrators as so-called "souvenirs." (Douglas et al., 1992, p. 10)

8. Other Crime Scene Indicators:
   a. The nature of the confrontation between the victim and the perpetrator is important in determining the motive and classification, for example, wounded victims, no escape plan, the probability of witnesses, etc.
   b. How did the perpetrator control the victim? Are restraints present?
   c. Did the perpetrator "blitz attack" to incapacitate the victim?
   d. Was the scene staged? "Staging" is the purposeful alteration of a crime scene. (Douglas et al., 1992, p. 10)

9. Forensic Evidence:
   a. The *primary* sources of physical evidence are the victim, the perpetrator, and the crime scene.
   b. *Secondary* sources include the home or work environment of a suspect.
   c. *Medical reports,* such as toxicology results, x-rays (and other medical imagery), and post-mortem autopsy results are forensic evidence.
      - *Cause of Death*—the mechanism of death:
        - Gunshot wounds
        - Explosive trauma—often associated with criminal competition or extremist murders
        - Strangulation—often associated with more personal crimes, such as domestic or sexual murders
      - *Trauma*—the type, extent, and focus of injury, such as overkill, facial battery, torture, bite marks, mutilation, etc., are examples of forensic findings.
      - *Sexual Assault*—the type and sequence of the assault, as well the timing (before, during, or after death) can also be revealing. (Douglas et al., 1992, p. 11)

Crime Classification by Type, Style, and Number of Victims

Classification of crimes is by the *type*, *style*, and *number of victims*. The number of victims is defined as:

- Single murder
- Double murder
- Triple murder
- Mass murder
- Spree murder—killing at two or more locations with no emotional cooling-off period
- Serial murder—three or more separate events with an emotional cooling-off period between

(Douglas et al., 1992, p. 12)

Crime Classification Worksheet

The Crime Classification Worksheet outlines the defining characteristics of each of the categories. Under each characteristic are some of the aspects that will assist investigators in classifying the offense (see Figure 9.1) (Douglas et al., 1992, pp. 12–14).

The basic code for the Crime Classification Numbering System uses three digits. The first digit represents the *major crime category* (homicide, arson, and sexual assault). The second digit represents further division of major crimes into *groups*. The third digit represents *specific classifications*

CRIME CLASSIFICATION WORKSHEET

I. Victimology: Why did this person become the victim of a violent crime?
  A. About the victim
- Lifestyle
- Employment
- Personality
- Friends (type, number)
- Income (amount, source)
- Family
- Alcohol/drug use or abuse
- Normal dress
- Handicaps
- Transportation used
- Reputation, habits, fears
- Marital status
- Dating habits
- Leisure activities
- Criminal history
- Assertiveness
- Likes and dislikes
- Significant events prior to the crime
- Activities prior to the crime

  B. Sexual Assault: Verbal Interaction
- Excessively vulgar or abusive
- Scripting
- Apologetic

  C. Arson and bombing: targeted property
- Residential
- Commercial
- Educational
- Mobile, vehicle
- Forest, fields

II. Crime Scene
- How many?
- Environment, time, place
- How many offenders?

- Organized, disorganized
- Physical evidence
- Weapon
- Body disposition
- Items left/missing
- Other (for example, witnesses, ecape plan, wounded victims)

III. Staging
- Natural death
- Accidental
- Suicide
- Criminal activity (i.e., robbery, rape/homicide)

IV. Forensic Findings
  A. Forensic analysis
- Hair/fibers
- Blood
- Semen
- Saliva
- Other

  B. Autopsy results
- Cause of death
- Trauma (type, extent, location on body)
- Overkill
- Torture
- Facial battery (depersonalization)
- Bite marks
- Mutilation
- Sexual assault (when, sequence, to where, insertion, insertional necrophilia)
- Toxicological results

V. Investigative considerations
  A. Search warrants
- Home
- Work
- Car
- Other

  B. Locating and interviewing witnesses

Figure 9.1 Crime Classification Worksheet.

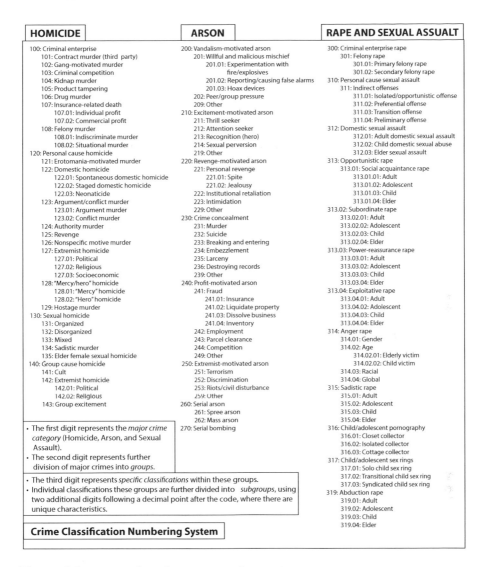

Figure 9.2 Crime Classification Numbering System.

within these groups. These groups are further divided into *subgroups*, using two additional digits following a decimal point after the code, where there are unique characteristics (see Figure 9.2) (Douglas et al., 1992, pp. 12–14).

Organized and Disorganized Crimes

Crime scenes and criminal personalities have been classified as "organized" and "disorganized." Profiler Robert Ressler wrote, "The organized versus disorganized distinction became the great divide, a fundamental way of separating two quite different types of personalities who commit multiple murders.... Some crime scenes, and some murders, display organized as well as disorganized characteristics, and we call these 'mixed'" (Ressler and Shachtman, 1992, p. 114) (see Figure 9.3).

Crimes are also divided into four phases. First, the *pre-crime stage* takes into account the "antecedent behavior" of the offender. Often, this is the last stage from which we infer information, although it is the first stage in temporal

A Comparison of
ORGANIZED NONSOCIAL TYPOLOGIES and DISORGANIZED ASOCIAL TYPOLOGIES

Profile Characteristics

• High intelligence	• Below average intelligence
	• High school dropout
• Socially adequate	• Socially inadequate
• Sexually competent	• Rarely dates
• Charming	• Poor personal hygiene
• Lives with partner	• Lives alone
• Geographically mobile	• Lives/works near crime scene
• Masculine image	• Nocturnal/night person
• Occupationally mobile	• Unskilled work
• Controlled mood	• Anxious mood during crime
	• Minimal use of alcohol
• Interest in media	• Minimal interest in news media
• Situational cause	• Significant behavioral change
• Model prisoner	• Secret hiding places
• High birth order status	• Low birth order status
	• Father's work unstable
• Harsh discipline	• Harsh/inconsistent discipline

Crime Scene
- Controlled crime scene
- Planned offense
- Targeted stranger
- Personalizes victim
- Controlled conversation
- Submissive victim
- Restraints used
- Aggressive acts
- Body moved
- Weapon taken
- Little evidence

Post-Offense Behavior
- May move body
- May dispose body to advertise crime
- Returns to scene of crime
- Police groupie
- Anticipates questioning
- Volunteers information

Interview Strategy
- Direct strategy
- Be certain of details
- Will only admit what he has to

Post-Offense Behavior
- May attend funeral
- Memorial in media
- Returns to scene of crime
- May keep diary or news clippings
- May change residence
- May change jobs
- May have personality change

Interview Strategy
- Counselor approach
- Empathize
- Indirectly introduce evidence
- Night time interview

Crime Scene
- Disorganized crime scene
- Spontaneous offense
- Victim known
- Depersonalizes victim
- Minimal conversation
- Sudden violence
- No restraints
- Sex after death
- Body not moved
- Weapon left
- Physical evidence

Figure 9.3 Comparison of Organized and Disorganized Typologies.

sequence. Second, the actual *commission of the crime stage* involves victim selection, as well as the criminal acts themselves, which may include abduction, torture, rape, as well as the killing. Third, the *disposal of the body stage* differentiates that some murderers do not seem to display any concern about having the victim found, while others go to great lengths to avoid its discovery. Fourth, the *post-crime behavior stage* can, in some cases, can be quite important, as some offenders attempt to inject themselves into the investigation of the murder, or otherwise "keep in touch with the crime in order to continue the fantasy that started it" (Ressler and Shachtman, 1992, pp. 114–115).

Author Brent Turvey does not agree with the organized–disorganized dichotomy, referring to it as "predictions masquerading as conclusions." He writes that the "dichotomy" can best be understood by the implication that organized offenders are inferred to be *psychopathic*, while disorganized offenders are inferred to be *psychotic*. Organized crime scenes, then, are characterized by behavior that is indicative of a psychopathic character disorder. Disorganized crime scenes, conversely, are evidenced by a psychotic deterioration of normal intellectual and social functioning and withdrawal from reality (Turvey, 1999, pp. 146–147).

Turvey's objections to the "false dichotomy" begin with his observation that crime scenes fall somewhere between two extremes on a continuum, rather than at one end or the other. He also asserts that a crime scene and the amount of evidence left behind must be viewed in the context of "a dynamic series of events," which may be the result of "non-psychotic or non-mental-illness-oriented events." He further notes that a crime scene lacking evidence of psychotic behavior does not necessarily infer the alternative of a psychopathic character disorder (Turvey, 1999, pp. 147–149).

Turvey goes on to opine that labeling an offender using the dichotomy may result in a failure to note an offender's development over time and that relying upon classifying offenders by *modus operandi* accounts only for *what* happened and not *why*. Finally, Turvey says that he has ethical issues with the "dichotomy" from a clinical perspective (Turvey, 1999, pp. 148–149). Regardless of these objections, it is important to understand this underlying theory of criminal behavioral analysis. Therefore, we will examine the organized (psychopathic) offender as the *organized nonsocial typology* and the disorganized (psychotic) offender as the *disorganized asocial typology*.

Organized Nonsocial Typology

Ressler says, "The major attribute of the organized offender is his planning of the crime" (Ressler and Shachtman, 1992, p. 115).

Organized nonsocial offenders are usually organized in their lifestyle, home or apartment, car or truck (automobile), personal appearance, etc. They are an anal personality type, requiring a place for everything and that everything is in its place. Organized nonsocials choose to be loners because no one is good enough for them. Their crimes usually involve real or imagined precipitating factors, leaving them "no choice" (Holmes, 1989, pp. 47–48).

Organized nonsocial offenders are usually of average intelligence, may have done well in school, and are socially competent. Some are married and most are intimate with someone, have sex partners, or have superficial relationships. Many are from middle-class families and are high in birth order. Their fathers usually held stable jobs, but discipline was inconsistent. They are more comfortable venturing away from home, are able to change jobs because they make a good first impression, and may hold a good position. They have little trouble making friends, are masculine and flashy dressers, and may drive a car that reflects their personality. Characterized as having a sociopathic character disorder, they are reluctant to accept constructive criticism because they perceive it as "destructive" and think they know best for everyone (Holmes, 1989, pp. 48–49).

The organized offender, like the disorganized offender, is also the stereotypic perpetrator who "returns to the scene of the crime" to relive the crime, but might not because of knowledge of the stereotype. These perpetrators should be confronted directly during interrogations and they tend to respect competence. If the investigator presents "the facts," they must truly and accurately reflect the facts because any false claims or misrepresentations will be noted by the perpetrators. They will know when they are being "conned" and "false evidence" will result in their knowing that there is no case. They will only admit what they have to admit, regardless of being confronted by the facts. They will not volunteer information that could result in a confession (Holmes, 1989, pp. 49–50).

Disorganized Asocial Typology

Disorganized asocial offenders are disorganized in their daily activities, including their home or apartment, employment (if they are employed at all), car or truck, clothing, demeanor, etc. This typology is disorganized in their appearance, lifestyle, and psychological state. They are usually non-athletic, white males with an introverted personality. Many have been victims themselves of physical or emotional abuse and are often loners with solitary hobbies or imaginary playmates. They also tend to have problems with educational pursuits and may have a below average IQ. They are likely to have few extracurricular activities, rarely date, are socially segregated, and tend toward menial, unskilled jobs (if they are employed at all) (Holmes, 1989, pp. 43–45).

The disorganized offender is likely to be a night person and the stereotypic perpetrator who "returns to the scene of the crime" to envision or relive the crime. He or she may even attend the funeral of the victim, place a memorial in the newspaper, or keep a diary or pictorial representation of his or her acts and fantasies (Holmes, 1989, p. 46).

The disorganized perpetrator may be more likely to respond to interrogation that employs a relationship-motivated strategy and empathy; for example, a *psychotic* killer who says a demon demanded the killing may respond better by suggesting that although the demon has not been seen, if the killer says that it exists, it must exist (Holmes, 1989, p. 46).

Assessment, Staging, and Personation

Speech patterns, writing styles, verbal and non-verbal gestures, and other traits and patterns make up human behavior. These combinations of behavior cause individuals to act, react, function, or perform in a unique and specific way. This individualized behavior usually remains consistent, whether it involves daily grooming, household chores, or rape and murder. The crime scene usually reflects this consistent behavior pattern and distinguishes between different perpetrators who commit the same offenses. There are three manifestations of perpetrator behavior at crime scenes: (1) *modus operandi* (M.O.), (2) personation (the perpetrator signature), and (3) staging (Douglas et al., 1992, p. 249).

The Assessment Phase of crime analysis should attempt to answer several questions, such as:

1. What is the sequence of events?
2. Was the victim sexually assaulted before or after death?
3. Was there mutilation before death?
4. How did the encounter between the perpetrator and the victim occur?
5. Did the offender "blitz attack" the victim or use verbal means to "con and capture" the victim?
6. Did the offender use restraints or ligatures to control the victim?
7. Were any items or artifacts left (added to) or taken from the crime scene (which require careful analysis)?

(Douglas et al., 1992, p. 250)

Modus Operandi (M.O.) and Victimology

Modus operandi (M.O.), or *modi operandi* in the plural, is the "method of operation" of a perpetrator. The term is used to describe the habits of a person or mode of working, particularly when referred to crime. It is learned behavior, but is also consistent behavior over long periods of time. It is commonly used to describe the methods employed by criminal perpetrators to identify clues about their identity.

Victimology involves the characteristics of victims and is an element in determining the M.O. of the perpetrator; for example, if the victims are all female professionals in their 20s or all elderly people living alone, this victimology information can be useful in determining the M.O. The M.O. is an important tool in linking cases together.

Turvey observes that profilers spend at least as much time examining victim histories as they do suspects. Victim profiles provide context, connections, and investigative leads or direction. Creating a timeline by retracing a victim's last known actions helps investigators understand the relationship between the victim, the environment, events, and how the victim came to be targeted or selected by the perpetrator. A "psychological autopsy" refers to the process of evaluating the state of mind of the victim before he or she died. This involves wound pattern analysis, the victim's state of mind, and the victim's mental health history (Turvey, 1999, pp. 106, 109, 110).

Personation (Signature)

Often violent crime activities begin with quiet, isolated thought within the offender's imagination. When these thoughts are translated into criminal actions, the perpetrator's needs compel him or her to exhibit unusual behavior during the crime. Unusual behavior by an offender that is not necessary to commit the crime is called "personation." The perpetrator vests intimate meaning into the crime scene, such as body positioning, mutilation, left or removed items or artifacts, or other "symbolic gestures involving the crime scene." When a serial perpetrator demonstrates repetitive ritualistic behavior from one crime to the next, it is called a "signature," which is repetitive personation. "Undoing" is a form of personation that occurs when there is a close association between the perpetrator and the victim by changing something, for example, changing the victim's clothing, washing the victim, covering the victim's face or body, etc. (Douglas et al., 1992, p. 251).

Staging

Staging is when someone intentionally alters the crime scene with the purpose of redirecting investigation away from the most logical suspect or to "protect" the victim or the victim's family. Staging may occur in rape–murder crimes and autoerotic deaths, such as when the apparatus of death is removed to protect the victim or family from embarrassment, whereas a sexual perpetrator often leaves the victim in a degrading position. Investigators should be alert to whether the perpetrator or some other interested party (e.g., a friend, family member, or first responder) altered the scene for protective purposes. It is also important to determine whether the crime scene is actually *disorganized* or whether the perpetrator *staged* the scene to appear "careless and haphazard." This is important in analyzing the motive and developing a perpetrator profile (Douglas et al., 1992, pp. 251–252).

When staging occurs, the perpetrator is usually someone who had some association or relationship with the victim, rather than someone who just happens upon the victim. When in contact with law enforcement, the perpetrator will attempt to direct the investigation away from him or her, while seeming to be cooperative. Inconsistencies will be present in staged crime scenes when perpetrators make mistakes while trying to stage the scene the way he or she thinks a crime scene should look. Investigators should ask themselves:

- Do these injuries fit the scene?
- Did the perpetrator take inappropriate items from the scene to make burglary appear to be the motive?
- Did the point of entry appear logical?
- Did commission of this crime pose a high risk to the perpetrator? (Douglas et al., 1992, pp. 251, 253)
- What looks out of place for the apparent crime or motive?

Investigators must understand the dynamics of human behavior displayed at crime scenes to diagnose such manifestations at the scene.

Conclusion

Profiling of behavior and crime scene patterns can be a powerful deductive and inductive resource for critical thinking and logical reasoning. It should not be considered a "crystal ball" for making predictions, but a forecasting tool for developing and exploiting leads.

Interviewing and Interrogation

10

Introduction to Interrogation

First, it is important to understand the legal limits and ramifications of interviews and interrogations. The legal requirements for interrogations and confessions are complex enough for a book entirely on that topic. The legal requirements are also ever evolving. Because that is beyond the scope of this book and the law changes from time to time, the reader should always seek competent legal counsel on this subject.

Make sure that both the investigator and the suspect know that the investigator is not merely seeking a confession or conviction, but is a fact-finder and truth seeker. It is also important for the investigator–interrogator to be thoroughly familiar with the case before starting any interview or interrogation.

The selection and preparation of the interview room is also important. It should provide privacy, with no distractions, and should have appropriate recording equipment. (Refer to state and federal case laws requiring the recording of confessions and interviews). Avoid barriers and distance between the interrogator and the suspect. Avoid overt note taking to the extent possible, but ensure that pertinent points are recorded.

Avoid words like "murder," "kill," "steal," "confess your crime," etc. and use more psychologically acceptable terms (for the suspect), such as "shoot," "take," "tell the truth," etc. Suspects will often tell the truth when terms that are more acceptable to them are used, rather than terms that they cannot psychologically accept. Rather than telling suspects that they are lying, tell them that they have not told the entire truth.

Treat suspects with common decency and respect. Adapt your language to their level so they will understand you and respond appropriately. Try to think the way the suspects would think and what you would say if you were in their place.

Types of questions used in an interrogation include (1) prepared questions, (2) control questions (used to check truthfulness), (3) non-pertinent questions (to conceal the true purpose), and (4) direct questions (which require a narrative reply). Avoid leading questions, which suggest the "correct" answers.

"Interrogation" (Interview) of Witnesses and Potential Informants

"Interrogations" of victims, witnesses, and potential informants are usually referred to as "interviews," rather than interrogations. Interviewing witnesses and informants is different from the interrogation of suspects in both objective and techniques.

An interview is a fact gathering process aimed at identifying who, what, when, where, why, and how. Unlike interrogations, the victim, witness, and informant interviews are dominated by the interviewee, who responds to questions from the interviewer. Once the victim, witness, and informant have completed their narrative, the interviewer returns to the beginning and leads them back through the areas that need clarification or more details. There may be times when an interviewer will want to conceal the areas that are of true interest, such as when the interviewee is trying to obtain as much information from the interviewer as the interviewer is from the interviewee. This is often accomplished by focusing on areas of interest to the interviewee and then coming back to the true areas of interest that are relevant (Zulawski and Wicklander, 1993, pp. 131, 157).

Here are a few suggestions for interviewing witnesses and potential informants:

1. Assure witnesses or potential informants that they will not be harmed by perpetrators or their friends or relatives. Assure them that they will receive any necessary protection (and keep that promise) (Inbau and Reid, 1970, p. 120).
2. When a witness or potential informant refuses to cooperate because he or she is defending a perpetrator's interests or because of anti-social or anti-police attitudes, try to break the bond of loyalty between the witness or informant and the perpetrator. In the alternative, accuse the witness or informant as if he or she is involved or is a suspect (Inbau and Reid, 1970, p. 122).

Deception Detection

Philip Houston and his associates say, "The idea here is that if you want to know if someone is lying, you need to ignore truthful behavior so that it is not processed. That seems counterintuitive to most people, and downright nonsensical to many. Yet it's one of the core principles underlying the model" (Houston, Floyd, and Carnicero, 2012, p. 48).

Houston and his associates write:

In order to determine whether a person is being untruthful, we need to look and listen for the first deceptive behavior to occur within the first five seconds after the stimulus is delivered.... Cognitive research, meanwhile, suggests that we think at least five times faster than we speak. What that tells us is the further in time we get away from the stimulus, the higher the likelihood that the brain has gone on to thinking about something else. Our experience has shown that if we can identify the first deceptive behavior within that first five seconds, we can reasonably conclude that the behavior is directly associated with the stimulus. (Houston et al., 2012, pp. 31–31)

Obstacles to deception detection include:

- The belief that people will not lie to you (Houston et al., 2012, p. 16)
- Reliance on behavioral myths (unsupported by research or evidence) (Houston et al., 2012, p. 17)
- The complexities of communication (Houston et al., 2012, p. 18)
- Inescapable biases (Houston et al., 2012, p. 19)
- The "global" influence (so much data coming in and so many tasks to perform to process that data that it cannot all be assimilated) (Houston et al., 2012, p. 21)

Interrogation of Suspects

The interview (used for victims, witnesses, and informants) and interrogation (used for suspects and perpetrators) process includes these steps:

1. Preparation and strategy—Know the case, know the legal restraints, and know why people make denials, resist admission, and lie.
2. Interviewing—Begin with non-accusatory fact finding; understand the cognitive psychology of interviewing and use neurolinguistics to evaluate the truth and deception.
3. Establish credibility—Convince the suspect that the investigation has clearly identified him or her as the perpetrator.
4. Reduce resistance—Stop denials. Denials may be *emphatic* (a physical behavior, such as shaking the head "no" in denial) or *explanatory* (any excuse or reason why the suspect could not be involved; usually following an emphatic denial).
5. Obtaining an admission—Once denials have been stopped, the suspect may be ready to be submissive to answering choice questions

(e.g., "Did you use the money for drugs or food?" or "Did you intend to hurt them or was it an accident?").

6. Developing an admission—An admission is not a confession, but an admission to certain facts; admissions alone are helpful, but they may also lead to a confession.

7. Professional close—Once the interrogation or interview is over, close with any appropriate written statements and summation.

(Zulawski and Wicklander, 1993, pp. 7–11)

Criminal offenders are often generally classified as *emotional* and *non-emotional* offenders. Emotional offenders often consist of those who have committed crimes against persons in the heat of passion, for revenge, anger, or by accident. Non-emotional offenders usually consist of those who have committed crimes for financial gain, such as theft, burglary, and other property crimes or crimes against persons (violence) for monetary gain. Understanding the classification often helps determine whether to use a sympathetic or emotional tactic or a factual analysis tactic (Inbau and Reid, 1970, pp. 25–26).

The *sympathetic* or *emotional* technique confronts the suspect, not about the details or circumstances of the suspect's involvement in the incident, but on the reasons why the suspect did what he or she did. Here, the interrogator rationalizes with the suspect by offering reasons or excuses that allow the suspect to save face, even when admitting involvement (Zulawski and Wicklander, 1993, pp. 2–3).

The *factual analysis technique* fails when the incident has not been adequately investigated and the interrogator has not prepared to counter the suspect's explanation or stories (Zulawski and Wicklander, 1993, p. 2).

When circumstances are right, *factual analysis* and *sympathetic* or *emotional* techniques or tactics can be modified and combined. Incorporating a "factual component" establishes the credibility of the investigation and reduces resistance. Combined with the "emotional interrogation," using rationalization to justify or minimize the seriousness of the suspect's actions in the incident is often more effective than using one or the other tactic alone (Zulawski and Wicklander, 1993, p. 3).

The interrogator should be flexible in using some or all of the following tactics and techniques when a suspect's guilt is reasonably certain.

1. Display an air of confidence in the subject's guilt. At various times throughout the interrogation the suspect should be reminded that the investigation has established the fact that the suspect committed the crime, that there is no doubt about this, and that his or her behavior patterns demonstrate that he or she is not telling the truth. If the suspect interrupts, avoid allowing them to make repeated denials

that become more and more fortified. The more suspects repeat a lie, the harder it is for them to recant it and tell the truth. They are often reluctant to admit lying after repeating a lie. Instead, direct their comments toward the reasons why they committed the offense, rather than whether they did so (Inbau and Reid, 1970, pp. 27–29).

2. Point out some, but not all, of the circumstantial evidence. Point out some evidence, but not all, that demonstrates the suspect's guilt. Avoid high-pressure, rapid-fire questions. Interrupt any explanation offered by the suspect and check anything the suspect says against known facts, especially those that have not been disclosed and are known only to the perpetrator (Inbau and Reid, 1970, pp. 31–32).

3. Draw attention to the subject's physiological and psychological symptoms of guilt. Offenders who believe that their appearance and demeanor betray their guilt destroy their confidence and make them vulnerable. Learn to recognize the physiological and psychological signs of stress (Inbau and Reid, 1970, p. 33).

4. Sympathize with the subject by telling him or her that anyone else under similar circumstances might have done the same thing. Offenders, particularly emotional offenders, may find mental comfort from an interrogator who assures them that others might have done the same thing or offer justification or excuses that seem acceptable (Inbau and Reid, 1970, p. 38).

5. Minimize the seriousness and moral implications of the offense. Use terms and explanations that minimize the seriousness of the offenses or acts in the suspects mind so the suspect can morally accept such terms or explanations (Inbau and Reid, 1970, p. 40).

6. Suggest a less stigmatizing and more morally acceptable motivation or reason for the offense than the one that is known or presumed. Suspects should be afforded an opportunity to save face by allowing them to offer an initial admission of guilt based upon a less offensive motivation, for example, accidental fire, intoxication, taking money for someone else (children, family, etc.), "everyone else was doing it," etc. The objective is to get the suspect to make an initial admission that connects him or her to the incident or the scene of the crime (Inbau and Reid, 1970, p. 43).

7. Sympathize with the subject by (a) blaming the victim, (b) blaming an accomplice, or (c) blaming anyone or anything else with a plausible causal connection (Inbau and Reid, 1970, p. 47).

8. Demonstrate sympathy and understanding when urging the subject to tell the truth. Some call this the "good cop–bad cop" technique. Ensure that no promises or threats are made when employing this method (Inbau and Reid, 1970, p. 59). Because this technique has been depicted in numerous movies and TV shows, it may not be

effective unless used in a more subtle way. It is also important that this technique not result in intimidation or coercion (Zulawski and Wicklander, 1993, p. 2).

9. Suggest possible exaggeration by the accuser or victim or exaggerate the nature and seriousness of the offense. Explain to the suspect that, while there is obviously some basis for the accusation, there is always the possibility that the accuser exaggerated. Explain that the suspect is not telling all of the truth, but that it may not be as serious as the accuser says and that is why he or she needs to tell everything (Inbau and Reid, 1970, p. 64).

10. Have the subject place himself at the scene of the crime or in contact with the victim or incident. If the suspect admits he or she was at the scene of the crime when the act occurred, or that he or she saw this missing item earlier, acceptance of full responsibility will come easier (Inbau and Reid, 1970, p. 70).

11. Try to obtain an admission that the subject lied about some incidental aspect of the incident. Once the suspects have been caught in a lie, it will be easy to remind them later that they have not been telling the truth (Inbau and Reid, 1970, p. 71).

12. Exploit the subject's sense of pride using flattery or a challenge to his or her honor. It is a common human characteristic to want the approval of others. Use this to build rapport (Inbau and Reid, 1970, p. 78).

13. Point out the futility of not telling the truth. You must not only convince the suspect that his or her guilt has been detected, but that it can be established by currently available evidence. Help the suspect to understand the futility of continued denial (Inbau and Reid, 1970, p. 77).

14. Point out the seriousness and futility of continuing criminal behavior. Often offenders will experience at least a fleeting desire or intention to reform or change their ways (Inbau and Reid, 1970, p. 77). Encourage this by encouraging them to clear everything up all at once.

15. Before asking for a general admission of guilt, first ask a question about some detail of the crime or about the reason for committing the offense. Begin by questioning the suspect about some detail of the incident or offense or the reason or excuse for committing the crime. You can move to more general admissions after obtaining specific admissions (Inbau and Reid, 1970, pp. 79–80).

16. When co-perpetrators are being interrogated (and all else fails), play one against the other. Co-defendants often share a fear that one will talk or confess, giving them some special consideration or advantage (Inbau and Reid, 1970, pp. 84–85). Remember not to make prom-

ises that you cannot keep. You can make suspects aware that their cooperation or lack of cooperation will be noted in your report and to the prosecutor, but make no promises.

Interrogation of Suspects Whose Guilt Is Uncertain

1. Ask the suspect if he or she knows why he or she is being questioned. A guilty subject is placed in a vulnerable and defensive position. If they say that they do not know, when circumstances make obvious the fact that they do, they are obviously lying at the outset. Both guilty and innocent subjects may start out by discussing offenses that the investigator or interrogator did not know about (Inbau and Reid, 1970, pp. 94–95).

2. Ask the suspect to relate everything he or she knows about the incident, victim, or possible suspects. Start out by asking a few general questions about the suspect's knowledge of the incident, victim, possible suspects, etc. If the suspect is innocent, this gives him or her an opportunity to reveal as much helpful information as he or she knows rather than restricting the suspect to specific questions (Inbau and Reid, 1970, p. 95).

3. Obtain details about the suspect's activities before, during, and after the incident. If the suspect's memory of details before and after an incident is good, it should be good for events during the incident (Inbau and Reid, 1970, p. 97).

4. Where certain facts suggest the subject's guilt, ask about him or her casually, as if the facts are not already known. This affords the suspect an opportunity to lie (or not) and provide an indication of lying or not lying or guilt or innocence (Inbau and Reid, 1970, p. 101).

5. Periodically ask relevant questions in a manner that implies that the correct answers are already known. This helps elicit information by creating an impression that the correct answer is known and that the interrogator is only interested in determining whether the suspect is willing to tell the truth (Inbau and Reid, 1970, p. 102).

6. Refer to some non-existing incriminating evidence to see if the suspect will attempt to explain it away. (If he or she does, this suggests that he or she is guilty.) A guilty person wants to "cover his tracks" and will often explain away the evidence. This is often asked as an "Is there any reason why . . ." question (Inbau and Reid, 1970, p. 103).

7. Ask the suspect if he or she ever "thought" about committing the crime or one similar to it. A guilty person may offer an explanation for why he or she "looks" guilty when answering this question (Inbau and Reid, 1970, p. 104).

8. Ask the suspect if he or she would offer to make restitution. (If he or she does, this suggests that he or she is guilty). Most innocent persons will not agree to pay a victim any part of restitution. Sometimes a perpetrator will offer to pay restitution for an actual amount, but not a fictional loss (Inbau and Reid, 1970, p. 106). For example, if three thefts of $100 occur, but the investigator asks about restitution for the three thefts of $100 each and a fourth theft of $150, the thief may offer to pay only the three and not the fourth fictitious theft.

9. Ask if the suspect is willing to take a polygraph (lie detector) or similar test. Most innocent people will agree to prove their innocence, while most guilty people will refuse or agree, then back out or make excuses not to (Inbau and Reid, 1970, p. 106). This is not always the case, as many people are afraid of "lie detectors" or opine that they are "not reliable."

10. Suspects who tell investigators or interrogators, "OK, I will tell you what you want to hear, but I didn't do it," are likely guilty. (However, watch for false confessions and corroborate them.) An innocent person usually persists in denying guilt, while a guilty suspect may try to placate an interrogator by offering to admit to committing the offense, while at the same time continuing to deny committing it (Inbau and Reid, 1970, p. 108). This often comes out something like, "I didn't do it; but if you want me to say I did, I'll say it." Do not accept this as a confession. Continue the interview.

Interrogation of Criminal Suspects

Here are a few more helpful tips for interrogating suspects:

1. Interview the victim, accuser, or discoverer of the crime before interrogating the suspect (Inbau and Reid, 1970, p. 108).

2. Be patient; do not be in a hurry. Take five more minutes (Inbau and Reid, 1970, p. 111).

3. Never make promises. Do not make promises when asked, "What will happen to me if I tell the truth?" Be skeptical of the so-called "conscience-stricken" confession (Inbau and Reid, 1970, p. 114).

4. When a suspect has made repeated denials to other interrogators, try asking the suspect about some other, unrelated offense of a similar nature (which he or she is also suspected of committing) (Inbau and Reid, 1970, p. 115).

5. Unintelligent, uneducated suspects should be questioned at the same psychological level employed to question a child about wrongdoing (Inbau and Reid, 1970, p. 116).

Written Confessions

1. Warnings of Constitutional rights (*Miranda* and similar warnings). Always follow the law when advising suspects of their Constitutional rights. This does not mean that you have to inform them of all of the Constitutional rights, but those referred to as *Miranda* rights. Videotaping the interview not only records the statement given, including admissions and confessions, but also demonstrates that the suspect was advised of his or her rights and that no promises, coercion, or force were used.

2. The form of the confession. Written confessions, even though recorded, may be taken following specific questions by the interrogator and narrative answers by the perpetrator. It should be typed, and then signed and dated by the perpetrator.

3. Readability and understandability. Handwritten confessions are also good, but only if they are legible (readable) and can be understood. For example, what does "it," "that night," "the place," etc. mean? Make sure that the perpetrator is specific.

4. Avoid leading questions. When ensuring that the perpetrator is specific, avoid leading questions. Avoid having the interrogator do most of the talking or using "yes" and "no" questions. It is better to ask, "What happened next?" or "What did you do with the gun" or "What happened to the money?"

5. Use the confessor's own words. Let the perpetrator tell the story his or her way, using his or her own language or expressions.

6. Personal history questions. Often the perpetrator will claim that he or she just said what he or she was told to say. It may be helpful to intersperse a few questions throughout the interview, which can only be answered by the perpetrator. For example, ask the perpetrator where he or she went to school or where he or she has lived (Inbau and Reid, 1970, p. 131)

7. Intentional errors for correction by the confessor. Sometimes placing intentional errors in the typed confession allows an opportunity for the perpetrator to initial or sign next to corrections. This demonstrates that he or she read it and approved the corrections (Inbau and Reid, 1970, p. 132).

8. Reading and signing the confession. You may also want to have the perpetrator write "OK" and his or her initials at the bottom of each page to verify that he or she approves the statement. The statement or confession should, of course, be signed and witnessed. It should include either a handwritten (by the perpetrator) or typed authentication statement similar to this:

I have read this statement and it is true. I gave this statement of my own free will, without any threats or promises being made to me by anyone.

> Do not tell the perpetrators to "sign here." Instead, tell them that if they agree that the statement is accurate, they should put their name "here."

9. Witnesses. A perpetrator may be reluctant to sign the statement in front of others. The interrogator should sign that he or she witnessed the statement. Another witness, perhaps an investigator or supervisor who is also a notary, can ask the perpetrator to authenticate his or her signature (Inbau and Reid, 1970, p. 133). A sworn statement can also be taken if the perpetrator will take an oath before the notary.

10. Only one written confession. Take a full and complete statement the first time, if possible.

11. One confession per crime. Unless the crimes are related, as in the case of a series of burglaries, the confession statement should cover one crime or related crimes. Do not refer in the statement to the fact that the perpetrator has been arrested for other crimes. If the perpetrator confesses to several unrelated crimes, it is best to take a separate statement for each confession (Inbau and Reid, 1970, p. 136).

12. Physical evidence, photographs, and sketches. If a weapon or some other physical evidence is recovered or the perpetrator is questioned about a photograph or sketch, it may be best to take a separate statement about that evidence, that is, that it is accurate, how it was used, etc. (Inbau and Reid, 1970, pp. 136–137).

More Suggestion for Confessions

1. Stenographic notes. In addition to preserving the signed or sworn statement, any stenographer notes should be preserved until final disposition of the case (Inbau and Reid, 1970, p. 138).

2. Notes on the circumstances and conditions under which the confession was obtained. The interrogator should not rely solely upon his or her memory about the circumstances and conditions under which the confession was obtained. He or she should note the date and time of *Miranda* warnings, the time the interrogation started and ended, and anyone who was present at the interrogation (Inbau and Reid, 1970, p. 138). The interrogator should also note if the perpetrator was afforded bathroom breaks or was given food or drinks.

3. Photographs and medical examination of the confessor. The video statement, as well as booking photos, should demonstrate that the police did not use force to obtain a confession. If the perpetrator

required any medical attention at the time of arrest or apprehension, this should also be documented (Inbau and Reid, 1970, p. 139).

4. The confession is not the end of the investigations. Inbau and Reid correctly opine, "A confession that is unsubstantiated by other evidence is far less effective at the trial than one which has been investigated and subjected to verification or supporting evidence" (Inbau and Reid, 1970, p. 139). Do not fall into the trap of thinking that once you have a confession the investigation is over. It is not. Follow up and verify the information obtained in the interrogation and confession.

5. Post-confession interview. Once the perpetrator has confessed, the interrogation is not over. Often the confessor is ready to give more details that will be useful in the follow-up investigation. Take your time. Keep talking. When it feels like the interview is over, go another five minutes or more.

Nine Steps of an Interrogation

In a brief summary, there are nine steps to follow in an interrogation. Here is an overview of these steps.

1. *Direct positive confrontation*—Presentation of facts synopsis to the subject (the file or dossier method). The suspect is told that he or she is involved in the incident and reference is made to real or fictitious evidence (but beware of bluffing).

2. *Theme development*—Propose reasons that will justify or excuse the act or incident after assessing the suspect's behavior. (Not "if," but "why" explanations.)

3. *Stop denials*—Recognize and stop denials before they are completed.

4. *Overcome objections*—Overcome the suspect's defenses to prove his or her innocence (e.g., moral or religious objections, economic objections, discrediting the facts ["I couldn't have done it because..."], emotional, etc.). Do not refute objections; this only leads to arguments. Explain how it would be if this were not true.

5. *Get the suspect's attention*—The themes will only work if the suspect is listening. Gestures and "moving in" may help the tense and confused suspect.

6. *The suspect quiets and listens*—Once you have the suspect's attention and he or she is quiet and listening, establish eye contact and shorten themes to lead toward alternatives.

7. *Alternatives*—Suggesting "alternatives" concerns some non-threatening, minor aspect of the incident and provides a choice between an acceptable reason and an unacceptable reason for committing the

crime. One alternative is stressed to allow the suspect to choose the more positive alternative.

8. *Bring the suspect into the conversation*—Reinforce the "alternative" and encourage the suspect to talk about aspects of the incident, using realistic words introduced by the interrogator, to obtain corroborating information known only to the suspect.

9. *The confession*—Reduce oral statements to a written or typed form (it should already be recorded), establishing the voluntariness of the statement along with the corroboration of details.

Houston and his associates write, "Ignoring truthful behavior helps us manage our biases, so we don't even have to think about them when the task at hand is detecting deception. Beyond that, it reduces—often dramatically—the amount of data we have to process in order to make a decision about a person's veracity. The more extraneous information that can be filtered out, the easier it is to spot behavior that's deceptive" (Houston et al., 2012, pp. 48–49). We will explore this further in the next chapter.

Formulating Questions

Here are a few tips to keep in mind as you formulate questions to ensure that they are as clear as possible and to manage deception to gain the advantage:

1. *Keep it short.* Remember that the person you are questioning is likely thinking ten times faster than you are speaking. If questions are too long, the subject has more time to develop misleading or deceptive answers (Houston et al., 2012, pp. 127–128).

2. *Keep it simple.* If the subjects do not understand, their responses are less likely to be behaviorally significant (Houston et al., 2012, p. 128).

3. *Keep questions singular in meaning.* If questions are ambiguous, you will not know how the subject understood the question (Houston et al., 2012, pp. 128–129).

4. *Keep it straightforward.* The more up front you are, the more likely the person will trust you, which may increase his or her cooperation (Houston et al., 2012, p. 129).

5. *Use prologues for key questions.* A prologue is a short, narrative explanation that precedes a question (Houston et al., 2012, p. 141).

6. *Broaden your focus.* By broadening the area of your focus in a particular line of questioning, you may steer the subject onto the path that provides additional information (Houston et al., 2012, p. 147).

7. *Always ask, "What else?"* When you think a subject has said every-thing, take five more minutes to ask, "What else?" There is usually more (Houston et al., 2012, p. 131).
8. *Overcome psychological alibis.* It is essential to avoid creating psychological entrenchment. Do not allow the subject to commit to a "psychological alibi" (Houston et al., 2012, p. 144).
9. *Avoid asking negative questions.* Once a person commits to a response, he or she is likely to become psychologically entrenched. Avoid allowing this to happen by asking negative questions (Houston et al., 2012, p. 141).

Legal Requirements for Interrogations and Confessions

As stated at the beginning of this chapter, the legal requirements for interrogations and confessions are complex enough for a book entirely on that topic. The legal requirements are also ever evolving. Because that is beyond the scope of this manuscript and the law changes from time to time, the reader should always seek competent legal counsel on this subject.

Kinesic Interviewing and Body Language

11

Introduction to Kinesic Interviewing and Interrogation

First, it is important to understand the legal limits and ramifications of interviews and interrogations. The legal requirements for interrogations and confessions are complex enough for a book entirely on that topic. The legal requirements are also ever evolving. As that is beyond the scope of this book and the law changes from time to time, the reader should always seek competent legal counsel on this subject.

Make sure that both the investigator and the suspect know that the investigator is not merely seeking a confession or conviction, but is a fact-finder and truth seeker. It is also important for the investigator-interrogator to be thoroughly familiar with the case before starting any interview or interrogation.

Nonverbal communication, often referred to as nonverbal behavior or body language, is a means of transmitting information—just like the spoken word—except it is achieved through facial expressions, gestures, touching (haptics), physical movements (kinesics), postures, and even body adornment (clothes, jewelry, hairstyle, tattoos, etc.). It can also include the tone, timbre, and volume of an individual's voice, but does not include the spoken content (what they say) (Navarro, 2008, pp. 2, 4).

Proxemics: Personal Zone Distances

- Public Zone: over 12 feet
- Social Zone: 4 to 12 feet
- Personal Zone: 18 to 48 inches
- Intimate Zone: 6 to 18 inches

Body Language

Stan Walters observes, "By combining the diagnostic system available to the interviewer for use during verbal analysis with the routine function of taking statements, the interviewer can now combine the two and obtain excellent insight into a suspect's areas of stress and deception" (Walters, 1996, p. 71). Basically then, the objective of kinesic interviewing is to combine the fundamentals of interviewing and interrogation (discussed in the previous chapter) with the perceptive diagnosis of nonverbal communications. Allan Pease and Barbara Pease write, "Being 'perceptive' means being able to spot the contradictions between someone's words and their body language" (Pease and Pease, 2006, p. 13). It is the perceptive ability to spot the contradictions between verbal and nonverbal communications that we will focus on here.

Being able to identify the critical cues of stress and deception can help an investigator turn a labor-intensive, yet uneventful, interview or interrogation into a treasure trove of information (Walters, 1996, p. 71). "Body language" is a topic of interrogation and interviewing that can take up an entire book itself. However, it is important enough to require further study on the subject. Body language can be divided into zones and can reveal truth or deception.

> "Research into the fortune-telling business shows that operators use a technique known as 'cold reading,' which can produce an accuracy of around 80 percent when 'reading' a person you've never met. While it can appear to be magical to naïve and vulnerable people, it is simply a process based on the careful observation of body-language signals plus an understanding of human nature and a knowledge of probability and statistics." (Pease and Pease, 2006, p. 15)

Seven out of ten people cross their left arm over their right. Evidence suggests that this may be a genetic gesture that cannot be changed, leading to research on whether nonverbal signals are inborn, learned, genetically transferred, or acquired in some other way. Research further suggests that some gestures fall into each of these categories (Pease and Pease, 2006, p. 17).

"A natural smile produces characteristic wrinkles around the eyes—insincere people smile only with their mouth" (Pease and Pease, 2006, p. 67). "When liars lie, the left side of the smile is usually more pronounced than the right" (Pease and Pease, 2006, p. 74).

The least dependable signs of lying are ones over which the liar has the most control, such as words and rehearsing lies. The most reliable clues to lying are gestures because people have little control over these automatic responses when they are lying. It is important to learn to differentiate gestures that indicate deceit, procrastination, boredom, and evaluation (Pease and Pease, 2006, pp. 143–144).

"Fleeting incongruencies in the face reveal conflicts in the emotions." "The difficulty with lying is that the subconscious mind acts automatically and independently of our verbal lie, so our body language gives us away." People who rarely lie are more easily caught because their body sends out contradictory signals. During lying, the subconscious mind sends out nervous energy as gestures that contradict the lies. "Professional" liars (you know to whom we are referring) learn to more easily to conceal such "tells" by practicing what "feels" like (acting) the right gestures and reducing their gestures while lying (Pease and Pease, 2006, pp. 146–147).

Ten Commandments for Observing and Decoding Nonverbal Communications

1. Be a competent observer of your environment (Navarro, 2008, p. 7).
2. Observing the "context" is the key to understanding nonverbal behavior (Navarro, 2008, p. 10). This involves what is expected, unexpected, and sudden.
3. Learn to recognize and decode behaviors that are universal (Navarro, 2008, p. 10). "Universal" refers to behavior that is similarly exhibited by most people.
4. Learn to recognize and decode idiosyncratic nonverbal behavior. This is behavior that is unique to a particular individual (Navarro, 2008, p. 12).
5. When you interact with others, try to establish their baseline behaviors. Note how they "normally" look and observe their posture, how they typically sit, where they place their hands, the usual position of their feet, their common facial expressions, the tilt of their head, where they place or hold their possessions, etc. (Navarro, 2008, p. 12).
6. Watch for multiple "tells"—behaviors that occur in clusters or in succession (Navarro, 2008, p. 13).
7. Look for changes in a person's behavior that can signal changes in thoughts, emotions, interest, or intent. Sudden changes help reveal how a person is processing information or adapting to emotional events (Navarro, 2008, pp. 13, 15).
8. Learn to detect false or misleading nonverbal signals (Navarro, 2008, p. 15).
9. Know how to distinguish between "comfort" and "discomfort" to help focus on the most important behaviors for decoding nonverbal communications (Navarro, 2008, p. 15).
10. Be subtle when observing others. Don't make your intentions obvious and don't stare (Navarro, 2008, p. 17).

Kinesic Interview and Interrogation

Kinesic interview and interrogation is a multiphase behavioral analysis of interpersonal communications (Walters, 1996, p. 1). It is based upon a few basic principles:

1. No single behavior, alone, proves anything.
2. Behaviors must be relatively consistent when the stimuli are repeated.
3. The interviewer must determine what is "normal" or "baseline" behavior for each subject and then identify changes in that norm or baseline.
4. Observed changes in the subject's "baseline" behavior are diagnosed in "clusters" and not individually.
5. Behaviors must be timely. (Do they occur when the fear-provoking questions are asked?)
6. Observing and interpreting behaviors is hard work. It takes a great deal of concentration and mental discipline. It requires watching, listening, and diagnosing kinesic behaviors.
7. The suspect is watching us while we are watching them. Suspects will detect when an interrogator or investigator is unprepared, distracted, bluffing, or fishing.
8. Kinesic interviewing is not as reliable with some groups as it is with the general population. Children, mentally deficient, psychotics, and persons under the influence of drugs or alcohol may not respond as most people do.

(Walters, 1996, pp. 9–13)

People normally have five "stress responses" and will likely display one or more of these during an interview or interrogation: (1) anger, (2) depression, (3) denial, (4) bargaining, and (5) acceptance. The first four are negative responses, while the fifth is a state in which admissions and confessions can occur (Walters, 1996, pp. 13–14).

Eight Common Lying Gestures

1. **The mouth cover**. The hand covers the mouth as the subconscious instructs it to try to suppress the deceitful words spoken. If they cover their mouth while *you* are speaking, it may indicate that they think *you* are hiding something (Pease and Pease, 2006, p. 148).
2. **The nose touch**. This may be several quick rubs or a quick, almost imperceptible touch. (It may also mean their nose itches, they have

allergies, or they have a cold.) However, researchers at the Smell and Taste Treatment and Research Center discovered that when you lie, chemicals known as *catecholamines* are released, causing tissue inside the nose to swell. The blood pressure also increases, inflating the nose and stimulating the nerve endings (known as the "Pinocchio Effect") (Pease and Pease, 2006, p. 150).

3. **The itchy nose**. The itchy nose is usually resolved by deliberate rubbing or scratching, rather than the light strokes of the aforementioned nose touch gesture. An itchy nose is usually an isolated repetitive gesture and is out of context with what the person is talking about (Pease and Pease, 2006, p. 151).

4. **The eye rub**. The "eye rub" is the brain's attempt to block out deceit, doubt, or distasteful things it sees or to avoid facing someone who is being lied to. The liar may even look away (Pease and Pease, 2006, p. 151).

5. **The ear rub**. Placing the hand over or around the ear or tugging at the earlobe are often symbolic attempts to block the words being heard. This and other variations may also indicate that the listener has heard enough or may want to speak (Pease and Pease, 2006, p. 152).

6. **The neck scratch**. The "neck scratch" usually involves the index finger of the dominant (writing) hand and usually occurs an average of five times (rarely more and rarely less). This gesture is indicative of doubt, uncertainty, or a person who may be saying, "I am not sure that I agree." Their verbal language may contradict this nonverbal language (Pease and Pease, 2006, p. 150).

7. **The collar pull**. Lies cause a tingling sensation in the facial and neck areas (eliciting a rub or scratch). Increased blood pressure because of deceitfulness causes sweat on the neck. This also occurs when the subject is angry or frustrated, resulting in a "pull" to relieve the pressure or air-cool the circulation area. Asking the subject to repeat what was said may allow for verification if the same behavior is repeated (Pease and Pease, 2006, p. 153).

8. **Fingers in the mouth**. This is thought to be an unconscious reversion to the "security of the child sucking" and may be manifested, not only by fingers in the mouth, but using glasses, pens, pipes, cigarettes, gum, etc. (Pease and Pease, 2006, p. 154).

(Pease and Pease, 2006, pp. 148–154)

Evaluation, Boredom, Impatience, and Procrastination Gestures

Evaluation is indicated by a closed hand resting on the chin or cheek, often with the index finger pointing upward. When the evaluator begins to lose interest, but still wants to appear interested, the position will change to the heel of the palm to support the head as boredom sets in. Boredom may be indicated when the listener uses his or her hand to support the head, beginning with a thumb, progressing to the fist, and finally to the entire hand. Drumming the fingers and tapping the feet are not indicators of boredom, but of impatience (the faster, the more impatient). If both are indicated, the audience is signaling that it is time to end (Pease and Pease, 2006, pp. 155–156).

True interest is indicated by the hand lightly resting on the cheek and not being used as a head support. When the index finger points vertically up, the thumb supports the chin, indicating the listener is having negative or critical thoughts about the speaker or the subject matter. The supporting thumb is the key signal. The index finger may even rub or pull the eye as negative thoughts continue. A "chin stroke," however, is a signal that the listener is engaged in the decision-making process (Pease and Pease, 2006, pp. 157–158).

Listen and Look for Deception

Philip Houston, Michael Floyd, and Susan Carnicero write, in their landmark book *Spy the Lie*, that the trick is to train our brains to *look* and *listen* simultaneously (the "L-squared mode") to process what is being communicated in both *visual* and *auditory* channels. Your brain will default to one or the other until you condition your brain to go into "L-squared mode." Another trick is to identify "*clusters* of deceptive behavior" (any combination of two or more deceptive indicators, which can be either verbal or nonverbal). This is the "Cluster Rule," which is very important to remember throughout the interview or interrogation. Combine these two guidelines to look and listen (in L-squared mode) for a cluster of two or more deceptive behaviors (Houston, Floyd, and Carnicero, 2012, pp. 32–33).

This "L-squared mode" is implemented by learning both "what deception sounds like" (listening) and "what deception looks like" (looking).

What Deception Sounds Like

Houston and his associates begin by listening to what deception "sounds like" by examining "the deceptive verbal behaviors that people use when the facts aren't their ally" (Houston et al., 2012, p. 55).

Failure to Answer. If you ask someone a question and you don't get an answer (to that question), there is a reason for that. One possible reason is that the facts are not on their side and the subject is trying to figure out how to respond. (Remember the Cluster Rule: We need more than one behavior to suspect lying.) (Houston et al., 2012, p. 55).

Denial Problems. The absence of an explicit denial of wrongdoing or an act with consequences, when questioned, is another behavior associated with deception (Houston et al., 2012, p. 56).

"The first type of denial problem, then, is an outright failure to deny. Instead of failing to answer the question, the person might simply fail to convey any sort of denial at all.... When the truth isn't an ally, the person is psychologically inclined to respond with information he feels more comfortable conveying" (Houston et al., 2012, p. 59).

Denial problems can take a couple of other forms:

- *Nonspecific denial.* If the "no" statement is delivered in a way that is more of a general focus than a specific expression of denial of the matter at hand (e.g., "I didn't do *anything*," "I would never do *something like that*"), that is also significant. It is subtle, but if a person says he didn't do *anything*, psychologically he's letting himself off the hook so he doesn't have to tell the bald-faced lie (e.g., "I didn't do it"). It is a nuance that is easily missed by an untrained ear (Houston et al., 2012, p. 59).
- *Isolated delivery of denial.* If in response to a question about wrongdoing, a person gives you a "no" response, but buries it in a long-winded answer, that is important. Consider it deceptive behavior (Houston et al., 2012, p. 59).

Reluctance or Refusal to Answer. A response like, "I'm not sure I'm the right person to talk to" may indicate that the subject does not want to be the "right person" to talk to. Another dodge or expression of reluctance may be, "I'm not sure I can answer that." This could, of course, be true (remember the Cluster Rule) (Houston et al., 2012, p. 60).

Repeating the Question. There may be legitimate reasons to repeat a question. (Again, remember the Cluster Rule.) The person may not have heard the question, may want to be sure he or she understands it, or may be in the habit of asking others to repeat. The person may be buying time to fill what would otherwise be an awkward moment of silence. While it may only take 2 to 3 seconds to repeat the question, because people think faster than they speak, the subject has given himself 20 to 30 seconds worth of time to gather a response (Houston et al., 2012, p. 60).

Non-Answer Statements. The psychology of the non-answer is similar to repeating the question—avoiding the awkward silence and buying time to figure out a response. It may be seen in statements like, "I'm glad you asked that," "That's a good question," "I knew you were going to ask me that," "That's a legitimate concern," etc. (Houston et al., 2012, p. 61).

Inconsistent Statements. When a person makes a statement that is not consistent with subsequent or previous statements and does not explain why the story has changed, that may be indicative of deception (Houston et al., 2012, p. 61).

Going into the Attack Mode. Being cornered by the facts of a situation can strain a deceptive person to the point of resulting in aggression. This may be manifested by attacking the investigator's credibility or competence, for example, "How long have you been doing this job?" or "Why are you wasting time on this stuff?" The subject is trying to get you to back off or question your path (Houston et al., 2012, p. 63).

Inappropriate Questions. Some schools of thought suggest that answering a question with a question is deceptive. Houston and his associates, however, find that it is much more significant when the question doesn't directly relate to the question asked (Houston et al., 2012, p. 63).

Overly Specific Answers. Deceptive people may be overly specific in two ways. First, they may answer a question too technically or narrowly. Second, they may go to the other extreme of over-specificity and give overly detailed information (Houston et al., 2012, p. 65).

Inappropriate Level of Politeness. Being nice is not always suspicious, but if, in response to a question, a person suddenly increases the level of "nicety," that is significant. The person may be using politeness as a means of promoting his or her likability (Houston et al., 2012, pp. 65–66).

Inappropriate Level of Concern. When the facts do not favor a person, he or she may try to diminish the importance of the issue. They will usually focus on the issue or the process. They may attempt to do the questioning by asking, "Why is this such a big deal?" or "Why is everybody worried about this?" They may even try to inappropriately joke about the issue (Houston et al., 2012, p. 66).

Process or Procedural Complaints. Sometimes the subject may go on the offensive by complaining about the process or the proceedings. They may question, "Why are you asking me?" or "How long is this going to take?" They may incorporate delaying tactics, make non-answer statements, or attempt to deflect the proceedings in a different direction (Houston et al., 2012, p. 66).

Failure to Understand a Simple Question. If particular wording (words or phrases that define the scope or magnitude) traps a subject, he or she may attempt to get you to change the phrasing or terminology to diminish the scope or magnitude of the question. An example of this was the infamous Bill Clinton quote, "It depends on what the meaning of the word '*is*' is" (Houston et al., 2012, p. 67).

Referral Statements. Sometimes in response to a question, a deceptive person will refer to having previously answered the question, for example, "As I said . . . ," "As we explained . . . ," "Like I told the last guy that asked that . . . ," etc. The objective is to build credibility through repetition (Houston et al., 2012, pp. 67–68).

Invoking Religion. When a person brings God into the situation (swearing to God or on a stack of Bibles, etc.), he or she is merely engaging in the psychology of "dressing up the lie" (Houston et al., 2012, p. 69).

Selective Memory. When a subject asserts, "I don't remember," it may be true or it may be a psychological alibi that is hard to disprove without irrefutable, tangible evidence. *Context* can be the key to identifying this behavior (Houston et al., 2012, p. 70).

Qualifiers. *Exclusive qualifiers* enable people who want to withhold information to answer truthfully without revealing specific information, for example, "basically," "for the most part," "probably," "most often," etc. *Perception qualifiers* are used to try to enhance credibility, for example, "frankly," "candidly," "to be perfectly honest," etc. Individual speech habits could account for this, so keep the cluster rule in mind (Houston et al., 2012, pp. 70–71).

Convincing Statements. Lies of influence are "convincing statements" (Houston et al., 2012, p. 72). If a person is unable to respond to a question with the facts because the facts are not his or her ally, he or she is likely to respond with these statements, which are designed to convince the questioner of something, rather than to convey truthful information (Houston et al., 2012, p. 74). For example, "I would never do that because . . . " or "That would be dishonest and I am not that kind of person." Other examples may be, "I have a good reputation . . . ," "Look at my record . . . ," or "Do you think I would risk that?" You may neutralize "convincing statements" by acknowledging them, rendering them ineffective, and staying on point and going in the original direction (Houston et al., 2012, p. 75).

What Deception Looks Like

Now that we have discussed what deception sounds like, we are ready to add what deception looks like. Houston and his associates write:

So-called body language "experts" tend to analyze nonverbal behaviors globally. Remember what we said about global behavior assessment? You don't want to go there, because you'd be trying to get that drink from the fire hose, and you'd be putting yourself in the position of having to guess at the meaning and significance of a particular posture or repetitive motion. You need to take the guesswork out of the equation, and filter out all of those global behaviors that do nothing to help you get to where you want to go: identifying deception. So you need to limit your analysis to only those behaviors that come in direct, timely response to stimulus, which is your question. (Houston et al., 2012, p. 95)

Experience has identified certain behaviors as being potentially deceptive when exhibited:

Behavior Pause or Delay. When you ask a question and you initially get nothing, how long it lasts (to be considered significant) depends upon a couple of factors. First, the delay should be considered in the *context* of whether it is appropriate for the question. For example, ask a friend what he or she did on a certain date seven years ago. The friend will likely pause before responding because the question does not evoke an immediate response. Then ask if, on a certain date seven years ago, he or she robbed a bank. You should get an immediate response (Houston et al., 2012, pp. 95–96).

Second, the delay should be *appropriate for the person*. A pattern should give you a sense of how much time elapses before the person responds to questions. If someone falls outside the established pattern, there may be cause for concern (Houston et al., 2012, pp. 95–96).

Hiding the Mouth or Eyes. A deceptive person will often hide his or her mouth or eyes when he or she is not being truthful. There is a natural tendency to want to cover a lie, so when a hand goes in front of the subject's mouth while responding to a question, that is significant. There is also a natural tendency to shield oneself from the reaction of those being lied to. If a person shields his or her eyes while responding to a question, that person may be subconsciously hiding from the reaction. Hiding or closing the eyes may indicate deception (Houston et al., 2012, pp. 97–98).

Throat-Clearing or Swallowing. If a subject clears his or her throat or significantly swallows before (rather than after) a question, psychologically the question may have created anxiety, which can cause discomfort or dryness in the mouth and throat (Houston et al., 2012, p. 98).

Hand-to-Face Activity. Watch for anything the subject does in the face or head area in response to a question. This includes biting or licking the lips and pulling on the lips or ears. The question causes a spike in anxiety because a truthful response would be incriminating. This anxiety triggers the autonomic nervous system to try to dissipate the anxiety. The fight-or-flight response may kick in. Blood rushing to major muscle groups causes diminished blood supply to the surface of the face, ears, and extremities, resulting in irritation of capillaries and a sensation of cold and itchiness. Hand wringing or rubbing and face touching may indicate deception (Houston et al., 2012, pp. 98–99).

Anchor-Point Movement. Anchor points of the body anchor someone in a particular spot or position. Anchor-point movement may be a physical activity that dissipates anxiety. When in response to a question, these movements may indicate deception (Houston et al., 2012, p. 100).

Grooming Gestures. Activity in the form of grooming oneself or the immediate surroundings may be another way of dissipating anxiety and indicating deception (Houston et al., 2012, p. 100).

Reanimation and Acceptance

One very significant gesture to be particularly aware of is *Memory Reanimation*. This involves subconscious gestures that illustrate memories. Investigators should remain aware of subjects' hands when they are describing something, such as the crime, a crime scene, their alibi, a location, etc. Some subjects subconsciously demonstrate a variety of visual information through their hand gestures of "reanimation." They may even inadvertently reenact something that they did, such as the use of a weapon or another act, during the course of a criminal act (Walters, 1996, p. 111).

Memory reanimation may involve retracing a route followed or taken to a particular location. While subjects may say that they have never been to a particular location, you may observe them tracing or drawing the location in the air, on their knees, or on a tabletop. Subjects have also been known to draw the shape of rooms or buildings and schematics, objects, landmarks, or locations, indicating intimate knowledge of them (Walters, 1996, pp. 113–114).

Acceptance gestures are very significant, indicating an admission or confession may be following. When a subject is in a state of "acceptance," the investigator should recognize the verbal cues along with the gestures that signal an opportunity. Be alert to movements of the hands to the chin. When subjects move their hands to their chin, such as rubbing or stroking their chin with the dominant hand, this is indicative of acceptance and readiness to confess. This touching occurs at the "knob of the chin" below the "facial touch target" (Walters, 1996, pp. 115–116).

If the subject's hand goes to the chin and face, such as the thumb under the chin and the finger against the side of the face and pointing toward the eye (in an "L" shape), this is *not* acceptance, but an indication of anger or antagonism (Walters, 1996, pp. 115–116).

Another indication of acceptance is a supplication gesture, such as the palms open or up in a bargaining gesture. Opening of the arms when they have been crossed may be another indicator (Walters, 1996, p. 116).

Behavioral Cautions

Use caution when relying on "common sense" behavioral signs. These "clues," which are assumed by most people, may be caused by something other than anxiety resulting from deception. So use extreme caution and never rely on only one "clue" or behavioral sign when using any of these signs as an indicator of deception:

- Eye contact
- Closed posture (crossed arms, legs, etc.)
- General nervousness or tension
- Preemptive responses
- Blushing or twitching
- Clenched hands
- Base-lining (control questions or behavioral signs used for comparison)

(Houston et al., 2012, pp. 151–152)

Neurolinguistic Eye Movement: The Three Sensory Channels

One aspect of kinesics interviewing that I have found to be very productive is the use of *neurolinguistic eye movement* or the "three sensory channels" to detect deception during an interview. Rabon refers to neurolinguistic eye movement as "three sensory channels," referring to sight, sound, and sensation. He observes that the eyes (the "windows to the soul") react to corresponding eye movements and positions for each of the senses of seeing, hearing, and touching. Essentially, when subjects recover data (information) stored in their visual memory, there are eye movement patterns associated with the data retrieval. The vocabulary the subject uses will also be correspondingly "visual" (Rabon, 1992, p. 25).

Zulawski and Wicklander (1993) observe that the eyes are used to **recall** or **create** information from the visual, auditory, or kinesic channels. The pattern of eye movements can be revealing. In most cases, pattern eye movements are such:

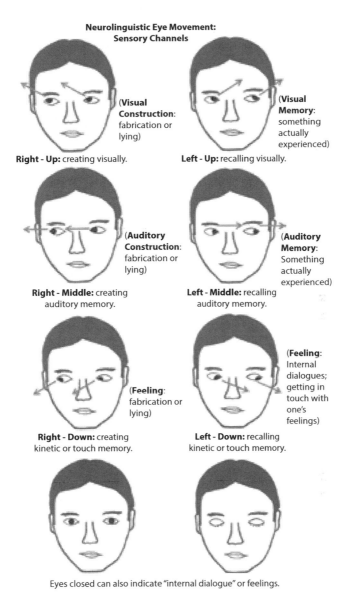

Figure 11.1 Neurolinguistic eye movement (sensory channels). (Illustration by Robert J. David Girod, Jr.)

Recall: Left

- When we **recall** something visually that we have actually **seen**, the eyes go *left* and *up*.
- When we **recall** something audible that we have actually **heard**, the eyes go *left* and *straight across*.

- When we **recall** something kenesically that we have actually **touched** (feel), the eyes go *left* and *down* (internal dialogues, getting in touch with one's feelings).

Create (Fabricate): Right

- When we **create** something visually that we have NOT **seen**, the eyes go *right* and *up*.
- When we **create** something audible that we have NOT **heard**, the eyes go *right* and *straight across*.
- When we **create** something kenesically that we have NOT **touched** (feel), the eyes go *right* and *down*.

(Zulawski and Wicklander, 1993, pp. 153–154) (See Figure 10.1 in Chapter 10.)

There are corresponding eye movements and positions for each of the senses of sight, hearing, and touch. If the subject is recovering data stored in his or her visual memory, there are certain eye-movement patterns that we expect to see. Rabon says that when the subject is recovering visual data, the "vocabulary of the subject will be correspondingly "visual" (Rabon, 1992, p. 25). Approximately 90% of individuals recall something from the left and create (lie) from the right. Moving the eyes left and down indicates an individual's internal dialogue or getting in touch with his or her feelings (Zulawski and Wicklander, 1993, p. 155).

Visual construction is the "building" of an image. When there is nothing to remember, the individual answering questions constructs (build or fabricate) the suggested image, evaluates what he or she "sees," and then answers the question. Because the event has not occurred, it must be constructed. Note that there may also be a change in the subject's speech pattern (Rabon, 1992, pp. 27–28).

Legal Requirements for Interrogations and Confessions

As stated at the beginning of this chapter, the legal requirements for interrogations and confessions are complex enough for a book entirely on that topic. The legal requirements are also ever evolving. As that is beyond the scope of this text and the law changes from time to time, the reader should always seek competent legal counsel on this subject.

Deception Detective
Discourse and
Content Analysis

12

Introduction

Investigators and interrogators not only conduct interviews and interrogations, but also look for signs of deception. Many methods of deception detection have been used throughout the history of criminal investigations. Polygraph and voice stress analysis are two methods using scientific instruments. Scientific content analysis (SCAN) or discourse analysis are methods that reply upon the content of language or discourse. We will discuss each of these here.

Deception Detection: Polygraph and Voice Stress Analysis

A discussion of interrogation and deception detection would not be complete without at least mentioning the polygraph and voice stress analysis ("lie detectors"). The *polygraph* is the best known of the "lie detector" equipment. It measures physiological changes, including the pulse rate, blood pressure, respiration rate and relative volume, and galvanic skin response (resistance). Test results are classified as (1) deception, (2) no deception, (3) inconclusive, or (4) no opinion. The *voice stress analysis (VSA)* and *psychological stress examination (PSE)* test variations of voice patterns due to stress and variations of voice patterns due to psychological factors, such as stress, respectively.

Polygraph and voice stress analysis require extensive training and are beyond the scope of this text. Each could comprise a text of its own. These are exceptional tools for the practitioner of deception detection and further training, education, study, and research in this area would be well recommended.

Scientific Content Analysis (SCAN)

Scientific content analysis (SCAN) is a linguistic investigative technique devolved by Avinoam Sapir, a former Israeli police official. SCAN does not rely on observing "kinesics" body language, but on the structure and contents of a subject's statements. It is a "cross-cultural" technique that can be used in any language that the user understands (Lesce, 1990).

```
┌─────────────────────────────────────┐
│  Discourse and Content Analysis     │
├─────────────────────────────────────┤
│                                     │
│  • Investigative Discourse Analysis │
│    (IDA)                            │
│                                     │
│  • Linguistic Statement Analysis    │
│    (LSAT)                           │
│                                     │
│  • Scientific Content Analysis      │
│    (SCAN)                           │
│                                     │
└─────────────────────────────────────┘
```

Figure 12.1 Scientific Content Analysis (SCAN).

Sapir has noted that 90% of all statements are truthful and that people do not attempt to lie directly, but do so by hedging, omitting crucial facts, feigning forgetfulness, or pretending ignorance. Some do this by answering a question with a question, giving cursory answers to critical points in a narrative, or bridging gaps in the details with useless information. SCAN analyzes speech patterns to detect signs of deception in the structure and content of statements. This begins with asking open-ended questions that avoid suggestiveness and encourage spontaneity. This technique does not give the suspect any information known by investigators and attempts to avoid the lack of objectiveness inherent in investigators who know the details of a case (Lesce, 1990) (Figure 12.1).

Speech pattern analysis helps distinguish between statements originating in the memory and those originating in the imagination. For example, *pronoun* use often reveals deception or a shift in a relationship (e.g., "we") being described. Gaps in narratives may indicate deception and even minor contradictions can indicate concealment of major omissions. Skipping over a critical point or asserting "I don't remember" may indicate avoidance of critical details. Posing his or her own questions, such as "Is that important?" may suggest that a suspect is uncomfortable with some point. Changes in *tense* (past tense, present tense, future tense) is indicative of a strong emotional response and may reveal that a subject is uncomfortable recalling "present" painful information (Lesce, 1990).

Content analysis looks for deception in changes or concealment of details that the suspect is "protecting" (hiding), which may leave traces, inconsistencies, or gaps. This is because the deceptive person works from imagination, rather than memory. In reality, many useless details go along with critical details to make up a truthful narrative. Deceptive statements can usually delete such details and contain mostly irrelevant information. Further, most deceptive stories place the critical issue at the end of the story and end there. Most deceptive stories are void of emotion and, if included at all, place emotions "logically" near the most threatening point. The most severe emotional reaction, in reality, is an "after-shock," taking place after the most threatening moment has passed. Lesce says, "Most deceptive stories... are governed by logic, while true stories are not necessarily logical" (Lesce, 1990).

SCAN differs from other interrogation and deception detection techniques in that it is based upon structure and content of language, rather than gestures, eye movements, physiological changes, etc. It is not a replacement for other techniques, but a supplement to them or another tool in the investigator's toolbox. It is a reasonably reliable method for probing for additional leads and, as with other methods, should be followed up with additional investigation and corroboration.

Investigative Discourse Analysis and Linguistic Statement Analysis

Investigative Discourse Analysis (IDA) and *Linguistic Statement Analysis (LSAT)* are other names given for SCAN. Investigative Discourse Analysis is the term used by Don Rabon in his book by the same title. Linguistic Statement Analysis is the term used for the course taught by the Public Agency Training Council (PATC). SCAN, IDA, and LSAT are all based upon the scientific analysis of the content of discourse in linguistic statements (both verbal and written). Therefore, what you call it is not so important (ironically, because the discipline is based upon the precise meaning of each word), but the science and methods are another important tool in logically conducting an investigation (Figure 12.2).

IDA, LSAT, and SCAN are a discipline that effectively detects deception and truthfulness and identifies concealed information in a subject's or suspect's spoken or written statements (discourse). It (IDA, LSAT, and SCAN) involves scientifically examining the *word choice*, *structure*, and *content* of a subject's statement to determine whether it is truthful or deceptive, as opposed to the traditional emotional method of rationalizing the events in the subject's or suspect's story. People use the same subconscious strategies

Scientific Content Analysis (Scan)
• *Speech pattern analysis* helps distinguish between   - statements originating in the memory and   - statements originating in the imagination.
• *Content analysis* looks for deception in changes or concealment of details that the suspect is " protecting" [hiding], which may leave traces, inconsistencies, or gaps.

Figure 12.2 Discourse and content analysis.

to deceive, by using different words and phrases, statement structure, and content in their statements than they use in truthful ones. Scientific research has identified trends in language that are referred to as "linguistic signals."

IDA, LSAT, and SCAN examine subject and suspect statements to identify these linguistic signals, which reveal specific points of these statements that are deceptive or truthful and reveal information that the subject or suspect did not intend to include. Using this scientific method, interviewers and interrogators can know prior to interviews and interrogations what and where the deception is. Using what is known as the Investigative Questionnaire (IQ), investigators can "interview" several subjects or suspects simultaneously.

Parts of Speech and Word Classes

Bear with me. We will discuss analysis and using these methods in a moment. First, as in report writing, a fundamental knowledge of the basic rules of language is important. Sentences are developed by combining some or all of the eight main parts of speech. These are:

1. **Nouns**—persons, places, things, actions, quality, etc.
2. **Verbs**—words expressing action, existence, or occurrences.
   - They denote *what is done* in a sentence.
   - Verb **tense** denotes when something is done (past, present, or future).
3. **Pronouns**—show relationship or signal words that assume the functions of nouns within clauses.
   - *Personal*: I, you, him, her, he, she, we, them, they, it
   - *Demonstrative*: this, these, those, that
   - *Relative*: what, whatever
   - *Interrogative*: who, what, which
   - *Indefinite*: one, some
   - *First person*: the speaker
   - *Second person*: the one spoken to
   - *Third person*: the one spoken about
4. **Adjectives**—limit or qualify a noun.
   - How many?
   - What kind?
   - Nouns and pronouns can function as adjectives (e.g., color, position, action taken, description, possessive, demonstrative, etc.)

5. **Adverbs**—modify a verb, adjective, another adverb, a phrase, or a clause, and express time, place, manner, degree, cause, etc.
   - When (time)
   - Where (place)
   - How (manner)
   - How often (frequency)
   - YES or NO (affirmation or negation)
6. **Conjunctions**—connect words, phrases, clauses, or sentences.
   - Connective conjunctions may be
     - *coordinating* (and, but, or)
     - *subordinating* (if, when, as, because, through, etc.)
     - *correlative* (either, or, both, and, etc.)
7. **Prepositions**—relation or function words that connect a *lexical word* (usually a noun or pronoun) or a *syntactic construction* to another element of the sentence (a verb, noun, or adjective), for example, at, by, in, for, from, off, on, above, below, over, under, around, before, behind, between, through, until, etc.
8. **Interjection**—an exclamation used to show emotion or sentiment.

Speech Pattern and Discourse Content Analysis: Word Choices

Each of these eight parts of speech is critical in discourse analysis of the meaning of spoken or written language. Within *discourse* (communication, expression, or interchange of thoughts), *words* are the smallest unit of analysis (the process of separating a "thing" into its component parts or elementary qualities) (Rabon, 1994, pp. 11, 14). Each word, whether spoken or written, is a *sign*. There are many different types of signs that can be read and interpreted. For discourse analysis, a sign is any linguistic unit that is the symbol of an idea.*

Discourse analysis (IDA, LSTA, and SCAN) is based on the science of signs, known as *semiotics*. Analysis involves the determination of the meaning and primary aim of the narrative. Word choices refers to the theory that every word used in a narrative is a matter of choice and that the selection process for each word is a form of behavior. Words form sentences. From the smallest unit of analysis (*words*), discourse analysis proceeds to the next level (*sentences*) (Rabon, 1994, p. 16). There are twelve linguistic signals to take note of when analyzing the content of discourse (spoken and written) (Figure 12.3):

* http://www.nuis.ac.jp/~hadley/publication/nuwritnanlysis/writtenanalysis.htm

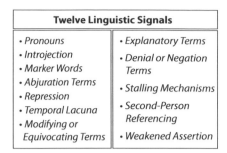

Twelve Linguistic Signals	

• Pronouns
• Introjection
• Marker Words
• Abjuration Terms
• Repression
• Temporal Lacuna
• Modifying or
  Equivocating Terms
	• Explanatory Terms
	• Denial or Negation
	  Terms
	• Stalling Mechanisms
	• Second-Person
	  Referencing
	• Weakened Assertion

Figure 12.3 Twelve linguistic signals.

1. **Pronouns**: "I" is a pronoun that refers to the speaker. Take note of where the "I" is present in the narrative and where it disappears from the narrative, particularly noting the content of the discourse at the point where this change occurs. The absence of the pronoun "I" may indicate the subject's loss of commitment to his or her own narrative or to what he or she is asserting at that point (Rabon, 1994, p. 17).

2. **Introjection**: the process by which "aspects of the external world are absorbed into or incorporated within the self." Uses of the possessive pronoun "my" are examples of *psychological introjection*. The word "my" refers to the speaker or self and indicates possession or possessiveness (Rabon, 1994, p. 17).

3. **Marker Words**: label or modify the word being marked, for example, "the," "a," "this," etc. Note the use of the pronoun "me" (the objective case of "I"). The frequent use of "me" may indicate that the subject perceives him or herself (or hopes to) as the "passive object of external actions or events" over which he or she has no control, but by which he or she has acted upon (Rabon, 1994, p. 18).

4. **Abjuration Terms**: serve to withdraw the assertion made in a previous clause of the sentence and are usually conjunctions, for example, "but" (Rabon, 1994, p. 18).

5. **Repression**: psychological repression is the mental process in which "anxiety-producing mental content is forcefully removed from the consciousness and prevented from reemerging," for example the clause [I] "have no recollection of...." Indicators of repression should always draw the attention of investigators who should take further notice of these (Rabon, 1994, p. 18).

6. **Temporal Lacuna**: a blank space or missing elements within the discourse; that is, something that has been skipped over or left out of the narrative, for example, "when," "later on," "after that," or "by and by" (Rabon, 1994, p. 19).

7. **Modifying or Equivocating Terms**: allow the speaker to "evade the risk of commitment" by undermining his or her own assertions, indicating "difficulty with committing to what is being said." Examples include "a little," "I believe," "I think," "I guess," "kind of," "sort of," "hopefully," "the best I/we can," etc. (Rabon, 1994, p. 20).

   • NOTE: Always take note of the use of "we," which is indicative of a collective reference to the speaker/writer and at least one other person (Rabon, 1994, p. 21).

8. **Explanatory Terms**: used to (a) give a reason or cause and (b) allow for an explanation of a cause and effect or justification or rationale. Examples include "since," "because," etc. (Rabon, 1994, p. 21).
9. **Denial or Negation Terms**: a defense mechanism that disavows or denies thoughts, feelings, wishes, or needs that cause anxiety, for example, "I didn't even know...." This is particularly notable when the speaker/writer is asked to relate what happened or how something occurred and he or she relates what did *not* happen, what is *not* involved, or what he or she did *not* know, do, or observe, etc. (Rabon, 1994, p. 21).
10. **Stalling Mechanisms**: pauses that allow the speaker to "hold back." This is a "change" that can be illustrated by a variety of linguistic factors, such as pauses in or between sentences, the abrupt onset of stuttering or stammering, and the use of terms such as "let's see," "okay now," "well," "oh well," "um," "ah," "uh," etc. (Rabon, 1994, p. 22).
11. **Second-Person Referencing**: the speaker/writer refers to himself or herself with the second-person pronoun "you," diverting attention from himself or herself. The speaker/writer is signaling that he or she feels no personal accountability or responsibility for whatever happened, for example, "You know, when you talk about it..." (Rabon, 1994, p. 22).
12. **Weakened Assertions**: the speaker/writer seems to feel the need for additional (but what should be unnecessary) support for what he or she said, for example, "to tell the truth...." They may also be used to allude to actions that were never actually carried out, for example, "We were going to play cards," "I needed to get my glasses," "I tried to ...," "I started to get...," "I most assuredly...," "As a matter of fact, I have never made this kind of mistake before...," etc.

   • "Try" or "tried" reflects an expectation of failure.
   • "Start to" and "started" are not the same as actually "doing" something.

(Rabon, 1994, p. 22)

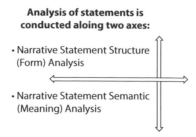

Analysis of statements is conducted aloing two axes:

- Narrative Statement Structure (Form) Analysis

- Narrative Statement Semantic (Meaning) Analysis

Figure 12.4 Two axes of statement analysis.

Analysis of Statements along two axes:

Narrative Statement Structure (Form) Analysis	Narrative Statement Semantic (Meaning) Analysis
1. *Identify the **formal organization** of the narrative in terms of balance or proportion.*	1. What the subject **actually** says or writes.
2. *Identify any **nonconforming statements.***	2. What the subject **intended** to say or write.
3. *Identify any **non-sequential statements**, which are statements that are out of place or chronological order.*	3. The **interpretation** of what the subject says or writes.

Figure 12.5 Two axes of statement analysis.

To analyze the content of speech, begin with open-ended, non-specific questions to obtain as much information as possible. If the questions are too specific, the subject's responses will also be too specific (Rabon, 1994, p. 30). Analysis of statements is conducted along two axes: (1) the structure (form) of the narrative and (2) the semantics (meaning) of the words used in the narrative. First, the *structure* or *form* of the narrative is indicative of truth or deceit. Second, *semantic (meaning)* analysis may be indicative of specific points where deception or inaccuracy occurs and where the subject needs to amplify or expand upon details (Rabon, 1994, p. 34) (Figure 12.4 and Figure 12.5).

Narrative Statement Structure (Form) Analysis

The structure or form of the narrative is indicative of truth or deceit. Analysis of the narrative structure (form) involves the identification of three features of the narrative:

1. Identify the formal organization of the narrative in terms of balance or proportion. This refers to the balance or proportion between the *prologue*, the *event*, and the *epilogue* of the narrative. The more balanced the narrative, the more indicative of truthfulness of the statement. The more lacking in balance the narrative is, the more indicative it is of *deception in its form*. The subject can mislead or deceive by leaving something out or by adding actions, conversations, events, etc. that did not actually occur (Rabon, 1994, p. 35).

Determining the Central Issue. To determine the "central issue" or event of the narrative, the investigator should identify the essential, principal element of the narrative's meaning or purpose (Rabon, 1994, p. 36).

2. Identify any nonconforming statements. Nonconforming statements are those in which the subject alludes to some action, procedure, or activity without saying that he or she has actually performed any of these. These statements indicate that the subject did *not* perform the action, procedure, or activity. *Weakened assertions* are indicative of these nonconforming statements (Rabon, 1994, p. 42).
3. Identify any *non-sequential statements*, which are statements that are out of place or chronological order. These statements may take the form of an aside (an out of the way statement that is not related to the topic), a second person reference, a statement that interrupts the orderly flow, or a statement that is incongruent (does not fit) with the rest of the narrative. Non-sequential statements are significant because they do not "fit," even though the speaker or writer included them for some reason (Rabon, 1994, p. 44).

Narrative Statement Semantic (Meaning) Analysis

After analysis of the structure/form of the narrative statement, analysis shifts to the individual words selected within the narrative. There are three parts to narrative statement semantic (meaning) analysis:

1. What the subject *actually* says or writes.
2. What the subject *intended* to say or write.
3. The *interpretation* of what the subject says or writes.

The objective is to align the first and third parts as closely as possible (Rabon, 1994, p. 47).

Every word, pause, and hesitation has meaning. If the subject's narrative is deceptive or contains misleading material, this will be reflected by one or

Semantic Indicators

1. *Lack of conviction about one's own assertions.*

2. *Use of present tense when describing a past occurrence.*

3. *Use of generalized statements.*

4. *Reduced or eliminated self-reference.*

5. *Reduced "mean length of utterance" (MLU) in relation to a particular unit of narration.*

MLU = Words ÷ Sentences

Figure 12.6 Semantic indicators.

more examples of *semantic indicators*, referring to the meaning of the words selected (Figure 12.6).

Semantic Indicators

1. Lack of conviction about one's own assertions. This lack of conviction will often be evinced by modifying or equivocating terms (Rabon, 1994, p. 48).
2. Use of present tense when describing a past occurrence. Deceptive persons are often reluctant to refer to past events as *past*, particularly about the subject matter of the investigation. They often begin referring to past events as if they were occurring in the present (Clikeman, 2012).
3. Use of generalized statements. Some deceptive individuals will relate events vaguely, with a series of actions or blocks of time summed up in phrases like "messed around," "talked for a while," "got my stuff together," etc. (Rabon, 1994, p. 50).
4. Reduced or eliminated self-reference. Such avoidance of self-referencing ("I" or "me") is apparent in sentences that begin with verbs or descriptions of activities in which the speaker was a participant, but which include no references to the speaker's involvement (Clikeman, 2012).
5. Reduced "mean length of utterance" (MLU) in relation to a particular unit of narration. The MLU consists of the number of words in a sentence or the number of sentences in a passage within a given section of the narrative. The "formula" for this process is MLU = Words ÷ Sentences and the steps are:
   a. Count the number of *words* in each sentence.
   b. Total the number of words in all of the sentences for a *total narrative word count.*
   c. Count the number of *sentences* in the narrative.

d. Divide the total word count by the number of sentences to obtain the MLU for sentences in the narrative.
e. Identify those sentences that are significantly above or below the MLU (Clikeman, 2012).

The *prologue* of the narrative contains an average word count. The *central event* or *issue* contains an average word count. Finally, the *epilogue* contains an average word count. Sentences that are significantly *above* the MLU may indicate the subject's *amplification*. Sentences that are significantly *below* the MLU may indicate the subject's *concealment*. The key here is "significant" deviations.

Parts of Speech and Semantic Analysis

Semantics is the study of "meanings" or the branch of linguistics and logic concerned with meaning. The two main areas are logical semantics, concerned with matters such as sense, reference, presupposition, and implication, and lexical semantics, concerned with the analysis of word meanings and relations between them. It is also defined as the historical and psychological study and the classification of changes in the signification of words or forms as factors in linguistic development. Linguistic semantics is the study of meaning that is used for understanding human expression through language.

The parts of speech considered in semantic (meaning) analysis include:

1. **Verbs** and **verb tense changes**: indicate action or state of being and are indicative of the subject, circumstances, or others involved (Rabon, 1994, p. 58).
2. **Pronouns**: can provide insight into the state of relationships and the labels that the subject places on events, actions, and circumstances (Rabon, 1994, p. 59).
3. **Nouns**: pay attention to nouns, particularly those referring to persons, when first introduced into a narrative. If nouns change, an antecedent has stimulated that change (Rabon, 1994, p. 60).
4. **Adjectives**: because of their limiting or qualifying role, analysis can be critically revealing (Rabon, 1994, p. 61).
5. **Adverbs**: verb-modifying, temporal-indicating, and degree-identifying words, which can also be critically revealing (Rabon, 1994, p. 62).
6. **Conjunctions**: connectives and their linking role makes them important to the "flow" of the narrative, in identification of components that have been left out of the narrative, and in determining cause and effect (Rabon, 1994, p. 63).

7. **Prepositions**: can provide a sense of the location or position of persons or objects, as well as the spatial relations between individuals, between individuals and objects, and between objects (Rabon, 1994, p. 67).

Semantic analysis is the basis for the next step in the process—the subject's amplification of the narrative (Rabon, 1994, p. 81).

Amplification of the Narrative

Once semantic analysis has been completed, the results can be examined in detail by trying to get the individual making the statement to amplify narrative details. Refer the subject to parts of the narrative and details that need to be amplified. Guide the subject toward areas that need amplification, emphasizing certain words and using open-ended questions, rather than structured responses (Rabon, 1994, pp. 89–90).

Analysis in the Form of Letters (Correspondence)

Pay particular attention to key terms (nouns, verbs, pronouns, etc.), including *repetition* and *changes* in their use. For example, *verbs* provide insight into the subject's perceived relationship to events or other persons. Letters (including e-mails), like narratives, indicate the author's goal in word choices, for example, to *convey* or *convince* (Rabon, 1994, pp. 103, 119).

Analysis of Interview and Interrogation Transcripts

The difference between discourse produced by interviews and interrogations and other forms of discourse is that the subject's words are responses to systematic inquiry, that is, the subject formulates a series of responses to a series of specific questions. Once again, the investigator must determine whether the subject's goal is to *convey* or *convince* (to be *truthful* or to *deceive*) (Rabon, 1994, p. 121). By systematically analyzing such discourse, more information can be gained from transcripts than by drawing conclusions based upon a "general reading of the interview" alone (Rabon, 1994, p. 151).

Conclusion

The polygraph or "lie detector," the voice stress analysis (VSA), and psychological stress examination (PSE) tests are all tools that can assist investigators in detecting deception and identifying the truthful facts. These can be power-ful tools in the logical investigation of crimes and other matters. Investigators should become as familiar with these tools as possible, possibly even becom-ing certified to operate such tools and equipment.

Other tools can be of assistance in logical investigations to help detect deception and identify truthful facts without the need for expensive or obtru-sive equipment. That does not imply that such equipment can be replaced but, rather, supplemented by other tools, which can be used with physiologi-cal deception detection devices or when such devices cannot be used or are impractical for whatever reasons or circumstances.

Scientific Content Analysis (SCAN), Investigative Discourse Analysis (IDA), and Linguistic Statement Analysis (LSAT) are such tools. The investi-gator who wants to conduct a thorough "logical investigation" should learn as much about these discourse and content analysis methods as possible, per-haps even attending one of the training courses offered by one of the versions of this methodology. This is very good and practical training and is available from a variety of sources. Using this as another tool will enhance the other investigative techniques discussed in this text.

Analytical Investigative Methods
Processing Data

13

Analytical Investigative Methods (AIM) are methods of helping others to "see" complex ideas and information in a more understandable way. They help investigators present information to prosecutors in a more graphic way and help prosecutors simplify cases for juries and judges who will be triers of fact and law. AIM involve basic analysis tools, such as CPM-PERT charts, Gantt charts, flow charts, etc., or may involve presentations of intelligence data and crime analysis charting that are more complex.

Visual Investigative Analysis (often abbreviated VIA) visually portrays information to aid in understanding complex financial, conspiracy, serial crimes, major crime cases, etc. As the old saying goes, "A picture is worth a thousand words." VIA pictorially presents information through presentation software using charts, graphs, diagrams, link analysis, etc.

CPM-PERT Network Diagrams

Network theory is not a new concept. Scientists and engineers have been using it for centuries. The history of PERT diagrams and charts is commonly associated, however, with Henry Gantt. Some of the earliest writings on network theory were papers on production scheduling and were associated with Gantt and Frederick W. Taylor (Stilian, 1962, pp. 9–10).

The need for improved planning and progress evaluation techniques for controlling the utilization of human resources, materials, and facilities became apparent in several industries at the same time during the 1950s. E.I. du Pont de Nemours and Company and the Sperry-Rand Corporation jointly sponsored the pioneering efforts to apply network or arrow diagrams and the critical path method (CPM) to project management. The initial efforts were aimed at improving planning, scheduling, and coordination of engineering projects (Baker and Eris, 1964, p. 1).

In 1957, a research team was established by the U.S. Navy Special Projects Office to develop a program evaluation technique for the Fleet Ballistic Missile System development effort. Through the efforts of this team, the Program Evaluation and Review Technique (PERT) was developed and implemented as a research and development project management tool for the Navy's Polaris Missile Program (Baker and Eris, 1964, p. 1).

CPM and PERT diagrams were not designed to replace Gantt (bar) charts, milestone charts, or line-of-balance techniques, but to supplement such planning tools and provide information management decisions. The *network plan* (central to CPM and PERT) has enabled progressive management information and control systems (Baker and Eris, 1964, p. 1).

Network Logic Techniques

- **The Milestone Approach:** The original PERT approach to networking was milestone or event-oriented. Under this system, important events were depicted on a chart and constraint lines drawn between events.
- **The Arrow-Diagramming Approach:** The original CPM approach to networking was entirely activity-oriented. Project activities were represented by arrows. The points between arrows were called *nodes*, though little concern was given to the precise definition of these nodes (see Figure 13.1).
- **The Start–Complete Approach:** Sometimes referred to as PERT-II, this technique is both event- and activity-oriented. Under this technique, all activities begin and end with dummy activities inserted between real activities.
- **The Combined PERT-CPM Approach:** Networks are activity-oriented, with even identification. Activities do not necessarily have starts and completes (beginnings and ends) in each case, but definitions of activity lines are unambiguous (see Figure 13.1).

(Baker and Eris, 1964, p. 17)

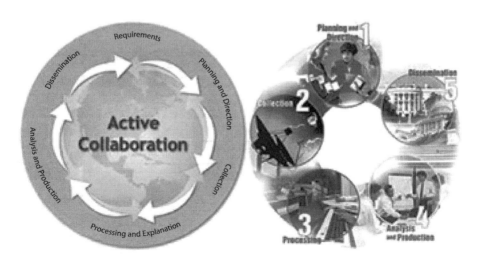

Figure 13.1 The intelligence cycle (FBI, left; CIA, right).

CPM and PERT are *management-by-exception* oriented systems, which emphasize the "pacing" or "critical" items of a project. Only 10 to 20% of the activities involved in most projects control the time required to complete the project. The "critical path" analytical tool of CPM and PERT identifies these pacing activities (Baker and Eris, 1964, p. 1).

Network-Based Project Management Methodology

CPM-PERT is a management planning and analysis tool that utilizes a graphic display, called a *network,* to depict the essential relationships between various tasks comprising a complex research and development program (Baker and Eris, 1964, p. 1). Network-Based Project Management Methodology is used for six purposes:

- Basic scheduling
- Time and resource estimation
- Time-cost trade-offs
- Project planning
- Resource allocation
- Project control

(Moder, Phillips, and Davis, 1983, p. 14)

PERT diagrams force *logical* thought and compel planners to recognize the relationship of parts to the whole (Stilian, 1962, p. 11). PERT networks may be described as flow charts made up of *events* that are joined by *activity lines* to depict their interdependencies and interrelationships (Baker and Eris, 1964, p. 2).

The *network* is the principal PERT display and involves two elements:

1. Events, which are symbolized on a network by a square, circle, rectangle, etc.
2. Activities, which connect events and are represented by a line or lines (Baker and Eris, 1964, p. 2).

An *event* is an instantaneous occurrence that is accomplished at some known and unambiguous point in time. Events represent meaningful accomplishments and signify the start or end of one or more *activities* (see Figure 13.2) (Baker and Eris, 1964, p. 2).

An *activity* is any portion of a project that consumes time or resources and has a definable beginning and ending. Activities are either (a) real activities or (b) dummy activities.

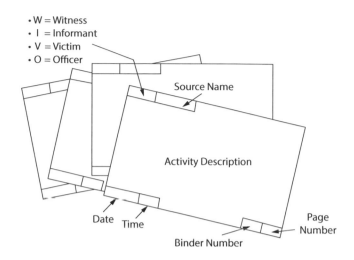

- W = Witness
- I = Informant
- V = Victim
- O = Officer

Source Name

Activity Description

Date　Time

Binder Number

Page
Number

Figure 13.2 VIA index cards.

- A *real activity* represents necessary work, which must be accomplished to progress from one event to another. Real activities expend time, money, equipment, and human resources. A real activity is represented by a solid line or arrow, which connects two events (Baker and Eris, 1964, p. 5).
- A *dummy activity* is represented by an arrow, which depicts dependency of one activity upon another. A dummy activity carries a zero time estimate often represented by dashed-line arrows or solid arrows with zero time estimates (Moder et al., 1983, pp. 23–24).

The *node scheme* uses nodes to represent activities and arrows merely as connectors, which denote precedence relationships (Moder et al., 1983, p. 37). Explanatory terms are included in each event symbol and each event is uniquely numbered for identification. Activities can be identified by referring to numbers of preceding and succeeding events.

The depiction of the sequencing of activities is a significant aid to communicating project interdependencies and interrelationships that exist between activities. Today, computers play a significant role in preparing and presenting sophisticated CPM and PERT systems. The use of computers not only aids in the preparation and presentation of networks, but also it allows for the integration, condensation, and interpretation of data and graphics. Simulations and analysis are also more practical using computer processing.

Elements of PERT

There are nine elements to PERT:

1. An **Event**—an identifiable *point in time* at which something has happened or a situation has come into existence.
2. An **Activity**—a clearly definable *task* to which a quantifiable amount of resources will be applied:
   - predecessor events and
   - successor events for the associated activity.
3. **Time Estimates**—association of an elapsed time with an activity:
   - optimistic (a = minimum),
   - pessimistic (b = maximum), and
   - most likely (m = normal) times.
4. **Expected Time**—the time estimates are combined mathematically in two formulas.
5. **Spread**—a manipulation of a measure of the *degree of certainty* associated with the expected event.
6. **Network**—analysis of component tasks and their interdependencies.
7. **Critical Path**—the longest path in a series of sequences:
   - from the *starting* event
   - to the *objective* event
8. **Slack**—time to spare along paths that are shorter than the critical path.
9. **Probability of Success**—a calculation on the three time estimates to obtain *a measure of the uncertainty* of the expected time for the activity. The time estimate (**te**) is a mean elapsed time, determined by the equation:

$$te = \frac{a + 4m + b}{6}$$

(Stilian, 1962, p. 61; Baker and Eris, 1964, p. 6)

Intelligence Cycle

The intelligence cycle is used in the intelligence, military, and law enforcement communities to describe the cycle of intelligence activities, which denotes that each step is a continuous and on-going process, rather than individual, terminal steps (see Figure 13.3). The five steps in the cycle are:

- Planning and Direction
- Collection
- Processing
- Analysis and Production
- Dissemination and Feedback

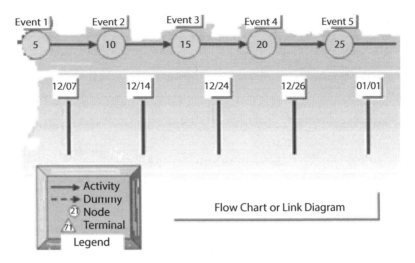

Figure 13.3 Flow chart or link diagram.

Planning and Direction

Intelligence requirements are determined by a decision maker to meet organizational objectives, sometimes called Essential Elements of Intelligence (EEIs). All other data are referred to as Other Intelligence Requirements (OIR). Directing intelligence requirements involves: (1) determine intelligence requirements (EEIs and OIRs); (2) determine indicators; (3) determine specific items of information required; (4) select collection agencies; (5) issue orders and requests; and (6) follow-up.

Collection

In response to requirements (EEIs), the intelligence staff develops an intelligence collection plan to task available sources and methods and request intelligence from other agencies. Sources may include ELINT (electronic intelligence), SIGINT (Signals Intelligence), EMINT (Emanations Intelligence), IMINT (imagery intelligence), HUMINT (human intelligence), and OSINT (open source or publicly available intelligence), etc.

Processing

Once collection is accomplished and raw information is available, it is processed for exploitation. This involves the translation of raw materials, evaluation of its relevance and reliability, and collation of the raw data in preparation for exploitation.

Analysis

Analysis integrates information by combining pieces of data with collateral information and patterns that can be interpreted to identify the significance and meanings of processed intelligence.

Dissemination and Feedback

Finished intelligence products are of little value if they do not meet the needs of the decision makers and intelligence consumers. Because the intelligence cycle is a closed loop, feedback is received from the decision maker or consumer and revised requirements (EEIs) are issued.

Intelligence Analysis

The analysis of intelligence can be conducted by two nearly identical processes, which were developed from scientific and engineering practices: AIM and VIA. Other methods of intelligence analysis are available, but AIM and VIA are commonly used by law enforcement, intelligence, and military analysts to present complex information with presentation media.

Analytical Investigative Methods (AIM)

AIM analyze large amounts of information using scientific concepts of investigation, data collection, and evaluation techniques, including:

- construction of association matrices and link analysis
- use of inductive and deductive logic from sources of information
- flow charting and construction of charts for analysis (see Figure 13.4, Figure 13.5, and Figure 13.6)
- the analytical process
- development of inferences from analysis
- the delivery of clear and concise briefings and presentation media

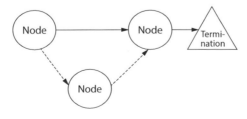

Figure 13.4 Nodes, activity lines, dummy lines, and termination.

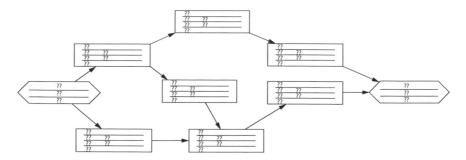

Figure 13.5 Network diagram. (Used with permission. http://en.wikipedia.org/wiki/File:Pert_example_network_diagram.gif)

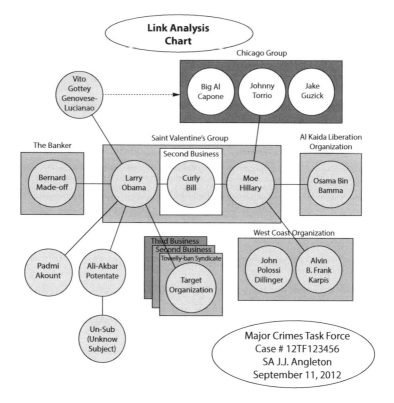

Figure 13.6 Example of a link analysis chart.

AIM, like VIA, emerged from using tools and techniques borrowed from science and engineering project management. Two such tools are CPM and PERT. CPM is used for scheduling, planning, and controlling projects with deadlines. Users decide which path in a network will take the most time. This patch then becomes a *critical path*. PERT is a scientific management information system for scheduling, planning, and controlling complex research and development projects. It is oriented to events and uses a network to display graphically the sequence of events, dependent relationships, and estimated duration of times for all the activities.

A network is a series of interconnected and interrelated symbols that graphically displays the sequence of occurrences and dependent relationships. Link Network Analysis shows associations while Time Flow Analysis shows sequential events.

Visual Investigative Analysis (VIA)

VIA was developed in the 1960s by the Los Angeles Police Department and named VIA by the California Department of Justice in the 1970s (Morris, p. iv). It was first used in trial support in Los Angeles in 1968 in the trial of Sirhan Sirhan for the murder of U.S. Senator (and former Attorney General) Robert F. Kennedy (Morris, p 5).

VIA makes complex investigations more controllable and makes it easier for supervisors and managers to monitor the hour-by-hour use of resources to avoid duplication. It also helps trial attorneys to quickly understand complex cases and large amounts of information by providing a sort of roadmap of critical events and essential elements. It helps judges and juries understand cases by allowing them to see and hear the progress of the events presented. Such analysis saves time, often reducing trial time by half, and clearly states essential facts.

VIA was also developed from concepts borrowed from engineering, construction, and shipbuilding, which used techniques such as CPM and PERT. CPM is similar to PERT and is geared toward scheduling and controlling projects. PERT is geared toward facilitating control of research activity in scientific tasks. The two can be integrated into one system. VIA is such an integration, with modifications that are responsive to the law enforcement or intelligence functions. VIA is a network approach to displaying graphically the sequences of events and the relationships of each element of an incident (Morris, pp. 3–4).

VIA can be performed manually or by use of computer graphics and tools. While computers are more practical today, understanding the manual system can aid in practice or be used in more remote or primitive environments. To perform VIA manually, the analyst needs a few tools and supplies:

1. **Index Cards**—3 × 5, using only one side, to tape or affix to the layout (Figure 13.7). Figure 13.2).
2. **Binders**—a case library for copies of all documentation supporting the VIA chart. Each binder is numbered and each page in each binder is numbered for quick reference (e.g., a document or informa-

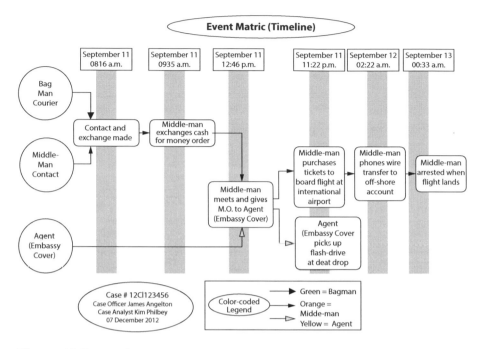

Figure 13.7 Timeline or event matrix.

tion in Binder 2 and on page 25 would be noted on an Index Card as 2-25).

3. **Highlighter Pens**—during the reading phase of the documentation, the analyst highlights items or information for transfer to the index cards. This can simply be in yellow highlight or various colors can be used to color-code specific aspects of information.

4. **Template**—symbols can be drawn using a template which includes circles, rectangles, arrows, triangles, and other symbols.

5. **Paper**—durable drafting paper can be used for the chart and tracing paper can be used for final drafts.

6. **Tape and Pins**—pins can hold index cards on the drafting paper during layout and tape can be used to affix them when finalized. Here, the index cards are taped down after the lines, circles, arrows, and triangles are added and the chart takes the shape and appearance of a story board.

7. **Pens and Pencils**—for compiling the index cards and drawing the chart. The final draft, of course, should be in ink.

8. **Copies of Reports and Documentation**—all material for the case should be copied (never the originals) because they will be hole-punched, page numbered, and highlighted.

The same process can be performed with a computer, using various Computer Aided Design (CAD) tools and programs (such as Visio©®, IntelliVIEW©®, and other commercially available programs). The important points of developing a VIA chart and library are:

1. Determine the important elements and data in reports, documents, and other information from the case library.
   a. Does this information relate to the incident in question?
   b. Does this information provide a Who, What, When, Where, Why, or How?
   c. Does this information build upon another known or suspected key element?
2. Summarize information into 50 words or less (for each element or key point).
   a. The index card's upper line might show "Who" gave the data (W = Witness, I = Informant, V = Victim, O = Officer, etc., followed by the name).
   b. The bottom line might show "When"—day, date, time, and binder and page numbers.
3. Link the nexus between activities when dates, times, and other elemental details are unclear, ambiguous, or missing.

The VIA process should not be viewed as individual steps, but as a continuous process like the Intelligence Cycle itself. However, the tasks in the VIA process include:

1. Confer with the client/consumer for planning and direction (trial attorney or intelligence consumer) on the EEIs.
2. Collect source documents (collection).
3. Develop the case library (documentation).
4. Conduct first reading of source documents.
5. Conduct second reading of source documents.
6. Create index cards (processing)
7. Compare and edit materials.
8. Conduct index card analysis (analysis).
   - Take the information from the reading and re-reading of the source documents of the case library and write each activity on an individual index card.
   - Study the index cards to determine which event and card most likely starts the network and which one is the logical conclusion.
   - Arrange the remaining cards in a logical chain of activity (sequential, if possible).
     - Activity flow (sequential and logical).

        – Parallel activity (simultaneous).
        – Activity display—nodes.
9. Create chart (attaching information from index cards) (analysis and production).
   - Use network logic to show each nexus.
   - What activities precede the next one (logical sequence)?
   - What activities are concurrent with this one (simultaneous)?
   - What activities follow this one (continuing logical sequence)? (Morris, p. 16)
10. Create arrows and nodes (arranged to show the logical sequence of activities and their relationship) and assign reference numbers (to source binders and pages from the case library) (analysis and production).
    - Use symbols to represent information in the network and on the chart.
    - Each arrow represents one activity (any portion of the case analysis that consumes time or resources and has a definable beginning and end).
    - A circle or node between the arrows denotes the start and stop of an activity. These event nodes consume no time or resources.
    - Every activity in a network must be preceded and succeeded by an event node (except the conclusion of the chart); there can only be one activity between every two nodes.
    - A burst (depicted by vertical sets of event nodes) is the initiation of two or more activities.
    - A merge depicts the completion of two or more activities.
    - The end of a VIA chart is signified by a triangle (the termination symbol) (Morris, pp. 19–20, 22) (see Figure 13.1).
11. Create Activity and Dummy Lines (analysis and production) (see Figure 13.1).
    - An activity arrow (mentioned previously) represents one activity.
    - A dummy line is represented by a dotted arrow and represents an activity that consumes no time.
      - It maintains network continuity and logic by indicating that, while a relationship exists between two activities, it does not warrant the strength of a solid line arrow.
      - The dotted dummy line completes a "straggler line" by attaching it to something—a continuing solid line (Morris, pp. 20–22).
12. Confer (again) with the client/consumer on the progress from the Planning and Direction phase (trial attorney or intelligence consumer).
13. Finish drafting and finalizing (inking, if manually constructed) the chart.

- Number each node or circle (in increments of five or more along the main line to allow for upgrades) for reference to points of interest.
- No two nodes should have the same number except fragnets and subnets (discussed later) (Morris, p. 22).

14. Attach information from index cards (with tape, if manually constructed).
15. Create a legend (of symbols), title, and credits (of who drafted the chart).
16. Develop fragnets and subnets, used to expand a complex chart.
    - *Fragnets* are an expansion that occurs as an appendage (for smaller amounts of information) on the face or surface of the original chart.
        - They are usually small (one to five activities) and always relate directly to one activity between two nodes on the original chart.
        - They are depicted by dotted lines, without arrowheads, attached to each end of the fragnet and to the nodes on the original chart.
        - Node numbering in the fragnet begins with the first node number to be fragneted on the original chart and ends with the next node number to the right (Morris, p. 23).
    - *Subnets* resemble a fragnet, but are displayed on an independent chart and usually represent large amounts of information or numbers of activities.
        - They are usually represented as a separate chart of their own, often after the completion of the original (main) chart. (When created on a computer, they may be imbedded and brought up, opened, or enlarged with a click).
        - They follow the numbering of the original chart (it begins with the first node number to be subnetted on the original chart and ends with the next node number to the right) (Morris, p. 23).
17. Conduct a final review with the client/consumer for Planning and Direction (trial attorney or intelligence consumer) (dissemination and feedback).

Use of computers can greatly simplify this process, especially the use of fragnets and subnets. The final draft of the chart can be copied using the trace paper or saved as a computer document, using overlays. Charts may then be presented using presentation software such as PowerPoint®.

Financial Information

Single-Entry Bookkeeping refers to the entry of information from all sources in one place without making an effort to balance the records. Double-Entry Bookkeeping refers to a system in which every transaction affects two or more accounts (with equal debits or credits) and is recorded in these accounts. Two or more adjustments must be made (never only one) and, in summary form, show the results of many transactions and the force affecting the organization.

The Fundamental Equation is:

$$A - L = C$$

Assets (items of value) = claims assets = Liabilities and Capital.

Accounting Cycle

1. **Journalizing**—analyzing and recording transactions in a *journal*.
2. **Posting**—copying the debits and credits of journal entries into the *ledger* accounts.
3. **Preparing a Trial Balance**—summarizing the ledger accounts and testing the recording accuracy.
4. **Constructing a Work Sheet**:
   a. affecting the adjustments without making entries in the account,
   b. sorting the account balances into
      - balance sheet and
      - income statement accounts, and
   c. determining the income or loss.
5. **Preparing the Statements**—rearranging the *work sheet* information into
      - a balance sheet and
      - an income statement.
6. **Adjusting the Ledger Accounts**—preparing *adjusting journal* entries from information in the Adjustments columns of the *work sheet* and posting the entries in order to bring the account balances up to date.
7. **Closing the Temporary Proprietorship Accounts**—preparing and posting entries to close the temporary proprietorship accounts and transfer the net income or loss to the capital account.
8. **Preparing a Post-Closing Trial Balance**—proving the accuracy of the adjusting and closing procedure.

Communicating Skills
Critical Documentation

14

Investigative Report Writing: "The Job's Not Finished 'til the Paperwork's Done"

Investigating crimes and report writing go hand in hand. Many officers lament that they are not English teachers, but neither are news reporters. Yet both deal in written reports of events and no one would expect to see a news report written in poor English. Investigators are people who look into events or situations to find the facts about what happened.

Do spelling, grammar, and punctuation really matter? A single comma was the deciding factor in one case because the rules of language matter when deciding the meaning of language.

In *United States v. Ron Pair Enterprises,* 489 U.S. 235 (1989), known as "the comma case," the court made its decision about the meaning of a document based upon a single comma. The court said, in part, "This reading of §506(b) is also mandated by its grammatical structure. Since the phrase 'interest on such claim' is set aside by commas, and separated from the reference to fees, costs, and charges by the conjunctive words 'and any,' that phrase stands independent of the language that follows." The U.S. Supreme Court was split 5-4 over the significance of a comma in a bankruptcy statute. Rules have reasons and language and punctuation matter (Wydick, 2005, p. 83).

Therefore, well-written reports may win cases and poorly written reports often lose cases. So, learn the basic rules of spelling, grammar, and punctuation. Use Spell Check on your computer, but do not assume that Spell Check always knows what you want to say or which word you mean to use. Spell Check will sometimes change a word without asking if it thinks it has found an error, which may not be. It also does not know how to spell everyone's names. Always make sure that if it changes something, you agree to the change. Keep a pocket dictionary in your car and on your desk. Remember the old saying posted on the outhouse door: "The job's not finished until the paperwork's done."

Don't Just Record—Investigate

Report writing is more than just writing down the basic information. It involves documenting your investigation of the facts, whether it is a fender-bender, vandalism, a "false" alarm call, a major financial investigation, a serial murder case, or an act of terrorism. Here are some important tips to remember:

- Allow persons being interviewed to tell their own stories.
- If you need to ask questions to get the interview started or to keep it going, ask very general open-ended questions (e.g., "What happened?" or "What did you see or hear?").
- Listen first, and then ask questions to fill in the details.
- Don't use "legalese" (or "policeese"); resist the temptation to try to sound like a lawyer or a legal document.
- Use the first person when writing, not "This officer," "Responding officer," "This unit," etc. Just use "I" or "we." Using third person language not only does not make the report sound more professional, it also makes report writers sound illiterate.

Do not waste the reader's attention by creating distractions or using "lawyerisms." Do not try to "sound like a lawyer" (or a cop) by using words that "smell" like legal words but have little or no legal substance or other purpose, for example, "said," as in, "That is a bright flashlight; where did you obtain said light?" In other words, do not try to be impressive, just be clear (Wydick, 2005, pp. 57–60).

Field Notes and Reports

Because few people have the ability to recall everything that they see, hear, or do, investigative note taking is an aid to short-term recall and the building blocks for a good report. News reporters take notes during interviews in order to develop their news stories later. In the same manner, investigators take notes of their interviews, observations, and actions to develop the narrative of their story—a factual police report. Narratives must be legible, accurate, and concise in order to be a memory aid sufficient to produce a clear and complete report. This also helps the investigator to clarify and organize facts before recording his or her official report of the investigation.

Tape recorders can be used as a notebook pad to record interviews and statements and to record phone calls (to which you are a party). In addition to everything that they see, hear, or do, investigators may want to record the weather and environmental conditions, measurements, exact quotes, critical and estimated times, etc. The notes can then be transformed into a report using simple but meaningful words.

Make a shopping list. Once you have taken notes on all of the information gathered during your investigation, put the information in a manageable form or order. List the facts into logical groups (e.g., victim's statement, witnesses' statements, etc.). Place these groups in order, arranging them in chronological order, if possible.

When necessary, make a list. Sometimes the best way to present a group of conditions, exceptions, or related ideas or elements is with an introductory clause followed by a list:

1. The elements of the list must be parallel in substance (related ideas or points).
2. The items in the list must be parallel in grammar (the same punctuation and grammar elements).
3. After each element in the list put a semicolon with "or" or "and" or a comma and an "and" before the last point or element (if short).
4. Put the list at the end of the passage or paragraph.
5. You may put a list within a list, that is, sub-points, but no more than two levels.

(Wydick, 2005, pp. 45–46)

Narrative

Use short sentences. Longer sentences are harder to understand. The first thing readers look for is the topic: what the report or brief is about. Long sentences strain the reader's memory of the points made (individual thoughts). Use one main thought per sentence. Keep the average sentence to 25 words or less (Wydick, 2005, pp. 33–36). Do not use redundant legal phrases (Wydick, 2005, pp. 17–18).

The narrative should be in chronological sequence (in the order that the events occurred, without flashbacks, flash-forwards, or flash-sideways). Do not overuse or misuse "stated," "related," or "indicated" when you mean "said." Avoid overused, stereotyped fillers such as:

- stated, related, and indicated
- the area
- submitted for your information
- pursuant to orders
- please be advised that
- the questions as to whether

Languages are precise. There are rules for language for a reason: to avoid miscommunications or misunderstandings. Misinterpretation often results from difficulty in reading form, for example, pronoun agreement (singular or plural) and the omission of information that is "unknown," "does not apply," or "none" (this should be noted so it does not appear that it was omitted or overlooked). When you feel like it does not matter or you just do not care about "good English," remember the famous "comma case," which turned on a single comma for the meaning of a contract.

Titles Describing People

- Complainant (or Complaining Party)
- Victim
- Witness
- Perpetrator
- Suspect
- Other Subject

Descriptions of Vehicles (CYMBL)

- Color (if two-tone, top over bottom colors, e.g., white over red)
- Year (year of manufacture)
- Make (manufacturer, e.g., Ford, Chevrolet, Pontiac, Chrysler, etc.)
- Body (4-door, 2-door, hatchback, pickup, van, etc.)
- License (year of issue, state of issue, tag number, type, etc.)

Solvability Factors

Solvability factors are known issues that reflect upon the probability of solving the crime. These factors are often listed in a report and determine how much and whether there will be follow-up investigation.

Automated Report Templates, Supplemental Reports, and the Narrative Summary

Computer-generated reports are becoming more common and in some cases are replacing written and typed reports. Templates are "fill-in" spaces of reoccurring fields. "Fields" is a computer term for the type of information listed in a particular space.

Supplements are reports written to add to or amend information from the main original report. Supplements may reflect follow-up information. Usually the investigation follows one chronological sequence, which is reflected in daily supplements.

A summary supplement is the responsibility of the lead investigator to take all reports written and compile a summary of the chronological sequence of events relevant to the entire investigation.

Elements of a Good Report: Helping Others Know What You Know

Be clear, complete, concise, and organize your information in chronological order (including an introduction, body, and conclusion). Here are the elements of a good report:

- **Clear**—legible and understandable (by readers other than the writer); keep it as simple as possible; other people must understand the complicated information you are conveying.
- **Complete**—all relevant facts and details (without unnecessary verbiage).
  - **Facts: The Five W's + H**—(1) Who, (2) What, (3) When, (4) Where, (5) Why, and (6) How
- **Concise**—thorough but brief; use simple, plain English and avoid police jargon or trying to sound like a lawyer. (Law schools are now teaching attorneys to use "plain English.") Be brief and avoid unnecessary wordiness. Writing in a natural form helps ensure this.
- **Organization: Chronological Order**—the order in which events occurred, not the order in which you investigated the facts (although this should be noted as well); organize the facts into a logical, chronological order.
  - Introduction (beginning)
  - Body (middle)
  - Conclusion (end)

Use the **A, B, C, D, E, F** system of organizing a report. Here are the elements:

- ACTIONS by officers
- BEHAVIOR of witnesses, suspects, and victims
- COMMUNICATION (dialog, questions, and answers)
- DESCRIPTION of the scene, suspects, and vehicles
- EVIDENCE (physical)
- FINAL disposition or resolution

Good organization is fundamental to effective legal writing. No matter how well you have done everything else, your work will be wasted unless it is organized intelligently. Although failure to communicate effectively can result from many causes, most such failures result from the writer's shoddy organization. Advance planning, outlining, and pre-writing a draft may help you think through a problem and avoid omitting important points (Dernbach et al., 2007, p. 115).

Apart from careful planning, there are five basic principles of good organization that enable you to create a document that is easy to read and easy to understand.

1. Discuss each issue separately.
2. Discuss each sub-issue separately.
3. For each issue or sub-issue, describe the applicable law before applying it to the factual situation. Each issue or sub-issue involves the application of a legal rule to specific facts. The relevant legal rules, therefore, provide a framework for your analysis and should be stated first. Stating the applicable law first enables you to be concise.
4. State the reasons supporting your conclusion on an issue or sub-issue before discussing counterarguments. The result of your thinking on an issue or sub-issue should be a legal conclusion expressed in your thesis.
5. When there is more than one issue, discuss the issues in a logical order.

(Dernbach et al., 2007, pp. 116–125)

Spelling Rules

Spelling is important; correct spelling (using Spell Check or a pocket dictionary) and ensure correct word usage. Not only does a misspelled report make the writer look less credible and more incompetent, but also misspelled words may convey an entirely different meaning that stays on the official record. Merely stating in courts, "What I meant was…" does not always solve this problem. Using a computer with Spell Check or a pocket dictionary is cheap and easy. Nevertheless, here are some tips to help with spelling:

- For words ending in *-ing* after a long vowel sound, drop the *e*, use a single consonant, and add *-ing* (e.g., rape becomes raping; the "*a*" in rape is a long vowel sound, so drop the *e*, use only one *p* [single consonant], and add *-ing*).
- Use *i* before *e* except after *c* or when pronounced *ay* (as in neighbor).
- Watch for nouns ending in *er, or,* and *ar.*
- Plurals are mostly made by adding *s,* but watch for the exceptions.

Parts of Speech

A sentence is a group of words that contains a *subject* and a *verb*. A sentence expresses a complete thought. A fragment is incomplete, does not express a complete thought, and lacks a subject and/or verb. If a line of words does not stand alone to complete the thought, it is not a sentence, but a fragment. Knowing what the parts of speech are is not merely a tool for your grade school and high school English teacher to bore you with sentence diagramming. Knowing the parts of speech helps you to identify whether your sentence and the complete report narrative correctly communicate what you need to say to win your case. Here are descriptions of the essential parts of speech:

Nouns name something, that is, a person, place, thing, action, quality, or belief.

- *Concrete nouns*—identify something tangible (perceived through the senses), that is, it can be observed through sight, sound, smell, taste, or touch.
- *Proper nouns*—identify specific persons, places, or things (i.e., titles may be capitalized when they identify a specific person, place, or thing, e.g., Chief Smith or City of Fort Wayne).
- *Common nouns*—identify a member of a larger group (e.g., "The sergeant read the report").
- *Collective nouns*—identify groups of people or a group of things that belong to a whole (e.g., team, squad, bureau, class, club, etc.); when the collective noun functions as a singular unit, the verb used is also singular.
- *Abstract nouns*—identify an idea, a belief, or a feeling.

Pronouns act as a substitute for a noun; they identify a person, place, or thing, but do not provide a specific name and are more general (e.g., I, me, my, mine, he, she, it, him, her, they, them, his, hers, their, theirs, you, your, yours, our, we, us, etc.).

Verbs illustrate action or activity, a state of being, and further describe the subject. Linking verbs (helping verbs) illustrate *being* (e.g., was, is, am, were, etc.).

- Present tense (e.g., ask, drive, come, etc.)
- Past tense (e.g., asked, drove, came, etc.)

Use base verbs, not nominalizations. Writers use action words (verbs) to express life in motion. A nominalization is a verb that has been turned into a noun. Lawyers and bureaucrats:

"take action," rather than "act"
"make assumptions," rather than "assume"
"draw conclusions," rather than "conclude"

Not all nominalizations are bad, but do not overuse them (Wydick, 2005, pp. 23–24).

Adjectives modify or limit nouns or pronouns (descriptive, such as blue, tall, dark, fast, etc.). They are used to describe nouns and pronouns (how much, what kind, which, how many, etc.) or to compare nouns and pronouns (fast, faster, fastest, etc.).

Adverbs modify or limit verbs, adjectives, or other adverbs or are intensifiers (e.g., very, too, quickly, carefully, etc.). They describe verbs, other adverbs, or adjectives (e.g., when, where, how, etc.) and usually (but not always) end in –ly (e.g., quickly, slowly, early, etc.).

Prepositions show the relationship or link between nouns or pronouns and other words in the sentence (e.g., about, above, across, against, along, at, before, behind, beside, beyond, during, except, from, into, like, onto, since, through, toward, up, etc.) and often indicate space or time (e.g., after, among, between, in, of, on, to, under, with, etc.).

Conjunctions join or connect words with other words, phrases, clauses and ideas, and either coordinates or subordinates (e.g., and, after, because, but, for, nor, or, so, yet, until, etc.) or FANBOYS (for, and, nor, but, or, yet, so).

Interjections are independent words used to express, show, or illustrate strong feeling or emotion and should be used (in reports) only in a direct quotation (e.g., Darn!, Wow!, Hey!, Help!, Duck!, etc.).

Definitions of Terms

- **Subject**—the word (or group of words) that a clause or sentence makes a statement about (e.g., "The *lawyer* objected to the evidence").
- **Predicate**—the word (or group of words) that makes a statement about the subject (e.g., "The lawyer *objected to the evidence*").
- **Phrase**—a group of closely related words that does *not* contain *both* a subject and a predicate.
- **Independent Clause**—a group of words that contains *both* a subject and a predicate and could stand alone as a sentence.
- **Dependent Clause**—a group of words that contains *both* a subject and a predicate, but could not stand alone as a sentence (usually begins with *who, which, when, that, since,* or *because*).

(Wydick, 2005, pp. 84–85)

Punctuation Rules (Made Easy)

Remember the "comma case," discussed previously? Punctuation may seem to be a useless technicality, but it makes a difference in the meaning of language and winning or losing. Those who feel that punctuation is merely a useless technicality are likely the same people who feel that case law is merely useless legal technicalities. Both of these attitudes lose cases. Therefore, here are a few quick, easy, and relatively painless rules to help with correct punctuation.

Capitalization

- Cities, states, and streets
- Organizations and buildings
- Days, months, and holidays
- Geographic locations but not the direction of travel
- Titles of professionals (e.g., Judge Ryan, Dr. Williams, Chief Ankenbruck, etc.)
- Academic subjects (e.g., Criminology, Criminal Law, Forensic Science, etc.)
- Brand names (e.g., Smith & Wesson, Motorola, Microsoft, etc.)
- Films, books, and poems (e.g., *Catch Me If You Can, Profiling the Criminal Mind, Invictus,* etc.)

Commas

Use a comma:

1. to link independent clauses, that is, to separate two complete sentences that are joined by a coordinating conjunction (*but, or, for, nor, yet, so, and* [sometimes]). If you do not use a conjunction, you may use a semicolon.
2. after introductory elements or an introductory clause (e.g., "At the time of the accident, the driver was intoxicated" or "Because he used a comma in his sentence, his reports were regarded as very precise").
3. to set off non-restrictive elements (which modifies or describes part of a sentence but is not essential to the meaning), for example, *which, although,* or *though.*
4. to set off parenthetical elements or separate nonrestrictive phrases in a sentence (one that is pertinent but is not essential to the meaning or unimportant phrases which the sentence reads well without), for example, *"to say the least," "after all,"* etc.

5. to separate items in a series (three or more). If the series is complicated or contains internal commas, use semicolons instead of commas.
6. to separate coordinate adjectives that are not joined by "and" (but not between the last adjective and the noun).
7. to set off transitional or interrupting words and phrases (e.g., *therefore, thus, furthermore, moreover,* etc.). If the transitional word is between two independent clauses, use a semicolon before it and a comma after it.
8. when writing dates or to set off dates, titles, geographic names, and short quotations, for example,
   a. On 07 December 1941, Pearl Harbor was attacked (or December 7, 1941, Pearl Harbor was attacked) [the first date is in military style]
   b. Robert J. Girod, Sr., Ph.D., was the professor (both "Sr." and "Ph.D." are titles)
   c. Washington, DC, is the seat of government (to separate cities, states and nations)
   d. The witness said, "He did it." (If more than three lines, use a block quote) (Wydick, 2005, pp. 85–90)
9. after the salutation of an informal letter (e.g., Dear Andy and Barney,).
10. to introduce a quote.

Colons

Use a colon to introduce:

- a series (the material that precedes the colon must be able to stand alone; do not use a colon between a verb or preposition and its object)
- a summary, elaboration, or illustration (e.g., "two types of crimes: felonies and misdemeanors)
- a long sentence or when introducing a formal quote, block quote, or a list (if a quote is longer than one sentence, use a colon rather than a comma) (Wydick, 2005, pp. 92–93)
- after the salutation of a formal letter (e.g., Mayor Pike:)
- when indicating time (e.g., 1:00 p.m., except when using military time, 1300 hours)

Semicolons

Use a semicolon:

1. to join two independent clauses (two complete sentences) without a conjunction, that is, that are not joined by a coordinating conjunction

2. when two independent clauses (two complete sentences) are joined by a transitional expression (a conjunctive adverb), that is, *then, therefore, however, furthermore, thus, indeed, in fact, as a result,* or *for example*); for example, "The judge signed the warrant; therefore, the perpetrator was arrested"
3. to separate items in a complicated series (separate clauses that already have commas; see **Commas** above)

(Wydick, 2005, pp. 90–91)

Dashes

Use dashes to signal an abrupt break. Commas, parentheses, and dashes are all used to set off material that interrupts a sentence. They differ in the emphasis they give:

- commas—tend to be neutral (neither emphasize nor de-emphasize material).
- parentheses—de-emphasize or play down the material.
- dashes—emphasize the material, especially to set off material in the middle of a sentence.

(Wydick, 2005, p. 93)

Quotation Marks

Quotation marks are used when quoting another's statements (but not when paraphrasing). Commas are placed inside quotation marks. Question marks and exclamation points are placed inside the quotation marks when they are a part of the quote, but outside when they are not.

Parentheses

Use parentheses:

- when you want to label the items in a series
- to introduce shorthand expressions or abbreviations
- to avoid ambiguities (clarify modifiers, state exceptions, or interject brief definitions or qualifications)
- to set off interjected or explanatory material (see **Dashes** above)

(Wydick, 2005, pp. 94–95)

Apostrophes

Use apostrophes to form possessives. To make the possessive of a singular noun, add *'s* (apostrophe "s") (e.g., Jones's), even if the word ends with an "s" sound. If that would make a triple "s" sound, then use an apostrophe only.

Do not use an apostrophe with pronouns (his, hers, its, yours, ours, theirs, whose). The possessive of the pronoun "it" is "its" (without an apostrophe). "It's" (with an apostrophe) is a contraction for "it is" (Wydick, 2005, pp. 95–97).

Hyphens

Hyphens are not the same as a dash. A hyphen looks like a shorter dash and has no space; a dash is longer and has spaces. Hyphens are used for compound numbers and fractions (e.g., twenty-one or two-fifths) and with some compound words. For example:

- brother-in-law (hyphenated)
- ice cream (written as two words, with no hyphen)
- textbook (written as one word, with no hyphens)

When in doubt, check a good dictionary (Wydick, 2005, pp. 97–99).

Periods, Question Marks, and Exclamation Points

- Periods end a declarative sentence, command, or indirect quotation and are used after abbreviations (e.g., Lt., Dr., or Prof.).
- Question marks end direct questions.
- Exclamation points show surprise or strong emotion. They should be used sparingly and almost never in formal writing.

(Wydick, 2005, pp. 99–100)

Quotations

Use quotations to enclose short, direct quotes of less than 50 words (then use a block quote, indenting both the left and right). Indicate alterations and additions to quoted material by surrounding it in square brackets [like these]. Ellipses (. . .) are used to indicate omissions (material left out) (Wydick, 2005, p. 101).

A Word on Word Usage

Arrange your words with care. Avoid big gaps between the subject, the verb, and the object. To make your writing easier to understand, most declaratory sentences should follow this order: subject, verb, and object (if there is one). You can decrease the gap between the subject and the verb by placing intervening words at the beginning or end of the sentence (Wydick, 2005, pp. 41–42).

Choose your words with care. Use "concrete words" that grip the readers' minds because they are not abstract or vague. Intentional vagueness, however, may be used when a writer cannot foresee every set of facts that may arise (but only if *both* necessary and intentional) (Wydick, 2005, pp. 56–57).

Homophones are words that are similar in sound but different in spelling and meaning. Make sure to use the correct word for the correct meaning and use the correct spelling of the correct word.

Misplaced phrases occur when word placement is not correct. The meaning of the sentence changes and makes the writer look foolish and incompetent. Here are some examples:

- "While patrolling, I parked my squad car behind the police station, which ran out of gas." (The police station ran out of gas?)
- "At the scene of the arson I observed behind the building, a suspect, which was burning." (The suspect was burning or the building was burning?)
- "Responding officer was sent to the robbery along with Officer Jones. When this officer arrived responding officer identified himself." (Who arrived and who identified whom? Avoid third person narratives!)

Use the Active Voice, Rather than the Passive Voice

The *active voice* is a clearer and precise way of showing "who" is doing an action versus the passive voice which shows "who" is having something done to them. The active voice style identifies the main subject at the beginning of the sentence and the subject performs the action.

"When you use a verb in the active voice, the subject of the sentence does the acting... When you use a verb in the passive voice, the subject of the sentence is acted upon" (Wydick, 2005, pp. 27–28). For example,

Passive: The perpetrator was arrested by the detective.
Active: The detective arrested the perpetrator.

The *passive voice* can create ambiguity and misunderstanding. The passive voice style identifies the main subject at the end of the sentence and the subject receives the action (usually using the words *was* and *by*). "The passive voice takes more words than the active voice [and] ... can be ambiguous. With the active voice, you can usually tell *who* is doing *what* to *whom*" [emphasis added]. The passive voice can hide the identity of the actor (a "truncated passive"), for example, "The perpetrator was arrested" (does not identify who arrested the perpetrator) (Wydick, 2005, pp. 30–32).

Use First Person: Use of "I" and "Me"

In first-person writing, an officer documents his or her actions by using the words "I" and "me." This is the most appropriate and least confusing form of simple communication. In third-person writing, the use of "this officer," "this unit," or "this reporter" can be confusing and does not sound professional.

Use of Who and Whom

Who is often the subject of a sentence (replace the word *who* with the word *he, she,* or *they* to check if you have used the word *who* correctly). *Whom* is often the object of a sentence (replace the word *whom* with the word *him, her,* or *them* to check if you have used the word *whom* correctly).

Focus on the Actor, the Action, and the Object

"*Who* {Actor} is doing *what* {Action} to *whom* or *which* (Object} in this sentence?" {emphasis added} Example: "Is it likely that the defendant will plead guilty to the offense?" Defendant = actor (who). Plead = action (what). Offense = object (whom/which). The first four words ("Is it likely that ... ") have no purpose. It is better to write (or say), "The defendant will likely plead guilty to the offense" (Wydick, 2005, pp. 15–16).

When the passive voice is appropriate:

- the thing done is important, but who did it is not or you don't know who did it
- you want the subject of the sentence to connect with words at the end of the preceding sentence
- to place a strong element at the end of the sentence for emphasis
- when a sense of detached abstraction is appropriate (e.g., "In the eyes of the law, all persons are created equal")

- when you want to muddy the waters (i.e., you do not want to say something outright; e.g., the defense does not want to say that the defendant knocked out the victim, but may say "the victim was knocked out").

Run-on Sentences

Run-on sentences or "fused sentences" lack punctuation and coordinating conjunctions (and, but, or, nor, for, yet, so, etc.), which indicate a break or pause in thought.

The *run-on sentence* goes on too long without having any clear connection between its many clauses and phrases. Errors include (1) punctuation—use, but don't overuse, commas and periods; (2) subject–verb agreement—describe who did or said what; and (3) dangling participles or modifiers—participles or participial phrases are often attached to the wrong noun or pronoun, for example, "Running down the street he saw the man he suspected of the burglary." (Who was running, the victim or the suspect; who is he?)

Incomplete Sentences or Sentence Fragments

A *sentence fragment* does not necessarily imply that the sentence is too short. An *incomplete sentence* may involve a long group of words introduced by a *subordinating word* (e.g., when, although, since, or because) without completing the thought. Subordinating words, such as "when," introduce a dependent clause, which must be completed to produce a complete thought. Reread the sentence to see if it makes sense and ends in a complete thought.

Surplus Words and Compound Constructions

In every English sentence there are two kinds of words: working words and glue words. The working words carry the meaning of the sentence. The others are glue words: *the...*, *of....* They hold the working words together to form a proper, grammatical sentence (Wydick, 2005, p. 7).

Avoid compound constructions. Compound constructions use three or four words to do the work of one or two words, for example, *With respect to...* instead of *on. For the reason that...* instead of *because* (Wydick, 2005, p. 11).

Here is a list of examples:

Compound	Simple
at that point in time	then
by means of	by
by reason of	because of

Compound	Simple
by virtue of	by, under
for the purpose of	to
for the reason that	because
in accordance with	by, under
inasmuch as	since
in connection with	with, about, concerning
in favor of	for
in order to	to
in relation to	about, concerning
in the event that	if
in the nature of	like
prior to	before
subsequent to	after
with a view to	to
with reference to	about, concerning

Avoid Word-Wasting Idioms

Verbose	Concise
The fact that . . .	
The fact that she had died	Her death
He was aware of the fact that	He knew that
Despite the fact that	Although, even though
Because of the fact that	Because
Case, instance, situation . . .	
In some instances	Sometimes
In many cases	Often
That was the situation in which the	There the (court)
Criminal prosecutions are now more frequent than was formerly the case	Criminal prosecutions are more frequent now
A warrant is required in the situation in which	A warrant is required when
Other examples . . .	
During the time that	During, while
For the period of	For
Insofar as the judge is concerned	The judge
There is no doubt but that	Doubtless, no doubt
The question as to whether	Whether, the question whether
This is a topic that	This topic
Until such time as	Until

(Wydick, 2005, pp. 13–14)

Put Conditions and Exceptions Where
They Are Clear and Easy to Read

The *beginning* of a sentence is usually the best place for conditions or exceptions that are *short* or need to be at the beginning to *avoid misleading* the reader (e.g., except for misdemeanors, all criminal offenses are . . .). The *end* of the sentence is the best place for a condition or exception that is *longer than the main clause* (e.g., a felony carries a sentence of more than one year, unless . . . a, b, c, d, e, etc.) (Wydick, 2005, p. 44).

Put Modifying Words Close to What They Modify

In some languages, the word order does not affect the meaning of the sentence, but in English it does. Modifiers are words like "often" or "only." You can usually avoid ambiguity (vagueness and confusion) by placing the relative pronoun (e.g., who, which, that) right after the word it modifies. Examples:

> Bad: Vehicles are inspected for the public only by a police officer.
> Better: Only police officers inspect vehicles for the public.
> Bad: Buy money, which must not exceed $100 a month, must be reported within 24 hours.
> Better: Buy money must not exceed $100 a month and must be reported within 24 hours (Wydick, 2005, pp. 47–49).

Avoid Nested Modifiers

Sentences are hard to understand when the reader must mentally supply brackets and parentheses to keep modifiers straight. The best remedy for this is to take the "nest of modifiers" apart and incorporate some of the information in a separate sentence. Example:

> Bad: The defendant, who was driving the white Ford van that was concealing the illegal drugs some of which was marijuana and some of which was cocaine, stopped in front of the house.
> Analysis: The defendant {who was driving the white Ford van [that was concealing the illegal drugs (some of which was marijuana and some of which was cocaine)]} stopped in front of the house.
> Better: The defendant was driving the white Ford van that was concealing the illegal drugs. Some of the contraband was marijuana and some of it was cocaine. The van stopped in front of the house (Wydick, 2005, p. 50).

Clarify the Reach of Modifiers

Example: "All male German Shepherds and Australian Shepherds over two years old." This is ambiguous because it is not certain if it means

- all "*male* German Shepherds *over two years old*" and all "*male* Australian Shepherds *over two years old*" (all male AND all over two years old; BOTH) OR
- all "*male* German Shepherds (of any age)" and all "Australian Shepherds *over two years old*" (of any gender) OR
- all "*male* German Shepherds" (of any age) and all "*male* Australian Shepherds *over two years old*" OR
- all "*male* German Shepherds *over two years old*" and all "Australian Shepherds *over two years old*" (of any gender)

To avoid ambiguity (vagueness and confusion), you must "clarify the reach of the modifiers" in the sentence. This may be as simple as changing the word order, repeating words, or making a list; for example,

- all women and all men over 35
- all male German Shepherds over two years old and all Australian Shepherds
- all (list):
  - male German Shepherds
  - male Australian Shepherds
- female Australian Shepherds over two years old

(Wydick, 2005, pp. 51–52)

Critique Checklist

It will be helpful to follow these steps in report writing: (1) Collect information at the crime scene and from witnesses and informants. (2) Take complete notes of relevant details. (3) Organize the information (volumes of information and details are useless if they are not in an understandable and orderly form). (4) Prepare, proofread, and evaluate the report (using the following checklist). Reports must contain specific facts about specific events. A *fact* is something that happened and can be proven. An *opinion* is someone's belief and is open to interpretation. Only note opinions when they are stated as an opinion. Here is a checklist to use as a format in report writing.

Proofread your reports before submitting them, correcting errors pertaining to:

- spelling
- grammar
- punctuation
- capitalization
- sentence structure
- READ:
  - **Review** for content.
  - **Evaluate** for errors.
  - **Analyze** for clarity.
  - **Determine** changes needed.

Revising and Editing

Almost everything you need to know about writing can be summarized in one principle: Write to communicate. Here are a few helpful tips to follow:

1. Be direct, precise, and concise (avoid lengthy phrases and unnecessary modifiers), combining precision with simplicity.
2. Use correct grammar, punctuation, and spelling. Use proper sentence structure. Do *not* use slang, jargon, or radio codes in the place of words (except in quotes). Write in the proper tense, which is usually past tense.
3. Whenever possible, use verbs to make writing forceful. Use the active voice and avoid excessive nominalization; that is, avoid expressing a key action with a noun instead of a verb, for example, "perform an operation" rather than "operate."
4. Eliminate unnecessary information and repetition (extraneous facts or useless details).
5. Edit intrusive or misplaced words and phrases.

(Dernbach et al., 2007, pp. 192–200)

Logical Presentation Methods
Conveying Information

15

Conveying Information: Telling the Story

Language involves speaking, listening, writing, and reading to communicate thoughts, ideas, information, feelings, etc. The first step in understanding (comprehending) language (communications) is speech perception, which involves translating sounds into speech units. Perception of speech also involves filling in missing sounds and determining "the boundaries between words" using *context*. Listeners process language as groups of words called "constituents," listen to "surface structure and determine the underlying, deep structure of a sentence." Sentences are harder to understand if they contain negatives, the passive voice, or ambiguities (Matlin, 1994, p. 260).

Reading involves perceptual processes such as eye movement and letter and word recognition. Context is important when we need to understand the meaning of an unfamiliar word. When we read, we frequently draw *inferences* that were not really actually stated in the written passage (or report), which is why logic, reasoning, deduction, induction, and inferences are so important to understand and utilize correctly.

Prepare to Tell Your Story in Court

Pre-trial preparation includes knowing what your case will sound like to those who will hear it in court—the jury, judge, attorneys (on both sides), the media, etc. Particularly, the jury and judge are your target audience. Here are 10 tips to determine if your "story" is ready to tell in court.

1. **Begin by believing in what you are saying.** To be compelling, you must believe in your own case, while looking at various angles to illustrate the truth.
2. **Start with a one-sentence version of your story.** What is the one sentence that states your case in a clear and compelling way? ("This case is about...")
3. **Choose an organizational structure.** Most attorneys default to storytelling in chronological order. Some, however, structure their

stories as either a flashback, a "before and after," or a "mystery to be solved." You should also choose your focus: (a) wide angle (big picture), (b) zoom-in (focus on one detail), or (c) start with a tight focus and zoom out to show the "big picture."

4. **Know your audience.** A successful story builds a bridge from teller to audience. Get to know your audience (juries) through *voir dire* questions that answer, "How can I reach this person?"

5. **Know the characters in the story (the parties involved, including the "bad guy").** While the characters can be conveyed through description, they are defined in a story by their roles (actions that convey who they are). Juries will look for the "bad guy," who gives a story shape and conveys a theme of a "battle between good and evil."

6. **Replace weak metaphors (descriptive comparisons).** Brainstorm for the right *analogy* (similarity between things upon which to base a comparison) and then reverse brainstorm to tear it down. If it stands up, it is a good one; if not, keep trying.

7. **Create compelling images in everyone's mind.** The images that stand out the most in your own mind will be the ones that you are best able to convey to a judge and a jury. Compelling imagery is most important in complex cases requiring complex understanding.

8. **Find the part of the story that makes listeners ask, "Then what happened?"** Good stories have a pause where you peak the listeners' interest. This is where you connect with a jury, draw them into the story, and make them ask themselves, "What happened next?"

9. **Answer the question, "Why should I care?"** It is an attorney's job (with the help of the lead detective) to make a jury care and seek justice. Help them to empathize (not merely sympathize, but truly "feel" the victim's pain). Who or what do they care about? How might this incident or issue affect them or the persons or things they care about?

10. **Tell your story to someone who is not an attorney (or a detective).** Ask someone to listen to your case, not as a series of arguments, but as a story. Try to identify weak points and the parts that are confusing, boring, or unbelievable. Strengthen the story until it reflects all of the necessary elements in a story that others will listen to and believe.

Storytelling: Theory and Themes

A *theory* is a judgment, conception, proposition, or formula formed by speculation, deduction, or abstraction and generalization from the facts. It is also a more or less plausible or scientifically acceptable general principle offered to explain observed facts.

A theory of the case refers to the facts and the law that lead a jury to a conclusion. It is a central theory that organizes all facts, reasons, and arguments, and forms the basic position from which to determine actions at trial. It functions as a litigator's "compass" or story synopsis and has three components:

1. Facts—acts, observations, real evidence, demonstrative evidence, etc.
2. Emotions—shock, confusion, fear, anger, etc.
3. Law—elements and defenses.

The theme of a case is an idea or principle that provides direction in a case and is dominant enough in a culture to control or direct beliefs and conduct. It is a brief and easily remembered word, phrase, or sentence that captures the essence or reality of the theory of the case. The elements of the theme of a case include:

1. Introducing the jury to the theory of the case.
2. Repetition that reinforces the theory of the case in the minds of the fact-finder (jury or court).
3. Labels and slogans that provide catchwords or catch phrases for jurors to remember during deliberations.
4. Vivid images and emotions that produce instant recall each time jurors hear them.
5. Necessity of the opponent to argue against the theory, rather than for his or her own case.
6. An unforgettable and memorable account.

The elements of a persuasive story include:

1. The plot—What is the story about? Will the fact-finder (jurors or court) empathize with it?
2. Cast of characters—Who are the characters (innocent or not)?
3. Character development—What are the characters like? What are their lifestyles?
4. Chronology and perspective—Does the story unfold in chronological order or flashbacks? Is it told from one individual's perspective or from the viewpoints of several witnesses?
5. Props—What physical objects will you need to tell the story (real evidence and demonstrative evidence)?
6. Dominant emotion—Is the dominant emotion of the story one that jurors can identify with and understand how it dominated or influenced the outcome of the story?

Storytelling and Opening Statements

Humans become involved in a story, even if they know it is fictional, through what is known as *suspension of disbelief.* Opening statements must tell a fascinating story to help listeners visualize events. "Let me tell you what happened." Litigation of lawsuits requires the re-creation of an event or events that occurred long before the suit was initiated. The process requires skillful storytelling that communicates to the jury and judge what happened and why. Successful storytelling in litigation comes from preparation and planning. A few elements include:

- Identifying the struggle between good and bad, the tragedy, the characters, and the life of the story.
- Identifying emotions, motives, results, consequences, the mood, sympathy, empathy, etc.
- Identifying the character traits of the parties and their virtues or flaws, truth or untruthfulness, honesty or dishonesty, courage or cowardice, generosity or greed, selflessness or selfishness, kindness or cruelty, loyalty or disloyalty, etc.
- Identifying the structure of the story; a logical presentation of the introduction, issues, personalization of the parties involved, narration of events, explanation of the weaknesses of the case, facts and evidence, and a conclusion.
- Describing details that help listeners visualize the story. Create a vivid mental image of events and incidents in the minds of the listeners (jurors and judges).
- Internalizing the story; know the story so well that you do not need to think about the content. This is not merely "memorized," but knowing and understanding the facts and details.
- Avoiding being argumentative in the opening statement. Direct the jury's attention to the story rather than the lawsuit.
- Using well-chosen words, pauses, pace, volume, and eye contact with each juror to make them feel personally spoken to, movement and position (don't pace or distract), and natural gestures that create mental images (but avoid trying to portray or act out actions).

Cross-Examination: Discrediting Testimony and Impeachment

There are five major areas to consider in evaluating testimony and witnesses:

1. **Memory.** While the witness may have had knowledge at the time, does the witness remember now or is his or her memory incomplete or inaccurate?

2. **Circumstantial impediments to perception.** Were there any objects or conditions at the scene that impeded the witness' observations or perceptions, such as lighting, distance, obstructions, noise, distractions, time, etc.?

3. **Physical impediments to perception.** Does the witness have any physical or mental impairment that could impede his or her perception of observations, such as eyesight, hearing, use of drugs, alcohol, or medication, illness, etc.?

4. **Truthfulness.** Reputation or opinion about the witness' character for truthfulness (**Rules 608** and **609**)* or impeachment by prior inconsistent statements (**Rules 612** and **801(d)(1)**).

5. **Bias and interest.** Are there any biases or interests that may affect the witness' ability or willingness to be truthful?

Some common types of questions and suggestions used by trial lawyers for formulating questions for cross-examination include (CLOSeDSS):

1. **Control** witnesses using good question formulation—when a witness won't cooperate in answering a question, ask it again or ask if there is a reason why the witness does not want to answer the question.

2. **Leading** questions—a statement or assertion presented as an inquiry by the tone of voice or by adding a question at the beginning or end ("Isn't it true" questions).

3. **One** fact per question—compound questions (which are also objectionable) and questions containing more than one fact give the witness room for argument.

4. **Separate** persons from their behavior—personal attacks may produce sympathy; focus on facts and demonstrate external behavior, influences, and errors.

5. **Don't** try to do too much—little pieces placed carefully build the case, not the big piece.

6. **Stick** to your story—know your case and tell your story through the cross-examination; try to have witnesses agree with your facts and show where the witness is wrong, is lying, lacks knowledge, or is biased about the things on which you disagree.

7. **Save** conclusions for closing argument—know what you want to argue on each point in closing, and then construct a set of questions on each point that breaks it down into facts with which the witness cannot disagree.

You are telling your story through your questions. Focus on the facts through good question construction.

---

* Federal Rules of Evidence (most states also follow the same or similar rules).

Logical Presentation Methods

Telling the story is not always enough. Sometimes you must "show" the story by using direct and demonstrative evidence or media presentation technology, such as PowerPoint®, Visio®, or other presentation software.

Presentation Software: The Power of Microsoft PowerPoint®

PowerPoint® is a presentation software package used to create and present slideshow presentations. It enables a presenter (instructor, attorney, or anyone presenting information) to present information in a neat, well-organized, legible manner with the capability of adding photos, diagrams, illustrations, audio, or video enhancements to make more information available in a shorter amount of time. I use PowerPoint in the classroom because I can present much more information in a shorter time than merely speaking it or writing it on a backboard or white board. My audience does not need to wait for me to write it, discern what I am writing in my "scratching," and I can illustrate a point with photos, charts, graphs, diagrams, or other illustrations. Indeed, "a picture is worth a thousand words!" I can get more across in less time, more efficiently, and more effectively using this presentation software.

PowerPoint® evolves with each new release, so the content, capabilities, enhancements, and methods of deploying it will vary, depending upon the version that you have. Therefore, a complete description of how to use PowerPoint® would not be practical here. There are many books on how to use PowerPoint® and all of the software applications that come stand-alone or as part of a Microsoft® Office Suite® package. The program itself also comes with a "Help" tutorial and much of the basics are self-explanatory. However, we can discuss some of the main features and applications here.

The "Tool bar" for the version of PowerPoint® that I am currently using is shown in Figure 15.1.

One of the first steps is to select a slide. You have options here. First, select the drop-down menu with the "New Slide Button" near the left of the Tool Bar (see Figure 15.2 and Figure 15.3). There are nine options in my current version of PowerPoint®:

Figure 15.1 Example of a PowerPoint® Tool Bar on one version.

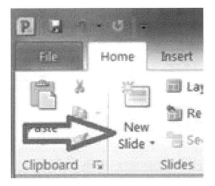

Figure 15.2 "New Slide" drop-down on Tool Bar.

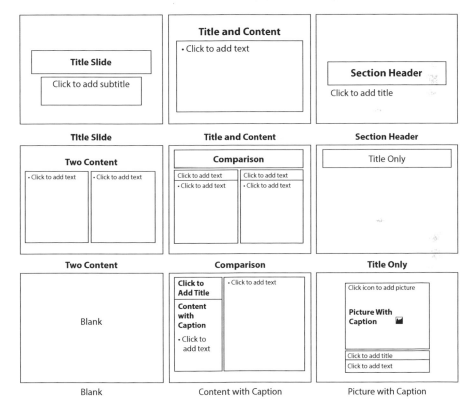

Figure 15.3 Slide choices from drop-down menu on Tool Bar.

1. **Title Slide** (used for an opening title and a block for additional information, such as instructor name, institution, etc.)
2. **Title and Content** (used to name a topic of information and then elaborate on the topic)
3. **Section Header** (used to name sections)

4. **Two Content** (a title block and two columns for information, graphics, charts, etc.)
5. **Comparison** (similar to Two Content, but with column titles on each side)
6. **Title Only** (used when you only want to display a title page)
7. **Blank** (used to insert pictures, illustrations, graphics, etc. with no text)
8. **Content With Caption** (a title section, a text box, and a column for text, pictures, graphics, charts, or other insertions)
9. **Picture With Caption** (used to insert pictures, graphics, charts, etc. with a title below and a box for text)

Next, you can use the "INSERT" drop-down menu to insert tables, pictures, clip art, screen shots, photo album images, shapes, "smart art," charts, links, text (various options), and video and audio media (Figure 15.4). You have several options, so I suggest just playing with it and seeing what you can create.

The Design Option drop-down Menu (Figure 15.5) allows you to select and alter various background designs for your presentation. You can also create unique designs.

The Transitions drop-down Menu (Figure 15.6) allows you to bring the presentation to life with a variety of transitions for each slide.

The Animation drop-down Menu (Figure 15.7) allows you to bring the presentation to life with a variety of animations for text, text boxes, pictures, illustrations, etc. Some examples are slip, fade-in, swivel, zoom, etc. Again,

Figure 15.4 The INSERT drop-down menu.

Figure 15.5 The Design Option drop-down menu.

Figure 15.6 The Transitions drop-down menu.

Figure 15.7 The Animation drop-down menu.

experiment with these to see what you can create. These also have automatic, manual, and timed options.

The Slide Show drop-down Menu (Figure 15.8) allows you to select various timing and audio-video options. This is worth exploring and experimenting with.

The Review drop-down Menu (Figure 15.9) includes Spell Check (very handy), translators, research options, new comments, linked notes, and other editing features.

The View drop-down Menu (Figure 15.10) includes various options for viewing your presentation, such as one slide, multiple slides, with or without notes, colors, etc.

Figure 15.8 The Slide Show drop-down menu.

Figure 15.9 The Review drop-down menu.

Figure 15.10 The View drop-down menu.

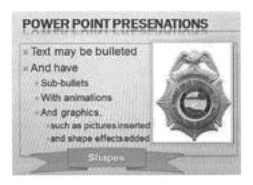

Figure 15.11 Example of a PowerPoint slide.

The major limitation of PowerPoint® presentations is your own imagination, so be creative and practice with the software by experimenting. (See Figure 15.11 for an example of a PowerPoint® presentation slide.)

Graphics and Reconstruction Software: Microsoft Visio Standard®

Other graphics software can be used to create and illustrate information on PowerPoint® presentations or as stand-alone packages. Such software applications can create crime scene and accident scene diagrams, animations, graphic presentation of analytical data, etc. Graphic reconstructions can be created. The Analytical Investigative Methods, discussed in Chapter 13, can be graphically displayed and presented using such applications software. There are other special purpose applications, but Visio is a general-purpose package that is less expensive and quite versatile. One such software package is Microsoft Visio Standard®.

Visio has a Tool Bar with several options:

1. Block Diagram (Figure 15.12)
2. Building Plan (Figure 15.13)
3. Flowchart (Figure 15.14)
4. Form and Charts (Figure 15.15)
5. Map (Figure 15.16)

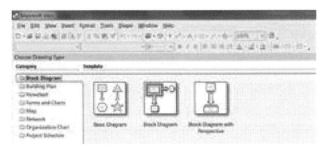

Figure 15.12 Visio Tool Bar and Block Diagram option.

Figure 15.13 Visio Tool Bar and Building Plan option.

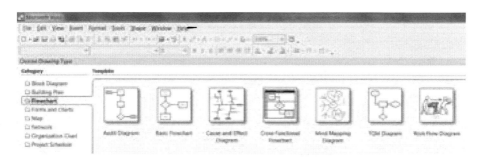

Figure 15.14 Visio Tool Bar and Flowchart option.

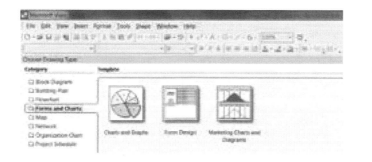

Figure 15.15 Visio Tool Bar and Form and Charts option.

Figure 15.16 Visio Tool Bar and Map option.

   6. Network (Figure 15.17)
   7. Organization Chart (Figure 15.18)
   8. Project Schedule (Figure 15.19)

While there are too many examples of Visio graphics to include here, a few are illustrated next, such as a Block Diagram (see Figure 15.20 and Figure 15.21). Other examples include a Flow Chart (Figure 15.22), a Map (Figure 15.23), and a Network (Figure 15.24).

Figure 15.17 Visio Tool Bar and Network option.

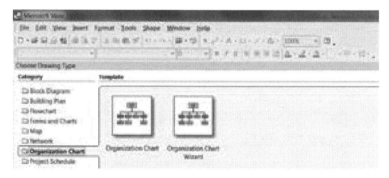

Figure 15.18 Visio Tool Bar and Organization Chart option.

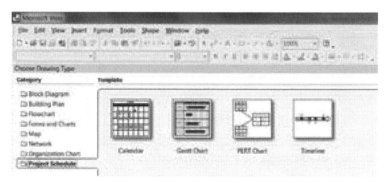

Figure 15.19 Visio Tool Bar and Project Schedule option.

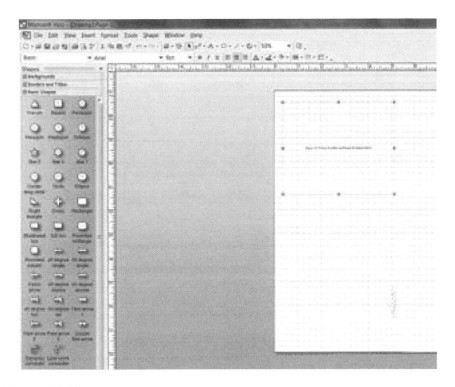

Figure 15.20 Block Diagram example.

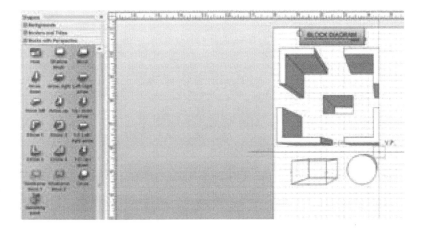

Figure 15.21 Block Diagram example.

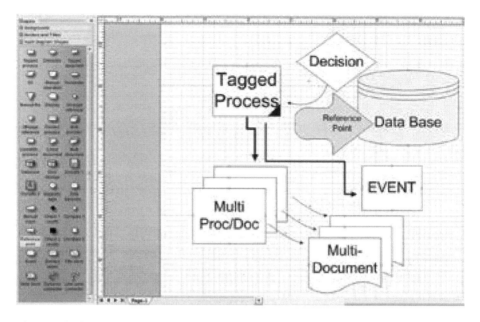

Figure 15.22 Flow Chart example.

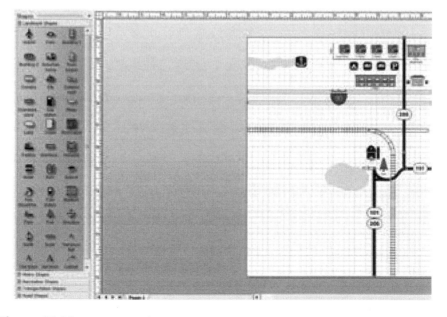

Figure 15.23 Map example.

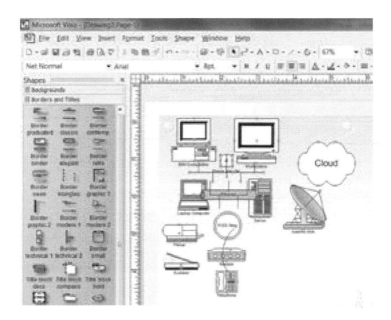

Figure 15.24 Network example.

Digital Imagery and Video Technology and Software

Technology is ever changing and evolving; however, it is worth at least mentioning the importance of incorporating digital photography and imagery, video imagery, and audio technologies into presentations where direct, demonstrative, and circumstantial evidence rules permit it. Software applications may be used to enhance or exploit such imagery, as long as it remains admissible as unaltered evidence. Rules of evidence should be consulted in the venue involved.

Court Testimony and Presentations

Presentation skills are not only the opportunity to present information and evidence, they are also The Big Game. That is, this is the one opportunity you may have to present your facts, evidence, and the theme and theory of the case. You must not only prepare the case and presentation materials, but also yourself. This includes your image, attitude, and skills in presentation.

A few books that you may want to consider adding to your library and from which to glean useful information include:

How to Win Friends and Influence People by Dale Carnegie; Simon & Schuster (Reissue edition; 2009): ISBN-10: 1439167346 and ISBN-13: 978-1439167342.

John T. Molloy's New Dress for Success by John T. Molloy; Gotham (2007): ISBN-10: 159240328X and 13: 978-1592403288.

The Power of Positive Thinking by Dr. Norman Vincent Peale; Orient Paperbacks, India (2006): ISBN-10: 8122204120 and ISBN-13: 978-8122204124.

Win Your Case: How to Present, Persuade, and Prevail—Every Place, Every Time by Gerry Spence; St. Martin's Griffin (Reprint edition; 2006): ISBN-10: 0312360673 and 13: 978-0312360672.

How to Argue & Win Every Time: At Home, At Work, In Court, Everywhere, Everyday by Gerry Spence; St. Martin's Griffin (Reprint edition; 1996): ISBN-10: 0312144776 and 13: 978-0312144777.

The Defense Never Rests by F. Lee Bailey; Signet (1995): ISBN-10: 0451126408 and 13: 978-0451126405.

To Be a Trial Lawyer by F. Lee Bailey; John Wiley & Sons, Inc. (1994): ISBN-10: 0471072567 and 13: 978-0471072560

Move Ahead with Possibility Thinking by Robert H. Schuller; Jove (1986): ISBN-10: 0515089842 and 13: 978-0515089844

The Best Defense, by Alan M. Dershowitz; Vintage Books (1983): ISBN-10: 039471380X and 13: 978-0394713809.

Melvin Belli: My Life on Trial by Melvin Belli, Morrow (1976); ISBN-10: 0688030858 and 13: 978-0688030858.

Using Logical Investigative Methods
Recapitulation

16

Recapitulation

This recapitulation is not redundant, but instead is a summary of main points in the form of a checklist. Use this summary as a checklist, not a shortcut.

Scientific Method: Fact Finding in Investigations

- Convince yourself first, then others.
- Fact finding and due diligence.
- Obviously a suicide—treat *all* deaths as a murder until proven otherwise.
- The Scientific Method—a method or procedure of systematic observation, measurement, and experiment, and the formulation, testing, and modification of hypotheses.

Steps of the Scientific Method

1. Observation
2. Question
3. Hypothesis (Prediction)
4. Method (Prediction)
5. Result (Testing)
6. Conclusion (Analysis)

Conclusion—two types of reasoning: (1) inductive reasoning and (2) deductive reasoning.

Cognitive Skills—perceptions and thought processes.

Logic: Deduction and Induction

- An introduction to logic—the study of *arguments* and methods of determining whether arguments are correct (*validated*) or incorrect (*flawed*).

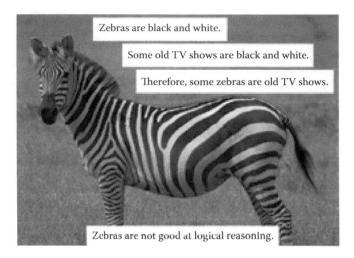

Figure 16.1 Zebras are not good at logical reasoning.

Deductive and Inductive Arguments

Formal Logic: The Logical Structure of Science

Deductive reasoning involves observing a set of characteristics that may be reasoned from a convergence of physical and behavioral actions or patterns within an event or a series of events, such as a crime or series of crimes. Inductive reasoning involves observing a set of characteristics based on a premise of broad generalizations and statistical analysis, which leads to the development of a hypothesis.

- The Psychology of Proof—reasoning is a psychological process.
- Deductive Validity

Deductive arguments may be (1) valid or invalid or (2) sound or unsound. There are three stages of deductive reasoning: (1) the premise, (2) the evidence, and (3) the conclusion.

- Science and hypothesis—an inductive argument is a valid argument if the degree of probability claimed for its conclusion is a reasonable degree of probability to attribute to the conclusion, relative to the given premises.
- Inductive analogy—an analogy is a parallel or resemblance between two different things. To use words in a *figurative* way is to stretch words beyond the bounds of literal use.

Legal Inferences and the Burdens of Proof

In inductive reasoning, there is enough of a link or a "nexus" to support or confirm a conclusion. The degree of probability of a conclusion must reach a degree of reasonable probability or rational credibility. In the law, this degree is referred to as the standard of proof or the burden of proof. Because inductive reasoning relies upon probabilities of the standard of proof, either a preponderance of evidence, clear and convincing evidence, or proof beyond a reasonable doubt, inferences are often relied upon.

- Circumstantial evidence and inferences—circumstantial evidence is evidence that, when presented with other evidence or facts, tends to establish a reasonable conclusion.

Critical Thinking: Fact Pattern Analysis

- Critical thinking (reasoning—a way of deciding whether a claim is always true, sometimes true, partly true, or false.
- Fact pattern analysis: what and why things go wrong.

Forty-three cases were examined to identify inadequate areas in a case. There arose 105 issues:

1. Interview/re-interview (inadequate interviews of witnesses or victims) 25.7%
2. Identify/interview suspects (no identification or interview of suspect) 16.1%
3. Report writing (poorly written reports failed to articulate understandable facts) 13.3%
4. Physical evidence and fingerprints (failure to attempt to collect) 10.4%
5. Documents (failure to provide available documents or documentation) 9.5%
6. Photos and videos (failure to provide available photos and videos) 7.6%
7. Identify witnesses (failure to identify witnesses or contact them) 7.6%
8. Property (failure to collect or account for property) 3.8%
9. Photo arrays (none conducted) 2.8%
10. Premises (lack of description or other necessary premises information) 2.8%

Six major problems or themes were identified by the Innocence Project.

1. Eyewitness misidentification
2. Unreliable or improper forensic science

3. False confessions
4. Government misconduct
5. Informants
6. Bad lawyering

Logical Reasoning: Legal Inferences

- Reasoning—the capacity for consciously making sense of things, applying logic, establishing and verifying facts.
- Convergent and divergent thinking—Convergent thinking reasons from very broad to very detailed; it identifies logical connectors and narrows the topic; divergent thinking reasons from very detailed to very broad, starting with facts and creating an explanation.
- Legal inferences—An inference is the act or process of deriving logical conclusions from premises known or assumed to be true. Because inductive reasoning relies upon probabilities of the standard of proof (a preponderance of evidence, clear and convincing evidence, or proof beyond a reasonable doubt), inferences are often relied upon. It is a "logical and reasonable conclusion of a fact" not presented by direct evidence but which, by process of logic and reason, a trier of fact may conclude exists.
- Types of fallacies—a fallacy is an argument that is incorrect, but may appear to be a correct statement.
  - Fallacies of ambiguity are generally deductive arguments that appear to be valid, but are not, due to a shift in meaning of a word, phrase, or sentence.
  - Material fallacies are incorrect for reasons other than ambiguity of language. There are two types of material fallacies: (1) *fallacies of relevance* (arguments that have premises that are irrelevant to the conclusion) and (2) *fallacies of insufficient evidence* (incorrect inductive arguments).
- There are two additional fallacies that do not fall into either of these categories.

Material Fallacies of Relevance

- **The Ad Hominem Fallacy** is an argument directed at the person, rather than his or her views.
- **The Tu Quoque Fallacy** is a fallacy committed when one tries to respond to a charge made by an opponent by making the same or similar charge against him.

- **The Ad Populum Fallacy** is an argument in which one bypasses relevant reasons and appeals to popular opinion, sentiment, pity, fear, or emotions to gain acceptance or rejection.
- **The Ad Verecundiam Fallacy** is an attempt to support a conclusion by citing another who asserts the same conclusion. This may or may not be a reliable authority to cite.
- **The Ad Ignorantium Fallacy** is an argument that asserts that because there is no proof that **A** is false, **A** is true, or because there is no proof that **B** is true, **B** is false.
- **The Petitio Principii Fallacy** involves circular arguments. For example: (1) **A** is true, therefore **A** is true, or (2) **A** is true because **B** is true; **B** is true because **C** is true and **C** is true because **A** is true. In both of these examples, the conclusion merely repeats the premise or reason.
- **The Fallacy of Inconsistency** is an argument of contradictory premises. It is a formally valid argument, but one that is faulty because it is necessarily unsound and necessarily an argument where the premises do not provide relevant reasons for affirming the conclusion.
- **Complex Questions** presuppose "facts" or make assumptions that may not be true.
- **Genetic Fallacy** occurs when the manner in which one acquires a view or source of a view is criticized with the purpose of casting doubt on the view itself.
- **The Straw Man Fallacy** is committed when a claim is misinterpreted (deliberately or accidentally) in an attempt to refute the misinterpreted claim. The argument is presented as a refutation of the original claim.

Material Fallacies of Insufficient Evidence

- **False-Cause Fallacy** occurs when in an argument one mistakes what is *not* the cause of a given effect for its real cause.
- **The Fallacy of Special Pleading** involves a failure to mention evidence that is unfavorable to a claim where all evidence is presumably mentioned. The Brady Rule (*Brady v. Maryland*) held that "the suppression by the prosecution of evidence favorable to an accused . . . violates due process where the evidence is material either to guilt or to punishment. . . ."
- **The Fallacies of Ambiguity** present "reasons" that are irrelevant to the truth or falsity of the conclusion.
- **The Fallacy of Equivocation** is the use of a word or words with different meanings than is appropriate in the present context. When a word or expression with two different meanings is used incorrectly and the correctness of the argument depends upon the word

or expression, maintaining the meaning throughout the argument results in a fallacy of equivocation.

- **The Fallacy of Syntactical Ambiguity** occurs where (a) a sentence can have different meanings because of its syntactical structure or (b) because it has a word or expression that can be understood in at least two ways.
- **The Division** and **Composition Fallacies** are similarly related. The *fallacy of division* occurs when one argues that something, which is true only of the whole, is true of its parts taken separately. The *fallacy of composition* occurs when one argues that what is true only of the parts of some whole is also true of the whole.
- **The Fallacy of Accent** occurs when one changes the meaning of a sentence by accenting some word or phrase.

Two Additional Fallacies

- **The Fallacy of Weak Analogy** is a material fallacy of insufficient evidence. In an *argument by analogy,* one argues that because two things are similar in some respects they are similar in other respects.
- **The Fallacy of False Dilemma** occurs when a dilemma is unrealistic because (a) the disjunctive premise is false or (b) one or both of the conditional premises are false.

Back to Basics: Criminal Investigations Skills

- Death investigations should be worked as murder cases until proven otherwise.
- Bank robbery investigations should be conducted like homicide investigations.
- A photo array should be conducted after selecting six to eight similar photos. The original photo array and the signed copies are evidence and should be stored in the property room.

Personality Profiling: The Compass

Dimensional Components of Personality
Types: Four Dimensional Components

1. How people are energized (motivated) (Tieger and Barran-Tieger, 1998, p. 68)
   a. Extroverted: "outer world"

    b. Introverted: "inner world (Tieger and Barran-Tieger, 1998, p. 39)
2. What kind of information people notice and remember (learning type) (Tieger and Barran-Tieger, 1998, p. 73)
    a. Sensing: being in the moment and seeing things realistically
    b. Intuition: seeing possibilities and implications (Tieger and Barran-Tieger, 1998, p. 39)
3. How people make decisions (decision-making) (Tieger and Barran-Tieger, 1998, p. 78)
    a. Feeling: understanding and relating to people
    b. Thinking: making logical, objective decisions (Tieger and Barran-Tieger, 1998, p. 39)
4. How people prefer to organize the world around them (organizational)
    a. Judging: planning
    b. Perceiving: winging it or adapting (Tieger and Barran-Tieger, 1998, p. 39)

Personality Type Combinations

- **ESTJ**: Extroverted, Sensing, Thinking, Judging (12–15%)
- **ISTJ**: Introverted, Sensing, Thinking, Judging (7–10%)
- **ESFJ**: Extroverted, Sensing, Feeling, Judging (11–14%)
- **ISFJ**: Introverted, Sensing, Feeling, Judging (7–10%)
- **ESTP**: Extroverted, Sensing, Thinking, Perceiving (6–8%)
- **ISTP**: Introverted, Sensing, Thinking, Perceiving (4–7%)
- **ESFP**: Extroverted, Sensing, Feeling, Perceiving (8–10%)
- **ISFP**: Introverted, Sensing, Feeling, Perceiving (5–7%)
- **ENTJ**: Extroverted, Intuition, Thinking, Judging (3–5%)
- **INTJ**: Introverted, Intuition, Thinking, Judging (2–3%)
- **ENTP**: Extroverted, Intuition, Thinking, Perceiving (4–6%)
- **INTP**: Introverted, Intuition, Thinking, Perceiving (3–4%)
- **ENFJ**: Extroverted, Intuition, Judging, Feeling (3–5%)
- **INFJ**: Introverted, Intuition, Feeling, Judging (2–3%)
- **ENFP**: Extroverted, Intuition, Feeling, Perceiving (6–7%)
- **INFP**: Introverted, Intuition, Feeling, Perceiving (3–4%) (Tieger and Barran-Tieger, 1998, p. 39)

Compass

The Korem Profiling System breaks profiles into two parts: (1) **talk** refers to how a person prefers to communicate and (2) **walk** refers to how a person performs and makes decisions. Marston's DISC theory also identified four measureable traits: (1) Dominance, (2) Inducement, (3) Submission, and (4) Compliance. The Korem "compass" provides four questions:

Communications Types (Talk)

1. CONTROL–EXPRESS: Does this person CONTROL or EXPRESS his or her emotions when he or she communicates? (Controlled or expressive emotions, e.g., quiet or outgoing)
2. ASK–TELL: Does this person prefer to TELL others what he or she thinks or does he or she prefer to be more indirect and ASK others what they think?

Performance Types (Walk) (How a person makes decisions and performs on the job)

3. CONFIDENT–FEARFUL: Is this person CONFIDENT or FEARFUL when he or she makes decisions? This is the only one of the four gauges with an inherently negative plot point; the others are neither positive nor negative.
4. PREDICTABLE–UNPREDICTABLE: Are this person's actions typically PREDICTABLE (conventional) or UNPREDICTABLE (unconventional)?

Characteristics of the Compass Points

Communications Types

Control–Express

Positive Control

- *Extreme:* control their emotions during a volatile crisis and provide stability to a group
- *Non-Extreme:* usually quiet, take it all in, and full of wisdom

Negative Control

- *Extreme:* cold, suspicious, recluse who refuses to help others for fear of having to express feelings
- *Non-Extreme:* reserved and, at times, indifferent to feelings of others

Positive Express

- *Extreme:* expressive, like a coach firing up the team before a game
- *Non-Extreme:* warm and makes people feel at home

Negative Express

- *Extreme:* short temper and explodes at inappropriate times
- *Non-Extreme:* philanthropic, but occasionally allows emotions to reject wise counsel (Korem, 1997, pp. 39–40)

Ask–Tell

Ask: inquisitive, curious, appears naïve or uninformed, agreeable, non-assertive, altruistic, weak, indirect, laid-back, etc.

Tell: strong, confident, overbearing, assertive, outgoing, unsympathetic, egotistical, directive, and fearful (Korem, 1997, p. 46)

Positive Ask
- *Extreme:* an example is a physician who always asks patients how they feel
- *Non-Extreme:* truth-seeker who asks questions but does not inject his or her own opinion into the story

Negative Ask
- *Extreme:* extremely weak, naïve, and uninformed (the office "brown nose" who obsessively asks about everything to "score points")
- *Non-Extreme:* subordinate who occasionally hesitates before offering an opinion when candor is needed

Positive Tell
- *Extreme:* a leader, for example a military leader
- *Non-Extreme:* an example is a salesperson who delivers a presentation that successfully matches his or her product or service with the client's needs and desires

Negative Tell
- *Extreme:* an example is a cult leader or dictator who tells and directs others with evil intent
- *Non-Extreme:* an example is the CEO who has occasional lapses of sensitivity when giving directions (Korem, 1997, p. 48)

Labels are useful to describe communication types and actions. These include:

- Sergeant: Control–Tell
- Salesman: Express–Tell
- Accountant: Control–Ask
- Artists: Express–Ask (Korem, 1997, pp. 63–64)

Labels are also useful to describe performance types and actions. These include:

- Manager: Confident–Predictable

- Innovator: Confident–Unpredictable
- Conformist: Fearful–Predictable
- Random Actor: Fearful–Unpredictable (Korem, 1997, pp. 111–112)

Performance Types
Confident–Fearful
Positive Confident
- *Extreme:* hard-charging, for example, a coach
- *Non-extreme:* a leader who demonstrates quiet confidence

Negative Confident
- *Extreme:* arrogance, for example, a tycoon
- *Non-extreme:* a "cocky" athlete (Korem, 1997, p. 96)

Positive Fearful
- *Extreme:* none (no positive attributes are associated with extreme "fearful")
- *Non-extreme:* operating with caution when caution is due because of the nature of the activity, for example, the operator of a fail-safe system for a nuclear warhead or a barge operator who navigates channels cautiously

Negative Fearful
- *Extreme:* unjustified paranoia, for example, a manager who is unjustifiably paranoid of those around him or her
- *Non-extreme:* avoiding confrontation when it is necessary (Korem, 1997, p. 96)

Predictable–Unpredictable   *Predictable* (Conventional) refers to persons who are usually characterized by regularity and conformity in their actions. They are described as consistent, conventional, dependable, formal, industrious, logical, orderly, organized, persistent, precise, punctual, rigid, reliable, self-disciplined, staid, or stuffy. (They may not be described by all of these adjectives.)

Unpredictable (Unconventional) refers to persons whose are infrequent, random, surprising, or unconventional and range from unconventionally creative to rebellious and reckless. They are described as unconventional, aimless, frivolous, forgetful, freewheeling, inconsistent, intemperate, irreverent, negligent, nonconforming, rebellious, reckless, and spontaneous. (They may not be described by all of these adjectives.)

Positive Predictable
- *Extreme:* a staunch defender
- *Non-extreme:* dependable support personnel

Negative Predictable
- *Extreme:* resists even admitted positive change
- *Non-extreme:* sometimes stuffy or staid (Korem, 1997, pp. 97, 101)

Positive Unpredictable
- *Extreme:* unconventional inventor
- *Non-extreme:* adapts well to changing trends and forecasts

Negative Unpredictable
- *Extreme:* reckless leaders and cult figures
- *Non-extreme:* absentminded or mind constantly wanders (Korem, 1997, pp. 97, 101)

Conformist Type A *predictable* trait may sometimes override a *fearful* trait, causing decision-making to be more predictable. This is referred to as a Conformist type (Korem, 1997, p. 103).

Personality Profiling: The Map

How to Communicate with Each Personality Type

Once you have determined a person's personality, using the four dimensional components, here are a few tips on how to communicate with each type:

- **Extraverts**: Communicate verbally, allowing them talk and think aloud. Include a variety of topics, but keep the conversation moving. Expect immediate action (Tieger and Barran-Tieger, 1998, p. 143).
- **Introverts**: Communicate in writing, when possible, or ask them to listen carefully when talking to them. Talk about one thing at a time and give them enough time to reflect. Do not finish their sentences for them (Tieger and Barran-Tieger, 1998, p. 143).
- **Sensors**: State the topic clearly. Be prepared with facts and examples and present information in a step-by-step fashion. Draw upon past, real experiences, emphasizing practical applications. Finish your own sentences (Tieger and Barran-Tieger, 1998, p. 143).
- **Intuitives**: Talk about the "big picture" and its implications, as well as about "possibilities." Brainstorm options and use analogies and meta-

phors, while engaging their imaginations. However, do not overwhelm them with details (Tieger and Barran-Tieger, 1998, p. 143).

Thinkers: Be organized and logical, taking into consideration cause and effect and focusing on the consequences. Appeal to their sense of fairness. Do not ask them how they "feel," but rather what they "think." Do not repeat yourself (Tieger and Barran-Tieger, 1998, p. 143).

Feelers: Mention first the points of agreement that you share and show appreciation for their efforts and contributions. Recognize the legitimacy of "feelings" and talk about "people" concerns. Be friendly and considerate, smiling and maintaining good eye contact (Tieger and Barran-Tieger, 1998, p. 143).

Judgers: Be on time, prepared, organized, and efficient. Do not waste their time. Come to conclusions and do not leave issues unresolved. Be decisive and definitive, while still allowing them to make decisions. Stick with plans that have been made (Tieger and Barran-Tieger, 1998, p. 143).

Perceivers: Expect several questions. Give them choices and do not force them to decide prematurely. Provide them with opportunities to discuss options and change plans. Focus on the process, not the product. Be open to new information (Tieger and Barran-Tieger, 1998, p. 143).

Map

There are 16 different profiles, each having strengths, weaknesses, and interaction suggestions. The comprehensive profile provides a "map" that shows how a person's communication type interacts with his or her performance type. Some performance types may share the same or similar actions because *types* that share a common *trait* may share some similar *tendencies* (Korem, 1997, p. 113, 149).

Traits by Associated Types

Manager–Confident/Predictable: described as an organizer or decision-maker who prefers to make decisions in methodical and standardized ways; most comfortable in steady, calm, and predictable environments (Korem, 1997, p. 108).

Innovator–Confident/Unpredictable: described as an idea-generator who will "try anything once," is motivated by change and variety, and is sufficiently self-confident to challenge situations and take risks (Korem, 1997, pp. 108–109).

Conformists–Fearful/Predictable: typically compliant, dutiful, reliable, and obedient, that is, a supporter or sustainer. Insecurity and fear, when making decisions, causes them to have an aversion to taking risks. They are often nervous and uninteresting (Korem, 1997, pp. 108–109).

Random Actor–Fearful/Unpredictable: described as typically deceptive, manipulative, scheming, and volatile, they act out of a strong perception of a need for self-defense and self-protection. They are often loyal to anyone who is able to control their fate or allay their fears, but are described as manipulators or public menaces. This is the least common, but potentially the most dangerous and volatile of the performance types. Some of those who are plotted high (5 points) on the gauge for this type may be psychotic (Korem, 1997, pp. 107–110).

Sixteen Combinations

You cannot tell what someone is thinking because in reality he or she is not thinking. Humans are forced into conclusions about how and what they see. What often passes for thought is actually a response based on *emotionally* preprogrammed choices. From the three primary colors—red, blue, and yellow—you can create millions of distinct and discernible colors. Similarly, when you understand the primary colors of the mind, all you need to know is how much of each "color" is present to tell the "shade" of the person's thoughts (Lieberman, 2007, pp. 114, 118–119). The "sixteen combinations" identified by the Korem system include the following:

Sergeant Types
- *Sergeant/Manager*—Control/Tell/Predictable/Confident
- *Sergeant/Innovator*—Control/Tell/Unpredictable/Confident
- *Sergeant/Conformist*—Control/Tell/Predictable/Fearful
- *Sergeant/Random Actor*—Control/Tell/Unpredictable/Fearful

Salesmen Types
- *Salesman/Manager*—Express/Tell/Predictable/Confident
- *Salesman/Innovator*—Express/Tell/Unpredictable/Confident
- *Salesman/Conformist*—Express/Tell/Predictable/Fearful
- *Salesman/Random Actor*—Express/Tell/Unpredictable/Fearful

Accountant Types
- *Accountant/Manager*—Control/Ask/Predictable/Confident
- *Accountant/Innovator*—Control/Ask/Unpredictable/Confident
- *Accountant/Conformist*—Control/Ask/Predictable/Fearful
- *Accountant/Random Actor*—Control/Ask/Unpredictable/Fearful

Artists Types

- *Artist/Manager*—Express/Ask/Predictable/Confident
- *Artist/Innovator*—Express/Ask/Unpredictable/Confident
- *Artist/Conformist*—Express/Ask/Predictable/Fearful
- *Artist/Random Actor*—Express/Ask/Unpredictable/Fearful

Combination Types

A person is a *combination type* when one of his or her plot points is near the middle of the gauge. He or she shares actions from both sides of the gauge (Korem, 1997, p. 65).

Profiling the Criminal Mind: Criminal Investigative Analysis

Where the perpetrator is a stranger and no victim–perpetrator relationship exists, investigators must assemble a list of suspects through a process known as "framing" or establishing the "circle of the investigation." The inability to recognize such connections has been described as "linkage blindness." When a bizarre crime has been discovered, rather than asking, "What kind of person would commit such an act?" we should ask, "What makes someone do something like this?"

Crime Classification

Questions asked when classifying crimes include:

1. Was the victim known to the offender?
2. What were the victim's chances of becoming a target for violent crime?
3. What risk did the offender take in perpetrating this crime? (Douglas et al., 1992, p. 7)

Crime Scene Analysis—Four Steps

1. The detection of staging and personation at the crime scene.
2. The *modus operandi* (method of operation) and signature aspects of violent crime.
3. Crime scene photography (documentation and evaluation of the scene).
4. Prescriptive interviewing—interfacing the interview/interrogation with crime classification witness typologies.

Crime Scene Indicators

1. How many crime scenes are involved? (Douglas et al., 1992, p. 8)
2. Environment/place/time—refers to the conditions or circumstances in which the offense occurred.
3. How many perpetrators were involved? This helps determine whether the offense should be categorized as (a) criminal enterprise or (b) group cause (Douglas et al., 1992, p. 9).
4. Organized or disorganized/physical evidence
5. Weapons
6. Body disposition
7. Missing or left items
8. Other crime scene indicators
9. Forensic evidence

Crime Classification Worksheet

Organized Nonsocial Typology and the Disorganized Asocial Typology

The organized nonsocial (psychopathic) typology is usually organized in his or her lifestyle, home or apartment, car or truck, personal appearance, etc. The disorganized asocial (psychotic) typology is disorganized in his or her daily activities, including home or apartment, employment (if employed at all), car or truck, clothing, demeanor, etc.

Assessment, Staging, and Personation

There are three manifestations of perpetrator behavior at crime scenes: (1) *modus operandi* (M.O.), (2) personation (the perpetrator signature), and (3) staging. Assessment phase:

1. What is the sequence of events?
2. Was the victim sexually assaulted before or after death?
3. Was there mutilation before death?
4. How did the encounter between the perpetrator and the victim occur?
5. Did the offender "blitz attack" the victim or use verbal means to "con and capture" the victim?
6. Did the offender use restraints or ligatures to control the victim?
7. Were any items or artifacts left (added to) or taken from the crime scene (which require careful analysis)? (Douglas et al., 1992, p. 250)

Modus Operandi and Victimology
M.O. is the "method of operation" of a perpetrator. Victimology involves the characteristics of the victims and is an element in determining the M.O. of the perpetrator and in linking cases together.

Personation (Signature)
Unusual behavior by an offender that is not necessary to commit the crime is called "personation." When a perpetrator demonstrates repetitive ritualistic behavior from one crime to the next, it is called a "signature," which is repetitive personation. "Undoing" is personation that occurs when there is a close association between the perpetrator and the victim.

Staging
Staging is when someone intentionally alters the crime scene with the purpose of redirecting investigation away from the most *logical* suspect or to "protect" the victim or the victim's family. Investigators should ask themselves:

- Do these injuries fit the scene?
- Did the perpetrator take inappropriate items from the scene to make burglary appear to be the motive?
- Did the point of entry appear logical?
- Did commission of this crime pose a high risk to the perpetrator?
- What looks out of place for the apparent crime or motive? (Douglas et al., 1992, pp. 251, 253)

Interviewing and Interrogation

Interrogation of Suspects

Interview (witnesses) and interrogation (suspects) steps:

1. Preparation and strategy—know the case and know the legal restraints.
2. Interviewing—begin with non-accusatory fact-finding.
3. Establish credibility.
4. Reduce resistance—stops denials.
5. Obtaining an admission—once denials have been stopped, the suspect may be ready to be submissive to answering choice questions (e.g., "Did you use the money for drugs or food?" or "Did you intend to hurt them or was it an accident?").
6. Developing an admission—an admission is not a confession, but an admission to certain facts; admissions alone are helpful, but they may also lead to a confession.

7. Professional close—close with any appropriate written statements and summation.

Interrogation of Criminal Suspects

1. Interview the victim, accuser, or discoverer of the crime before interrogating the suspect.
2. Be patient; do not be in a hurry. (Take five more minutes.)
3. Never make promises.
4. When a suspect has made repeated denials to other interrogators, try asking the suspect about some other, unrelated offense of a similar nature (which he or she is also suspected of).
5. Unintelligent, uneducated suspects should be questioned at the same psychological level employed to question a child about wrongdoing.

Interrogation of Suspects Whose Guilt Is Reasonably Certain

1. Display an air of confidence in the subject's guilt.
2. Point out some, but not all, of the circumstantial evidence.
3. Draw attention to the subject's physiological and psychological symptoms of guilt.
4. Sympathize with the subject by telling him or her that anyone else under similar circumstances might have done the same thing.
5. Minimize the seriousness and moral implications of the offense.
6. Suggest a less stigmatizing and more morally acceptable motivation or reason for the offense than the one that is known or presumed.
7. Sympathize with the subject by (a) blaming the victim, (b) blaming an accomplice, or (c) blaming anyone or anything else with a plausible causal connection.
8. Demonstrate sympathy and understanding when urging the subject to tell the truth ("good cop–bad cop"). Never use promises or threats when employing this method.
9. Suggest that (while there is obviously some basis for the accusation) there is the possibility that the accuser exaggerated the nature and seriousness of the offense.
10. Have the subject place himself at the scene or in contact with the victim (an admission).
11. Try to obtain an admission that the subject lied about some incidental aspect of the incident. (It will be easy to remind him or her later that he or she has not been telling the truth.)
12. Exploit the subject's sense of pride using flattery or a challenge to his or her honor.

13. Point out the futility of not telling the truth (that his or her guilt has been detected and can be established by evidence).
14. Point out the seriousness and futility of continuing criminal behavior. Encourage this by encouraging them to clear everything up all at once.
15. Before asking for a general admission of guilt, ask a question about some detail of the crime or about the reason for committing the offense.
16. When co-perpetrators are being interrogated (and all else fails), play one against the other. They often fear that one will "talk," giving them some advantage. Make suspects aware that their cooperation will be noted to the prosecutor, but make no promises.

Interrogation of Suspects Whose Guilt Is Uncertain

1. Ask the suspect if he or she knows why he or she is being questioned. (If the suspect says that he or she does not know, when circumstances it make obvious, the suspect is obviously lying.)
2. Ask the suspect to relate everything he or she knows about the incident, victim, or possible suspects. (Start out by asking a few general questions about the suspect's knowledge of the incident, victim, possible suspects, etc.)
3. Obtain details about the suspect's activities before, during, and after the incident. (If the suspect's memory of details before and after an incident is good, it should be good for events during the incident.)
4. Where certain facts suggest the subject's guilt, ask about him or her as if the facts are not already known (affording an opportunity to lie).
5. Periodically ask relevant questions in a manner that implies that the correct answers are already known (creating an impression that the answer is known and that the interrogator is only interested in determining whether the suspect is willing to tell the truth).
6. Refer to some non-existing evidence to see if the suspect will attempt to explain it away. (If he or she does, this suggests that he or she is guilty; e.g., "Is there any reason why . . .".)
7. Ask the suspect if he or she ever "thought" about committing the crime or one similar to it (a guilty person may offer an explanation for why he or she "looks" guilty when answering).
8. Ask the suspect if he or she would offer to make restitution. (If he or she does, this suggests that he or she is guilty; most innocent persons would not agree to pay any part. Sometimes a perpetrator will offer to pay restitution for an actual amount, but not a fictional loss.)
9. Ask if the suspect is willing to take a polygraph (lie detector) or similar test. (Most innocent people will agree to prove their innocence,

while most guilty people will refuse or agree, then back out or make excuses not to.) This is not always the case, as many people are afraid of "lie detectors" or opine that they are "not reliable."

10. Suspects who tell investigators or interrogators, "OK, I will tell you what you want to hear, but I didn't do it," is likely guilty. (However, watch for false confessions and corroborate them. An innocent person usually persists in denying guilt, while a guilty suspect may try to placate an interrogator by offering to admit to committing the offense.) This often comes out something like, "I didn't do it; but if you want me to say I did, I'll say it." Do not accept this as a confession. Continue the interview.

Written Confessions

1. Warnings of Constitutional rights (*Miranda* and similar warnings) and videotaping.
2. Written confessions, even though recorded, may be taken following specific questions by the interrogator and narrative answers by the perpetrator. It should be signed and dated.
3. Handwritten confessions are also good, but only if they are legible (readable) and can be understood. For example, what does "it," "that night," "the place," etc. mean?
4. When ensuring that the perpetrator is specific, avoid leading questions. Avoid having the interrogator do most of the talking or using "yes" and "no" questions. Instead ask, "What happened next?" or "What did you do with the gun" or "What happened to the money?"
5. Let the perpetrator tell the story his or her way, using his or her own words or expressions.
6. Often the perpetrator will claim that he or she just said what he or she was told to say. Intersperse a few questions throughout the interview which can only be answered by the perpetrator, for example, ask the perpetrator where he or she went to school or where he or she has lived.
7. Placing intentional errors in the typed confession allows the perpetrator to initial or sign next to corrections. This demonstrates that he or she read it and approved the corrections.
8. Reading and signing the confession.
   - Have the perpetrator write "OK" and his or her initials at the bottom of each page to verify that he or she approves the statement.
   - The statement should be signed and witnessed. Do not say "sign here." Tell him/her that if he/she agree that the statement is accurate, he/she should "Put your name here."

- It should include either a handwritten or typed authentication statement similar to this: "I have read this statement and it is true. I gave this statement of my own free will, without any threats or promises being made to me by anyone."

9. A perpetrator may be reluctant to sign the statement in front of others. The interrogator should sign that he or she witnessed the statement. Another witness (another investigator or supervisor) can ask the perpetrator to authenticate his or her signature. A sworn statement can also be taken if the perpetrator will take an oath before a notary.

10. Only one written confession—full and complete statement the first time, if possible.

11. One confession per crime. Unless the crimes are related, the confession statement should cover one crime or related crimes. Do not refer in the statement to the fact that the perpetrator has been arrested for other crimes. If the perpetrator confesses to several unrelated crimes, it is best to take a separate statement for each confession.

12. If a weapon or some other physical evidence is recovered or the perpetrator is questioned about a photograph or sketch, it may be best to take a separate statement about that evidence, that is, that it is accurate, how it was used, etc.

More Suggestion for Confessions

1. Stenographic notes should be preserved until final disposition of the case.

2. The interrogator should not rely upon memory about the circumstances and conditions under which the confession was obtained. Note the date and time of *Miranda* warnings, the time the interrogation started and ended, and anyone who was present at the interrogation. Note if the perpetrator was given bathroom breaks, food, or drinks.

3. The video statement, as well as booking photos, should demonstrate that the police did not use force to obtain a confession. If the perpetrator required any medical attention at the time of arrest or apprehension, this should also be documented.

4. The confession is not the end of the investigation. Do not fall into the trap of thinking that once you have a confession that the investigation is over. Follow up and verify the information obtained in the interrogation and confession.

5. Once the perpetrator has confessed, the interrogation is not over. Often the confessor is ready to give more details that will be useful in the follow-up investigation. Take your time. When it feels like the interview is over, go another five minutes or more.

Nine Steps of an Interrogation

1. **Direct Positive Confrontation**—presentation of facts synopsis to the subject (the file or dossier method, but beware of bluffing).
2. **Theme Development**—propose reasons that will justify or excuse the act or incident after assessing the suspect's behavior. (Not "if," but "why" explanations.)
3. **Stop Denials**—recognize and stop denials before they are completed.
4. **Overcome Objections**—overcome the suspect's defenses to prove his or her innocence (e.g., moral or religious objections, discrediting the facts ["I couldn't have done it because ... "], emotional, etc.) Do not refute objections; this only leads to arguments.
5. **Get the Suspect's Attention**—the themes will only work if the suspect is listening. Gestures and "moving in" may help the tense and confused suspect.
6. **The Suspect Quiets and Listens**—once you have the suspect's attention and he or she is quiet and listening, establish eye contact and shorten themes to lead toward alternatives.
7. **Alternatives**—suggest some non-threatening "alternative" that provides a choice between an acceptable reason and an unacceptable reason for committing the crime. Allow the suspect to choose the more positive alternative.
8. **Bring the Suspect into the Conversation**—reinforce the "alternative" and encourage the suspect to talk about aspects of the incident, using realistic words introduced by the interrogator, to obtain corroborating information known only to the suspect.
9. **The Confession**—reduce oral (recorded) statements to a written or typed form, establishing the voluntariness of the statement along with the corroboration of details.

Formulating Questions

1. Keep it short.
2. Keep it simple.
3. Keep questions singular in meaning.
4. Keep it straightforward.
5. Use prologues for key questions.
6. Broaden your focus.
7. Always ask, "What else?"
8. Overcome psychological alibis.
9. Avoid asking negative questions.

Kinesic Interviewing and Body Language

Ten Commandments for Observing and Decoding Nonverbal Communications

1. Be a competent observer of your environment.
2. Observing the "context" is the key to understanding nonverbal behavior.
3. Learn to recognize and decode universal behaviors.
4. Learn to recognize and decode idiosyncratic nonverbal behavior.
5. When you interact with others, try to establish their baseline behaviors.
6. Watch for multiple "tells"—behaviors that occur in clusters or in succession.
7. Look for changes in a person's behavior that can signal changes in thoughts, emotions, interest, or intent.
8. Learn to detect false or misleading nonverbal signals.
9. Know how to distinguish between "comfort" and "discomfort" to help focus on the most important behaviors for decoding nonverbal communications.
10. Be subtle when observing others.

Kinesic Interview and Interrogation

1. No single behavior, alone, proves anything.
2. Behaviors must be relatively consistent when the stimuli are repeated.
3. The interviewer must determine what is "normal" or "baseline" behavior for each subject and then identify changes in that "norm" or "baseline.
4. Changes in "baseline" behavior are diagnosed in "clusters," not individually.
5. Behaviors must be timely. (Do they occur when the fear-provoking questions are asked?)
6. Observing and interpreting behaviors is hard work. (It takes a great deal of concentration and mental discipline. It requires watching, listening, and diagnosing kinesic behaviors.)
7. The suspects are watching us while we are watching them. Suspects will detect when an interrogator or investigator is unprepared, distracted, bluffing, or fishing.
8. Kinesic interviewing is not as reliable with some groups as it is with the general population. (Children, mentally deficient, psychotics, and persons under the influence of drugs or alcohol may not respond as most people do.)

Eight Common Lying Gestures

1. The mouth cover
2. The nose touch
3. The itchy nose
4. The eye rub
5. The ear rub
6. The neck scratch
7. The collar pull
8. Fingers in the mouth (Pease and Pease, 2006, pp. 148–154)

Evaluation, Boredom, Impatience, and Procrastination Gestures

Evaluation is indicated by a closed hand resting on the chin or cheek, often with the index finger pointing upward. Boredom may be indicated when the listener uses his or her hand to support the head, beginning with a thumb, progressing to the fist, and finally to the entire hand. Drumming the fingers and tapping the feet are not indicators of boredom, but of impatience.

Listen and Look for Deception

The trick is to train our brains to (1) *look* and *listen* simultaneously (the "L-squared mode") to process what is being communicated in both *visual* and *auditory* channels and (2) to identify "*clusters* of deceptive behavior" (combinations of indicators).

What Deception Sounds Like

- Failure to answer
- Denial problems
- Reluctance or refusal to answer
- Repeating the question
- Non-answer statements
- Inconsistent statements
- Going into the attack mode
- Inappropriate questions
- Overly specific answers
- Inappropriate level of politeness
- Inappropriate level of concern
- Process or procedural complaints
- Failure to understand a simple question
- Referral statements
- Invoking religion

- Selective memory
- Qualifiers
- Convincing statements

What Deception Looks Like

- Behavior pause or delay
- Hiding the mouth or eyes
- Throat-clearing or swallowing
- Hand-to-face activity
- Anchor-point movement
- Grooming gestures

Reanimation and Acceptance

Memory reanimation involves subconscious gestures that illustrate memories. A subject's hands may be used to describe something, such as the crime, a crime scene, an alibi, a location, etc. Acceptance gestures are also significant, indicating an admission or confession may be following.

Behavioral Cautions

Use caution when relying on "common sense" behavioral signs. These "clues" may be caused by something other than anxiety resulting from deception.

- Eye contact
- Closed posture (crossed arms, legs, etc.)
- General nervousness or tension
- Preemptive responses
- Blushing or twitching
- Clenched hands
- Base-lining (control questions or behavioral signs used for comparison)

Neurolinguistic Eye Movement: The Three Sensory Channels

The use of neurolinguistic eye movement or the "three sensory channels" (sight, sound, and sensation) to detect deception during an interview is effective. The eyes indicate whether one recalls or creates information from the visual, auditory, or kinesic channels.

Recall: Left

- When we **recall** something visually that we have actually **seen**, the eyes go *left* and *up*.

- When we **recall** something audible that we have actually **heard**, the eyes go *left* and *straight across*.
- When we **recall** something Kenesically that we have actually **touched** (feel), the eyes go *left* and *down* (internal dialogues, getting in touch with one's feelings).

Create (Fabricate): Right (Right Is Wrong)

- When we **create** something visually that we have NOT **seen**, the eyes go *right* and *up*.
- When we **create** something audible that we have NOT **heard**, the eyes go *right* and *straight across*.
- When we **create** something kenesically that we have NOT **touched** (feel), the eyes go *right* and *down*.

Deception Detection: Content and Discourse Analysis

Deception Detection: Polygraph and Voice Stress Analysis

Results are classified as (1) deception, (2) no deception, (3) inconclusive, or (4) no opinion.

Scientific Content Analysis (SCAN), Investigative Discourse Analysis (IDA), and Linguistic Statement Analysis (LSAT)

Speech pattern analysis helps distinguish between statements originating in the memory and those originating in the imagination. Content analysis looks for deception in changes or concealment of details. The deceptive person works from imagination, rather than memory.

All are based upon the scientific analysis of the content of discourse in linguistic statements.

Parts of Speech and Word Classes

There are eight main parts of speech:

1. **Nouns**—persons, places, things, actions, quality, etc.
2. **Verbs**—words expressing action, existence, or occurrences, denoting what is done in a sentence. Verb tense denotes when something is done (past, present, or future).
3. **Pronouns**—show relationship or signal words that assume the functions of nouns within clauses.

4. **Adjectives**—limit or qualify a noun: (a) how many, (b) what kind, (c) nouns and pronouns can function as adjectives (e.g., color, position, action taken, description, possessive, demonstrative, etc.).
5. **Adverbs**—modify a verb, adjective, another adverb, a phrase or a clause, and expresses time, place, manner, degree, cause, etc.
6. **Conjunctions**—connect words, phrases, clauses, or sentences.
7. **Prepositions**—relation or function words that connect a lexical word (usually a noun or pronoun) or a syntactic construction to another element of the sentence (a verb, noun, or adjective), for example, at, by, in, for, from, off, on, above, below, over, under, around, before, behind, between, through, until, etc.
8. **Interjection**—an exclamation used to show emotion or sentiment.

Speech Pattern and Discourse Content Analysis: Word Choices

1. **Pronouns**—take note of where the "I" is present in the narrative and where it disappears from the narrative, particularly noting where this change occurs. The absence of the pronoun "I" may indicate the subject's loss of commitment to his or her own narrative.
2. **Introjection**—aspects of the external world incorporated within the self. Uses of the possessive pronoun "my" are examples of psychological introjection, referring to the speaker or self, and indicating possession or possessiveness.
3. **Marker Words**—label or modify the word being marked, for example, "the," "a," "this," etc. Note the use of the pronoun "me" (the objective case of "I"). The frequent use of "me" may indicate that the subject perceives himself or herself (or hopes to) as the "passive object of external actions or events" over which he or she has no control, but by which he or she has acted upon.
4. **Abjuration Terms**—serve to withdraw the assertion made in a previous clause of the sentence and are usually conjunctions, for example, "but."
5. **Repression**—psychological repression is the mental process in which "anxiety-producing mental content is forcefully removed from the consciousness and prevented from reemerging," for example, the clause [I] "have no recollection of. . . ." Indicators of repression should always draw the attention of investigators.
6. **Temporal Lacuna**—a blank space or missing elements within the discourse, that is, something skipped over or left out of a narrative, for example, "when," "later on," "after that," or "by and by."
7. **Modifying or Equivocating Terms**—allow the speaker to "evade the risk of commitment" by undermining his or her own assertions or indicating difficulty with committing to what is being said.

Examples include "a little," "I believe," "I think," "I guess," "kind of," "sort of," "hopefully," "the best I/we can," etc. (*Note*: Always take note of the use of "we," which is indicative of a collective reference to the speaker/writer and at least one other person.)

8. **Explanatory Terms**—used to (a) give a reason or cause and (b) allow for an explanation of a cause and effect or justification or rationale. Examples include "since," "because," etc.

9. **Denial or Negation Terms**—a defense mechanism that disavows or denies thoughts, feelings, wishes, or needs that cause anxiety, for example, "I didn't even know," which relates to what happened or how something occurred but they relate what did *not* happen, what is *not* involved, or what he or she did *not* know, do, or observe, etc.

10. **Stalling Mechanisms**—pauses, which allow the speaker to hold back. This is a change that can be illustrated by a variety of linguistic factors, such as pauses in or between sentences, the abrupt onset of stuttering or stammering, and the use of terms, such as "let's see," "okay now," "well," "oh well," "um," "ah," "uh," etc.

11. **Second-Person Referencing**—the speaker/writer refers to himself or herself with the "second-person" pronoun "you," diverting attention from himself or herself. The speaker/writer is signaling that he or she feels no personal accountability or responsibility for whatever happened; for example, "**You** know, when **you** talk about it. . . ."

12. **Weakened Assertion**—the speaker/writer seems to feel the need for additional (but what should be unnecessary) support for what he or she said, for example, "to tell the truth. . . ." They may also be used to allude to actions that were never actually carried out, for example, "We were going to play cards," "I needed to get my glasses," "I tried to . . . ," "I started to get . . . ," "I most assuredly . . . ," "As a matter of fact, I have never made this kind of mistake before . . . ," etc. "Try" or "tried" reflect an expectation of failure. "Start to" and "started" are not the same as actually "doing" something.

Analysis of statements is conducted along two axes: (1) the structure (form) of the narrative and (2) the semantics (meaning) of the words used in the narrative. The structure or form of the narrative is indicative of truth or deceit. Semantic (meaning) analysis may be indicative of specific points where deception or inaccuracy occurs and where the subject needs to amplify or expand upon details.

Narrative Statement Structure (Form) Analysis

1. Identify the formal organization of the narrative in terms of balance or proportion.
2. Identify any nonconforming statements.
3. Identify any non-sequential statements, which are statements that are out of place or chronological order.

Narrative Statement Semantic (Meaning) Analysis

1. What the subject *actually* says or writes.
2. What the subject *intended* to say or write.
3. The *interpretation* of what the subject says or writes.

Semantic Indicators

1. Lack of conviction about one's own assertions.
2. Use of present tense when describing a past occurrence.
3. Use of generalized statements.
4. Reduced or eliminated self-reference.
5. Reduced "mean length of utterance" (MLU) in relation to a particular unit of narration.

Amplification of the Narrative

Once semantic analysis has been completed, the results can be examined in detail by trying to get the individual making the statement to amplify narrative details. Refer the subject to parts of the narrative and details that need to be amplified. Guide the subject toward areas that need amplified, emphasizing certain words and using open-ended questions.

Analytical Investigative Methods: Processing Data

Analytical Investigative Methods (AIM) or Visual Investigative Analysis (VIA) help others to "see" complex ideas and information and visually portray information to understand complex financial, conspiracy, serial crimes, major crime cases, etc.

Intelligence Cycle

- Planning and direction
- Collection

- Processing
- Analysis and production
- Dissemination and feedback

Accounting Cycle

- Journalizing
- Posting
- Preparing a trial balance
- Constructing a work sheet
- Preparing the statements
- Adjusting the ledger accounts
- Closing the temporary proprietorship accounts
- Preparing a post-closing trial balance

Communicating Skills: Critical Documentation

Investigative Report Writing: "The Job's Not Finished 'til the Paperwork's Done"

A single comma was the deciding factor in one case because the rules of language matter when deciding the meaning of language. In *United States v. Ron Pair Enterprises*, 489 U.S. 235 (1989), known as "the comma case," the court made its decision about the meaning of a document based upon a single comma. Well-written reports may win cases and poorly written reports often lose cases. Remember: "The job's not finished until the paperwork's done."

Don't Just Record, Investigate

Field Notes and Reports
Make a shopping list; list the facts into logical groups (e.g., victim's statement, witnesses' statements, etc.). Place these groups in order, arranging them in chronological order, if possible.

The Narrative
Use short sentences; longer sentences are harder to understand. Use one main thought per sentence. The narrative should be in chronological sequence (in the order that the events occurred). Don't overuse or misuse "stated," "related," or "indicated" (when you mean "said"), "the area...," "submitted for your information," "pursuant to orders...," "please be advised that...," "the questions as to whether...."

Titles Describing People

- Complainant (or Complaining Party)
- Victim
- Witness
- Perpetrator
- Suspect
- Other Subject

Descriptions of Vehicles (CYMBL)

- Color (if two-tone, top over bottom colors, e.g., white over red)
- Year (year of manufacture)
- Make (manufacturer, e.g., Ford, Chevrolet, Pontiac, Chrysler, etc.)
- Body (4-door, 2-door, hatchback, pickup, van, etc.)
- License (year of issue, state of issue, tag number, type, etc.)

Solvability Factors—issues that reflect upon the probability of solving the crime and determine how much and whether there will be follow-up investigation.

Automated Report Templates, Supplemental Reports, and the Narrative Summary

Templates are "fill-in" spaces of reoccurring fields. Supplements are reports written to add to or amend information from the original report. A summary supplement is a summary of all reports written and the chronological events of the entire investigation.

Elements of a Good Report—Helping Others Know What You Know

- Clear, Complete (Who, What, When, Where, Why, and How), Concise
- Organization: Chronological Order
- Use the *A, B, C, D, E, F* system of organizing a report. Here are the elements:
  - **A**CTIONS by officers
  - **B**EHAVIOR of witnesses, suspects, and victims
  - **C**OMMUNICATION—dialog, questions, and answers
  - **D**ESCRIPTION of the scene, suspects and vehicles
  - **E**VIDENCE (physical)
  - **F**INAL disposition or resolution

A Word on Word Usage

Choose your words with care. Arrange your words with care. Homophones are words that are similar in sound but different in spelling and meaning. Misplaced phrases occur when word placement is not correct and changes the meaning of the sentence. For example:

- "While patrolling, I parked my squad car behind the police station, which ran out of gas." (The police station ran out of gas?)
- "At the scene of the arson I observed behind the building, a suspect, which was burning." (The suspect was burning or the building was burning?)
- "Responding officer was sent to the robbery along with Officer Jones. When this officer arrived responding officer identified himself." (Who arrived and who identified whom? Avoid third person narratives!)

Use the Active Voice, Rather than the Passive Voice

The active voice is a clearer and precise way of showing "who" is doing an action versus the passive voice, which shows "who" is having something done to them. For example:

> Passive: The perpetrator was arrested by the detective.
> Active: The detective arrested the perpetrator.

Use First Person: Use of "I" and "Me"

In first-person writing, an officer documents his or her actions by using the words "I" and "me." This is the most appropriate and least confusing form of simple communication. In third-person writing, the use of "this officer," "this unit," or "this reporter" can be confusing and does not sound professional.

Use of Who and Whom

Who is often the subject of a sentence (replace the word *who* with the word *he, she,* or *they* to check if you have used the word *who* correctly). *Whom* is often the object of a sentence (replace the word *whom* with the word *him, her,* or *them* to check if you have used the word *whom* correctly).

Focus on the Actor, the Action, and the Object

"**Who** {Actor} is doing **what** {Action} to **whom** or **which** (Object) in this sentence?"

Run-On Sentences
Run-on sentences lack punctuation and coordinating conjunctions (and, but, or, nor, for, yet, so, etc.), which indicate a break or pause in thought.

Incomplete Sentences or Sentence Fragments
An incomplete sentence may involve a long group of words introduced by a subordinating word (e.g., when, although, since, or because) without completing the thought. Subordinating words such as "when" introduce a dependent clause, which must be completed to produce a complete thought.

Put Modifying Words Close to What They Modify
Modifiers are words like "often" or "only." You can usually avoid ambiguity (vagueness and confusion) by placing the relative pronoun (e.g., who, which, that) right after the word it modifies. For example:

- Bad: Vehicles are inspected for the public only by a police officer.
- Better: Only police officers inspect vehicles for the public.
- Bad: Buy money, which must not exceed $100 a month, must be reported within 24 hours.
- Better: Buy money must not exceed $100 a month and must be reported within 24 hours.

Avoid Nested Modifiers
Sentences are hard to understand when the reader must mentally supply brackets and parentheses to keep modifiers straight. The best remedy for this is to take the "nest of modifiers" apart and incorporate some of the information in a separate sentence. For example:

- Bad: The defendant, who was driving the white Ford van that was concealing the illegal drugs some of which was marijuana and some of which was cocaine, stopped in front of the house.
- Analysis: The defendant {who was driving the white Ford van [that was concealing the illegal drugs (some of which was marijuana and some of which was cocaine)]} stopped in front of the house.
- Better: The defendant was driving the white Ford van that was concealing the illegal drugs. Some of the contraband was marijuana and some of it was cocaine. The van stopped in front of the house.

Clarify the Reach of Modifiers
For example, "All male German Shepherds and Australian Shepherds over two years old." This is ambiguous because it is not certain if it means

- all "*male* German Shepherds *over two years old*" and all "*male* Australian Shepherds *over two years old*" (all male AND all over two years old; BOTH) OR
- all "*male* German Shepherds (of any age)" and all "Australian Shepherds *over two years old*" (of any gender) OR
- all "*male* German Shepherds" (of any age) and all "*male* Australian Shepherds *over two years old*" OR
- all "*male* German Shepherds *over two years old*" and all "Australian Shepherds *over two years old*" (of any gender).

To avoid ambiguity (vagueness and confusion), clarify the reach of modifiers in the sentence. This may be as simple as changing the word order, repeating words, or making a list:

- all women and all men over 35;
- all male German Shepherds over two years old and all Australian Shepherds;
- all (list):
  - male German Shepherds,
  - male Australian Shepherds, and
  - female Australian Shepherds over two years old.

Critique Checklist
A fact is something that happened and can be proven. An opinion is someone's belief and is open to interpretation. (Only note opinions when they are stated as an opinion.)

Proofread your reports before submitting them, correcting errors pertaining to:

- spelling, grammar, punctuation, capitalization, and sentence structure
- **READ**—**Review** for content, **Evaluate** for errors, **Analyze** for clarity, **Determine** changes needed

Logical Presentation Methods: Conveying Information

Prepare to Tell Your Story in Court

Pre-trial preparation includes knowing what your case will sound like to your audience.

1. Begin by believing in what you are saying.
2. Start with a one-sentence version of your story.

3. Choose an organizational structure (chronological order).
4. Know your audience.
5. Know the characters in the story (the parties involved, including the "bad guy").
6. Replace weak metaphors (descriptive comparisons).
7. Create compelling images in everyone's mind.
8. Find the part of the story that makes listeners ask, "Then what happened?"
9. Answer the question, "Why should I care?"
10. Tell your story to someone who is not an attorney (or a detective).

Storytelling: Theory and Themes

"Theory of the case" refers to the facts and the law that lead a jury to a conclusion. "Theme of a case" is an idea or principle that provides direction in a case and may be a brief and easily remembered word, phrase, or sentence that captures the essence of the theory of the case. The Elements of the Theme of a Case include:

1. Introducing the jury to the theory of the case.
2. Repetition that reinforces the theory of the case in the minds of the fact-finder.
3. Labels and slogans that provide catchwords or catch phrases for jurors to remember during deliberations.
4. Vivid images and emotions that produce instant recall each time jurors hear them.
5. Necessity of the opponent to argue against the theory, rather than for his or her own case.
6. An unforgettable and memorable account.

The elements of a persuasive story include:

1. The Plot—what is the story about; will the fact-finder (jurors or court) empathize with it?
2. Cast of Characters—who are the characters (innocent or not)?
3. Character Development—what are the characters like; what are their lifestyles?
4. Chronology and Perspective—does the story unfold in chronological order or flashbacks? Is it told from one individual's perspective or from the viewpoints of several witnesses?
5. Props—what physical objects will you need to tell the story (real evidence and demonstrative evidence)?

6. Dominant Emotion—is the dominant emotion of the story one that jurors can identify with and understand how it dominated or influenced the outcome of the story?

Storytelling and Opening Statements

Opening statements must tell a fascinating story to help listeners visualize events and communicate what happened and why.

Cross-Examination: Discrediting Testimony and Impeachment

Five major areas to consider in evaluating testimony and witnesses are as follows:

1. Memory
2. Circumstantial impediments to perception
3. Physical impediments to perception
4. Truthfulness
5. Bias and interest

Suggestions for formulating questions for cross-examination include (CLOSeDSS):

1. **Control** witnesses using good question formulation.
2. **Leading** questions—a statement or assertion presented as an inquiry by the tone of voice or by adding a question at the beginning or end ("Isn't it true" questions).
3. **One** fact per question—compound questions (which are also objectionable) and questions containing more than one fact give the witness room for argument.
4. **Separate** persons from their behavior—personal attacks may produce sympathy; focus on facts and demonstrate external behavior, influences, and errors.
5. **Don't** try to do too much—little pieces placed carefully build the case, not the big piece.
6. **Stick** to your story—know your case and tell your story through the cross-examination; try to have witnesses agree with your facts and show where the witness is wrong, is lying, lacks knowledge, or is biased about the things on which you disagree.
7. **Save** conclusions for closing argument—know what you want to argue on each point in closing, then construct a set of questions on each point that breaks it down into facts with which the witness cannot disagree.

Logical Presentation Methods

Sometimes you must "show" the story by using direct and demonstrative evidence and media presentation technology, such as PowerPoint®, Visio®, or other presentation software. Presentation skills are not only the opportunity to present information and evidence, but also the one opportunity to present your facts, evidence, and the theme and theory of the case.

Bibliography

Baker, Bruce N., and Rene L. Eris. *An Introduction to PERT-CPM*. Richard D. Irwin, Inc., 1964.

Baker, Stephen F. *The Elements of Logic*, 2nd ed. McGraw-Hill Book Company, New York, 1974.

Carney, James D., and Richard K. Scheer. *Fundamentals of Logic*, 3rd ed. Macmillan Publishing Co., New York: 1980.

Clikeman, Paul M. The 10 Telltale signs of deception. *Fraud Magazine*, January/February 2012. http://www.fraud-magazine.com/article.aspx?id=4294971184.

Dauer, Francis Watanabe. *Critical Thinking: An Introduction to Reasoning*. Oxford University Press, New York: 1989.

Dernbach, John C., Richard V. Singleton II, Cathleen S. Wharton, Joan M. Ruhtenberg, and Catherine J. Wasson. *A Practical Guide to Legal Writing & Legal Method*, 3rd ed. Aspen Publishers (Wolters Kluwer Law & Business), New York: 2007.

Davidson, Dan E., Kira S. Gor, and Maria D. Lekic, *Russian Stage One: Live from Moscow—Volume 1*. Kendall/Hunt Publishing Company, Dubuque, IA: 1996.

Douglas, John E., Ann W. Burgess, Allen G. Burgess, and Robert K. Ressler. *Crime Classification Manual: A Standard System for Investigating and Classifying Violent Crimes*. Lexington Books, New York: 1992.

Eysenck, Michael, and Mark T. Keane. *Cognitive Psychology: A Student's Handbook*, 6th ed. Psychology Press (Taylor & Francis Group), New York: 2010.

Goldstein, E. Bruce. *Cognitive Psychology: Connecting Mind, Research, and Everyday Experience*. Wadsworth, Belmont, CA: 2011.

Greive, Donald. *A Handbook for Adjunct/Part-time Faculty and Teachers of Adults*. Info-Tec, Inc., Cleveland, OH: 1995.

Hare, Robert D. *Without Conscience: The Disturbing World of the Psychopaths Among Us*. The Guilford Press, New York: 1993.

Hawking, Stephen W. *The Theory of Everything: The Origin and Fate of the Universe*, New Millennium Press, Beverly Hills, CA: 2002.

Hemingway, Ernest. On the blue water, *Esquire*, April 1936.

Holmes, Ronald M., and Stephen T. Holmes. *Mass Murder in the United States*. Prentice Hall, Upper Saddle River, NJ: 2001.

Holmes, Ronald M. *Profiling Violent Crimes: An Investigative Tool*. Sage Publications, Newbury Park, CA: 1989.

Houston, Philip, Michael Floyd, and Susan Carnicero. *Spy the Lie: Former CIA Officers Teach You How to Detect Deception*. St. Martin's Griffin, New York: 2012.

Inbau, Fred E., and John E. Reid. *Criminal Interrogation and Confessions*. Williams & Wilkins, Baltimore, MD: 1970.

Jason, Gary. *Introduction to Logic*. Jones and Bartlett Publishers, Boston, MA: 1994.

Korem, Dan. *The Art of Profiling: Reading People Right the First Time*. International Focus Press, Richardson, TX: 1997.

Lesce, Tony. SCAN: Deception detection by scientific content analysis. *Law and Order*, 38(8), August 1990.

Lieberman, David J. *You Can Read Anyone: Never Be Fooled, Lied To, or Taken Advantage Of Again*. Viter Press, Lakewood, NJ: 2007.

Matlin, Margaret W. *Cognition*, 3rd ed. Harcourt Brace Publishers, Orlando, FL: 1994.

Moder, Joseph J., Cecil R. Phillips, and Edward W. Davis. *Project Management with CPM, PERT and Precedence Diagramming*, 3rd ed. Blitz Publishing Co., Middleton, WI: 1983.

Morris, Jack. *Crime Analysis Charting—An Introduction to Visual Investigative Analysis*. Palmer Press; Loomis, CA: 1982.

Navarro, Joe. *What Every Body is Saying: An Ex-FBI Agent's Guide to Speed-Reading People*. William Marrow (Harper Collins Publishers), New York: 2008.

O'Conner, Joseph, and John Seymour. *Introducing Neuro-Lingusitic Programming: Psychological Skills for Understanding and Influencing People*. Thorsons (Harper Collins Publishers), New York: 1990.

Pease, Allan, and Barbara Pease. *The Definitive Book of Body Language*. Bantam Books (Random House), New York: 2006.

Rabon, Don. *Interviewing and Interrogation*. Carolina Academic Press, Durham, NC: 1992.

Rabon, Don. *Investigative Discourse Analysis*. Carolina Academic Press, Durham, NC: 1994.

Ressler, Robert K., and Tom Shachtman. *Whoever Fights Monsters: My Twenty Years Hunting Serial Killers for the FBI*. St. Martin's Press, New York: 1992.

Rips, Lance J. *The Psychology of Proof: Deductive Reasoning in Human Thinking*. The MIT Press, Cambridge, MA: 1994.

Sagan, Carl. *Carl Sagan's Cosmic Connection: An Extraterrestrial Perspective*, Cambridge University Press, Cambridge, UK: 2000.

Samenow, Stanton E. *Inside the Criminal Mind*. Times Books, New York: 1984.

Schaeken, Walter, Gino DeVooght, and Gery d'Ydewalle. *Deductive Reasoning and Strategies*. Lawrence Erlbaum Associates, Mahwah, NJ: 2000.

Solso, Robert L., Otto H. MacLin, and M. Kimberly Maclin. *Cognitive Psychology*, 8th ed. Pearson Education, Inc. (Allyn and Bacon), Boston, MA: 2008.

Stilian, Gabriel. *PERT: A New Management Planning and Control Technique*. American Management Association, New York: 1962.

Tieger, Paul D., and Barbara Barran-Tieger. *The Art of SpeedReading People: Harness the Power of Personality Type and Create What You Want in Business and in Life*. Little, Brown and Company, Boston, MA: 1998.

Turvey, Brent. *Criminal Profiling: An Introduction to Behavioral Evidence Analysis*. Academic Press, San Diego, CA: 1999.

Walters, Stan B. *Principles of Kinesic Interview and Interrogation*. CRC Press, Boca Raton, FL: 1996.

Wydick, Richard C. *Plain English for Lawyers,* 5th ed. Carolina Academic Press, Durham, NC: 2005.

Zulawski, David E., and Douglas E. Wicklander. *Practical Aspects of Interview and Interrogation*. CRC Press, Boca Raton, FL: 1993.

Index

A

A,B,C,D,E,F system, 183
Abel and Cain (biblical), 6
absoluteness, 28
abstractedness, 93
abstract nouns, 185
abusive ad hominem fallacy, 56
accent, fallacy of, 57, 219
acceptance
    checklist, 238
    kinesic interviewing, 147–148
    stress response, 140
Accountant types
    checklist, 227
    communication type and actions, 86, 88
    overview, 103–104
accounting cycle, 178, 243
accuracy, 34, 105–106
actions, 192–193, 245
active *vs.* passive voice
    checklist, 245
    critical documentation, 191–192
    word usage, 191–192
activities, 167–169
actors, 192–193, 245
ad hominem fallacy, 56, 218
ad ignorantium fallacy, 219
adjectives
    parts of speech, 154, 186
    semantic analysis, 161
adjuration terms, 156
admissions, 125
ad populum fallacy, 56, 219
adverbs
    parts of speech, 155, 186
    semantic analysis, 161
ad verecundiam fallacy, 56, 219
"after-shock," 152
AIM, *see* Analytical investigative methods
ambiguity, fallacies of, 54, 57–58, 219
amplification
    checklist, 242
    deception detection, 162
    mean length of utterance, 161
analogies
    arguments, 52
    overview, 32
    preparation, 200
analysis
    intelligence cycle, 171
    scientific method, 11–12
Analysis (IRAC acronym), 51
analytical investigative methods (AIM)
    accounting cycle, 178
    analysis, 171
    checklists, 242–243
    collection, 170
    CPM-PERT network diagrams, 165–167
    direction, 170
    dissemination, 171
    feedback, 171
    financial information, 178
    intelligence analysis, 171
    intelligence cycle, 169–171
    network-based project management
        methodology, 167–168
    network logic techniques, 166
    overview, 165, 171–173
    PERT elements, 168–169
    planning, 170
    processing, 170
    visual investigative analysis, 173–177
anchor-point movement, 147
anger, stress response, 140, 147
answering, deception, 143, 144
antagonism, 147
apostrophes, 190
appearance, 28
apprehension, 93
arguments
    analysis diagram, 53, 59
    deductive, 26–28
    inductive, 26–28, 30–32

legal inferences, 32
logic, 25
logical reasoning, 52
psychology of proof, 28
Army example, 1
arrow-diagramming approach, 166
arson, 76
Artist types
    checklist, 228
    communication type and actions, 86, 88
    overview, 104–105
assessment, 119, 229
assets, 178
assumptions, 26
attack mode, 144
automated report templates, 182–183, 244
auto theft, 77
axioms, 37–38

B

bad lawyering, 45–46
Barbara, Allen, 138
bargaining, stress response, 140
basics, *see* Criminal investigation skills
"before and after," 200
behaviors
    cautions, 148, 238
    clusters, 142
    common sense signs, 148
    of deception, 145–147, 238
    past and future, 107
    pause or delay, 146
    ritualistic, 120
Ben-Porath, Ben, 94
beyond a reasonable doubt, 33, 51
bias, 202
Bible, referring to, 145
bibliography, 251–252
binders, VIA, 173
blitz attack, 112
blueprints to the mind, 99
body disposition, 112, 117
body language, 137–139, *see also* Kinesic
        interviewing
Bond, Nicholas A., Jr., 95
boredom gestures, 142, 237
Brady Rule, 57
Brady v. Maryland, 57
Brombard, Jimmy Ray, 46
burdens of proof
    checklist, 217
    legal inferences, 32–34
    overview, 32–34
burglary, 76–77
business burglaries, 76
business records, 63

C

CAD, *see* Computer Aided Design
Cain and Abel (biblical), 6
calculation, arguments, 52
calculus of probability, 32, *see also*
        Probability
California Psychological Inventory (CPI),
        94
canons, 37
capital, 178
capitalization, 187
Carnicero, Susan, 142
case studies
    Brombard, Jimmy Ray, 46
    Dominguez, Alejandro, 41–42
    Godschalk, Bruce, 44–45
    Lloyd, Eddie Joe, 43
    Peterson, Larry, 45
    Willis, Calvin, 40
Cattell, Raymond B., 93
cause of death, 113
CCM, *see* Crime Classification Manual
"central issue," 159, 161
change, 94, 162
characteristics, law enforcement profession,
        7
characters, persuasive elements, 201
checklists, 215–250
chin stroke, 142
Christensen, Paul R., 95
chronology, persuasive elements, 201
CIA, *see* Criminal investigative analysis
circumstantial ad hominem fallacy, 56
circumstantial evidence, 34–35, 217
claims, 30–32
Clarke, Walter Vernon, 83
classifications, crime, 110, 113–115, 228–230
clear and convincing evidence, 33, 51
CLOSeDSS, 203
closing temporary proprietorship accounts,
        178
clusters, behavior, 142
cognitive neuroscience and psychology,
        16–17
cognitive skills

cognition and reasoning, 23
cognitive neuroscience and psychology,
        16–17
    explicit *vs.* implicit memory, 20–21
    eyewitness testimony, 20–21
    learner types, 14–16
    logic, 23
    memory, 18–20
    overview, 13
    perceptions, 17–18, 23
    tachistoscopic training, 21–22
    thought processes, 17–18
    trained observer, 21–22
cold reading, 138
collar pull gesture, 141
collection, intelligence cycle, 170
colons, 188
colors example, 101
Combination types, 105, 228
combined PERT-CPM approach, 166
"comma case," 187
commas, 187–188
commission of crime stage, 117
common nouns, 185
common sense, 3
communication, 97–98, 225–226
communication types, 85–90, 222–224
compass, 83–87, 220–225, *see also*
        Personality profiling
complaints, 144
complex questions, 56, 219
composition fallacy, 57, 219
compound constructions, 193–194
Comprehensive Profile, 98, 106
Computer Aided Design (CAD), 175
computer crimes, 70, 77
concealment, 161
concern, inappropriate level, 144
Conclusion (IRAC acronym), 51
conclusions, *see also* Analysis
    arguments, 52
    cross-examination, 202
    deductive arguments, 26
    general premise to specific, 29
    inductive arguments, 26, 30
    logic, 25
    logical reasoning, 58–59
    prediction masquerading as, 117
    psychology of proof, 28
concrete nouns, 185
conditions, word usage, 195
confidential informants, 64–66

conformists-fearful/predictable type,
        226–227
Conformist type
    checklist, 225
    communication type and actions, 90
    interaction tips, 101–105
    performance type and actions, 87
    personality profiling, 92
    traits, 99–100
confrontation, 112
conjecture, 11
conjunctions, 155, 161, 186
Connery, Sean, 1
Consulting Psychologists Press, 94
content analysis, 152, *see also* Discourse and
        content analysis
context, conveying information, 199
control, cross-examination, 202
control-express type, 84, 85–86
control of victim, 111
convergent thinking, 50–51
conveying information
    checklists, 247–249
    court testimony, 213–214
    cross-examination, 202–203
    digital imagery, 213
    discrediting testimony, 202–203
    graphics and reconstruction software,
            208–213
    impeachment, 202–203
    Microsoft PowerPoint software, 204–208
    Microsoft Visio Standard software,
            208–213
    opening statements, 202
    overview, 199
    preparation, 199–200
    presentation software, 204–208
    theory and themes, 200–201
    video technology and software, 213
conviction, lack of, 160
convincing statements, 145
correspondence and letters analysis, 162
corroborating evidence, 34
counterintelligence, 70, 78
court testimony, 213–214
CPI, California Psychological Inventory
        (CPI)
CPM, *see* Critical Path Method
creation, arguments, 52
credibility, *see also* Rational credibility
    building through repetition, 145
    interrogation of suspects, 125

Crime Classification Manual (CCM), 110
crime classifications, 110, 113–115, 228–230
crimes against persons
    death investigations, 71–72
    overview, 70
    robbery investigations, 72
    sex crimes, 72–73, 75
crimes against property
    arson, 76
    auto theft, 77
    burglary, 76–77
    larceny, 77
    overview, 70, 76
crimes against public morals, 70, 77–78
crime scene indicators
    additional indicators, 112
    body disposition, 112
    environment, 111
    forensic evidence, 113
    left items, 112
    missing items, 112
    number of crime scenes, 111
    organized/disorganized physical
            evidence, 111
    perpetrators, number of, 111
    physical evidence, 111
    place, 111
    time, 111
    weapons, 112
crime scenes
    analysis, 110–111, 228
    indicators, 111–113, 229
criminal investigation skills
    business records, 63
    checklist, 220
    computer crimes, 70, 77
    confidential informants, 64–66
    counterintelligence, 70, 78
    crimes against persons, 70, 71–75
    crimes against property, 70, 76–77
    crimes against public morals, 70, 77–78
    economic crimes, 70, 77
    financial, 70, 77
    fraud, 70, 77
    government records, 63
    importance, 61
    information sources, 62–69
    interrogation, 69
    interviews, 69
    investigation types, 69–78
    juvenile and family crimes, 70, 78
    law enforcement, 62

    methodical technique, 61–62
    narcotics, 70, 77–78
    overview, 62, 69, 78
    physical surveillance, 68
    security, 70, 78
    technical surveillance, 68
    throughness, 61–62
    undercover operations, 66–68
    vice, 70, 77–78
criminal investigative analysis (CIA)
    additional indicators, 112
    assessment, 119
    body disposition, 112
    checklist, 228–230
    crime classification, 110, 113–115
    crime scenes, 110–113
    deductive reasoning, 109–110
    disorganized asocial typology, 118–119
    environment, 111
    forensic evidence, 113
    indicators, crime scenes, 111–113
    inductive reasoning, 109–110
    left items, 112
    missing items, 112
    modus operandi, 119–120
    number of crime scenes, 111
    organized/disorganized crimes, 115–119
    organized/disorganized physical
            evidence, 111
    organized nonsocial typology, 117–118
    overview, 121
    perpetrators, number of, 111
    personation, 119, 120
    physical evidence, 111
    place, 111
    signature, 120
    staging, 119, 120–121
    time, 111
    victimology, 119–120
    weapons, 112
criminal minds, profiling
    additional indicators, 112
    assessment, 119
    body disposition, 112
    crime classification, 110, 113–115
    crime scenes, 110–113
    deductive reasoning, 109–110
    disorganized asocial typology, 118–119
    environment, 111
    forensic evidence, 113
    indicators, crime scenes, 111–113
    inductive reasoning, 109–110

left items, 112
missing items, 112
modus operandi, 119–120
number of crime scenes, 111
organized/disorganized crimes, 115–119
organized/disorganized physical
    evidence, 111
organized nonsocial typology, 117–118
overview, 121
perpetrators, number of, 111
personation, 119, 120
physical evidence, 111
place, 111
signature, 120
staging, 119, 120–121
time, 111
victimology, 119–120
weapons, 112
critical documentation
    active *vs.* passive voice, 191–192
    actor, action, object, 192–193
    apostrophes, 190
    automated report templates, 182–183
    capitalization, 187
    checklists, 243–247
    colons, 188
    commas, 187–188
    compound constructions, 193–194
    conditions, 195
    critique checklist, 196–197
    CYMBL, 182
    dashes, 189
    editing, 197
    elements of report, 183–184
    ellipses, 190
    exceptions, 195
    exclamation points, 190
    field notes and reports, 180–181
    first person, 192
    hyphens, 190
    incomplete sentences, 193
    modifiers, 195–196
    narrative, 181–182
    narrative summary, 182–183
    nested modifiers, 195
    overview, 179
    parentheses, 189
    parts of speech, 185–186
    periods, 190
    punctuation rules, 187–190
    question marks, 190
    quotation marks, 189

    quotations, 190
    recording *vs.* investigation, 180–183
    report elements, 183–184
    revisions, 197
    run-on sentences, 193
    semicolons, 188–189
    sentence fragments, 193
    solvability factors, 182
    spelling rules, 184
    supplemental reports, 182–183
    surplus words, 193–194
    terms defined, 186
    titles describing people, 182
    vehicle descriptions, 182
    who and whom, 192
    word usage, 191–196
    word-wasting idioms, 194
critical path, PERT element, 169
Critical Path Method (CPM)
    analytical investigative methods, 172
    network diagrams, 165–167
    visual investigative analysis, 173
critical thinking
    axioms, 37–38
    bad lawyering, 45–46
    Brombard, Jimmy Ray, 46
    checklist, 217–218
    Dominguez, Alejandro, 41–42
    eyewitness misidentification, 39–40
    false confessions, 42–43
    forensic science, unreliable/improper,
        40–42
    Godschalk, Bruce, 44–45
    government misconduct, 44–45
    informants, 45
    Lloyd, Eddie Joe, 43
    logical reasoning, 46–47
    overview, 38–39
    Peterson, Larry, 45
    problems, 38–46
    reasoning, 37
    Willis, Calvin, 40
critique checklist, 196–197, 247
cross-examination, 202–203, 249
CYMBL acronym, 182, 244

D

dashes, 189
data, *see* Processing data
death investigations, 71–72

deception
    amplification of narrative, 162
    behaviors of, 145–147, 238
    checklists, 237–242
    correspondence and letters analysis, 162
    interviewing and interrogation,
        124–125, 162
    investigative discourse analysis, 153–154
    linguistic statement analysis, 153–154
    narrative statement semantic analysis,
        159–162
    narrative statement structure analysis,
        158–159
    obstacles to, 125
    overview, 142, 151, 162–163
    parts of speech, 154–155
    polygraphs, 151
    scientific content analysis, 151–153
    sounds of, 143–145, 237–238
    speech pattern and discourse content
        analysis, 155–158
    transcript analysis, 162
    voice stress analysis, 151
    word choices, 155–158
    word classes, 154–155
decoding nonverbal communications, 139
deduction
    certainty, 12
    checklist, 215–217
    defined, 3
    legal inferences, 34
    reasoning, 50
deductive arguments, 26–28, 216
deductive criminal profiling, 109
deductive infereneces, 52
deductive logic, 52
deductive reasoning
    criminal investigative analysis, 109
    deductive and inductive arguments, 26
    defined, 12
    logic, 28–29, 30
    logical structure of science, 28
    overview, 50
    profiling, criminal mind, 109–110
deductive validity, 29–30, 52
degree of probability, 28, 33, see also
        Probability
delay, behavior, 146
demon directives, 119
denial
    analyzing content of discourse, 157
    deception, 143
    stress response, 140

dependent clause defined, 186
depression, stress response, 140
DFS, see Dynamic Factors Survey
digital imagery, 213
dimensional components, 79–80, 220–221
direction, intelligence cycle, 170
disarrayment, 111
DISC assessment theory, 83
discourse and content analysis, see also
        Deception
    amplification of narrative, 162
    checklists, 239–242
    correspondence and letters analysis, 162
    interviews and interrogation transcript
        analysis, 162
    investigative discourse analysis, 153–154
    linguistic statement analysis, 153–154
    narrative statement semantic analysis,
        159–162
    narrative statement structure analysis,
        158–159
    obstacles to, 125
    overview, 151, 162–163
    parts of speech, 154–155
    polygraphs, 151
    scientific content analysis, 151–153
    speech pattern and discourse content
        analysis, 155–158
    voice stress analysis, 151
    word choices, 155–158
    word classes, 154–155
discrediting testimony, 202–203, 249
disorganized asocial typology, 118–119
dissemination, intelligence cycle, 171
divergent thinking, 50–51
division fallacy, 57, 219
DNA, 40–46
documentation copies, VIA, 174
dominance, 93
dominant emotion, persuasive elements,
        201
Dominguez, Alejandro, 41–42
double-entry bookkeeping, 178
doubt, see Beyond a reasonable doubt
Doyle, Sir Arthur Conan, 25
DSM-IV comparison, 110
due diligence, 7–8
dummy activities, networks, 168
dumpster diving, 63
Dynamic Factors Survey (DFS), 95

E

ear rub gesture, 141
Eastwood, Clint, 6
Eber, Herbert, 93
economic crimes, 70, 77
Edwards Personality Profile Scale (EPPS), 95
EEI, *see* Essential Elements of Intelligence
electronic intelligence (ELINT), 170
ellipses, 190
Emanations Intelligence (EMINT), 170
EMINT, *see* Emanations Intelligence
emotions
    emotional/nonemotional offenders, 126
    persuasive elements, 201
    sixteen combinations, 100
    Sixteen Personality Factor
        Questionnaire, 93
enthymemes, 26
environment, crime scene indicators, 111
epilogue, 159, 161
EPPS, *see* Edwards Personality Profile Scale
equivocating terms, 157
equivocation, fallacy of, 57, 219
Essential Elements of Intelligence (EEI),
        170, 171, 175
estimator variables, 40
evaluation gestures, 142, 237
events, 168–169
evidence, 33–35
exceptions, word usage, 195
exclamation points, 190
exclusive qualifiers, 145
expected time, PERT element, 169
explanatory terms, 157
explicit memory, 20–21
extroverts
    combination types, 82–83
    communication with, 97, 225
    dimensional components, 79
eyes
    hiding, 146
    movements, 149–150, 238–239
    rub gesture, 141
eyewitnesses, *see also* Witnesses
    misidentification, 39–40
    testimony, 20–21

F

fabrication, 150
facial incongruencies, 138–139

fact finding, 7–8, *see also* Scientific method
fact pattern analysis
    axioms, 37–38
    bad lawyering, 45–46
    Brombard, Jimmy Ray, 46
    checklist, 217–218
    Dominguez, Alejandro, 41–42
    eyewitness misidentification, 39–40
    false confessions, 42–43
    forensic science, unreliable/improper,
        40–42
    Godschalk, Bruce, 44–45
    government misconduct, 44–45
    informants, 45
    Lloyd, Eddie Joe, 43
    logical reasoning, 46–47
    overview, 38–39
    Peterson, Larry, 45
    problems, 38–46
    reasoning, 37
    Willis, Calvin, 40
factual analysis technique, 126
fallacy types
    false dilemma, 56, 58
    material fallacies of insufficient
        evidence, 55, 57
    material fallacies of relevance, 55, 56–57
    overview, 53–55, 58
    weak analogy, 56, 58
false-cause fallacy, 57, 219
false confessions, 42–43
false dichotomy, 117
false dilemma fallacy, 56, 58, 220
feedback, 171
feelers
    combination types, 82–83
    communication with, 97, 226
    dimensional components, 79
field notes and reports, 180–181, 243
figurative words, 32
fillers, stereotyped, 181
financial information, 70, 77, 178
fine-tuned read, 105
fingers in mouth gesture, 141
first person, 192, 245
flashbacks, 200
flaws, 25, 32
fleeting incongruencies, 138–139
Floyd, Michael, 142
forensic evidence/science
    crime scene indicators, 113
    unreliable/improper, 40–42

formal fallacy, 53
formal logic, 28, 216
formal reasoning, 50
four rules, systematic accuracy, 106
fragnets, 177
framing, 109
fraud, 70, 77
fused sentences, 193
fuzzy thinking, 46

G

Gantt, Henry, 165
Geier, John, 83
genetic fallacy, 56, 219
gestures
    acceptance, 147–148
    boredom, 142
    evaluation, 142
    impatience, 142
    lying, 140–141
    memory reanimation, 147–148
    procrastination, 142
    supplication, 148
God, 145
Godschalk, Bruce, 44–45
Gough, Harrison, 94
government
    misconduct, 44–45
    records, 63
graphics software, 208–213
grooming gestures, 147
group excitement killing, 111
Guilford, J.P., 95
Guilford-Zimmerman Temperament
        Survey, 95

H

hand-to-face activity, 146–147
Hare, Robert, 100
Hawking, Stephen, 5–6
Hemingway, Ernest, 6–7
hiding mouth or eyes, 146
highlighter pens, VIA, 174
high-quality reasoning, 46
historical developments, logic, 25
Holmes, *see Sherlock Holmes*
Holmes, Ronald, 100, 109–110
Holmes, Stephen, 100
homicides *vs.* murder, 8–9
Houston, Philip, 124–125, 142, 145–146

human intelligence (HUMINT), 4, 64, 170
hyphens, 190
hypothesis/hypotheses
    defined, 9
    inductive reasoning, 50
    logic, 30–32
    scientific method, 11

I

identification, 75
idioms, 194
imagery intelligence (IMINT), 170
IMINT, *see* Imagery intelligence
impatience gestures, 142, 237
impeachment, 202–203, 249
impermissible inferences, 51
implicit memory, 20–21
improbability
    deductive and inductive arguments, 27
    legal inferences, 32
incomplete sentences
    checklist, 246
    communication skills, 193
    word usage, 193
incongruencies, fleeting, 138–139
inconsistency, fallacy of, 56, 219
inconsistent statements, 144
independent clause defined, 186
index cards, VIA, 173
indicators, crime scenes
    additional indicators, 112
    body disposition, 112
    environment, 111
    forensic evidence, 113
    left items, 112
    missing items, 112
    number of crime scenes, 111
    organized/disorganized physical
        evidence, 111
    perpetrators, number of, 111
    physical evidence, 111
    place, 111
    time, 111
    weapons, 112
induction
    arguments, 52
    checklist, 215–217
    uncertainty, 12
inductive analogy, 32
inductive arguments, 26–28, 216
inductive evidence, 34–35

inductive logic, 30–32, 52
inductive reasoning
    arguments, 52
    deductive and inductive arguments, 26
    defined, 12
    legal inferences, 32–33, 51
    logical structure of science, 28
    profiling, criminal mind, 109–110
inference rule, 29
inferences
    circumstantial evidence, 34
    convergent/divergent thinking, 50
    conveying information, 199
    defined, 3
    legal, 32–34, 218
    logic, 34–35
    reasoning, 50
informal fallacy, 53
informants
    confidential, 64–66
    fact pattern analysis, 45
    interviewing and interrogation, 124
information, conveying
    checklists, 247–249
    court testimony, 213–214
    cross-examination, 202–203
    digital imagery, 213
    discrediting testimony, 202–203
    graphics and reconstruction software,
        208–213
    impeachment, 202–203
    Microsoft PowerPoint software, 204–208
    Microsoft Visio Standard software,
        208–213
    opening statements, 202
    overview, 199
    preparation, 199–200
    presentation software, 204–208
    theory and themes, 200–201
    video technology and software, 213
information sources
    business records, 63
    confidential informants, 64–66
    government records, 63
    interrogation, 69
    interviews, 69
    law enforcement, 62
    overview, 62
    physical surveillance, 68
    technical surveillance, 68
    undercover operations, 66–68
Innocence Project, 39, 41, 43, 45

innovator-confident/unpredictable type, 226
Innovator type
    communication type and actions, 89
    interaction tips, 101–104
    performance type and actions, 87
    traits, 99
intelligence analysis, 171
intelligence cycle
    analysis, 171
    checklist, 242–243
    collection, 170
    direction, 170
    dissemination, 171
    feedback, 171
    overview, 169
    planning, 170
    processing, 170
IntelliVIEW software, 175
interest, cross-examination, 202
interjections, 155
interrogation of suspects, 125
interviewing and interrogation, see also
        Kinesic interviewing
    checklists, 230–236
    criminal suspects, 130
    deception detection, 124–125, 162
    information sources, 69
    mandatory electronic recordings, 43
    overview, 110
    potential informants, 124
    questions, formulation of, 134–135
    steps of interrogation, 133–134, 235
    suspects, 125–130
    transcript analysis, 162
    uncertain guilt of suspects, 129–130
    witnesses, 124
    written confessions, 131–133
introjection, 156
introverts
    combination types, 82–83
    communication with, 97, 225
    dimensional components, 79
intuition, basis of, 3
intuitives
    combination types, 83
    communication with, 97, 225–226
    dimensional components, 79
investigation types
    computer crimes, 70, 77
    counterintelligence, 70, 78
    crimes against persons, 70, 71–75
    crimes against property, 70, 76–77

crimes against public morals, 70, 77–78
economic crimes, 70, 77
financial, 70, 77
fraud, 70, 77
juvenile and family crimes, 70, 78
narcotics, 70, 77–78
overview, 69
security, 70, 78
vice, 70, 77–78
investigative discourse analysis (IDA),
          153–154, 163
IRAC acronym, 51
isolated delivery, denial, 143
Issue (IRAC acronym), 51
itchy nose gesture, 141
iteration, 12

J

Jack the Ripper, 25
journalizing, accounting cycle, 178
judgers
          combination types, 82–83
          communication with, 97–98, 226
          dimensional components, 80
Jung, Carl, 94
juvenile and family crimes, 70, 78

K

kinesic interviewing
          acceptance gestures, 147–148
          behavioral cautions, 148
          behaviors of deception, 145–147
          body language, 137–139
          boredom gestures, 142
          checklists, 236–239
          deception, 142–147
          decoding nonverbal communications, 139
          evaluation gestures, 142
          eye movements, 149–150
          impatience gestures, 142
          left eye movement, 149–150
          lying gestures, 140–141
          memory reanimation gestures, 147–148
          neurolinguistic eye movement, 148
          observing nonverbal communications, 139
          overview, 137, 140
          personal zone distances, 137
          procrastination gestures, 142
          proxemics, 137
          reanimation gestures, 147–148

right eye movement, 149–150
sounds of deception, 143–145
ten commandments, 139
three sensory channels, 148–150
zone distances, 137
Korem Profiling System
          levels of information, 105–106
          map, 98
          overview, 79, 83–85

L

language, *see also* Parts of speech
          compound constructions, 193–194
          lawyerisms, 180
          nominalizations, 185–186
          precise, 182
          stereotyped fillers, 181
          surplus words, 193–194
larceny, 77
law enforcement, 7, 62
lawyerisms, 180, 185–186
leading questions, 202
"leakage," 106–107
learner types, 14–16
ledger account adjustments, accounting
          cycle, 178
left eye movements, 149–150, 238–239
left items, 112
legal inferences
          argument analysis diagram, 53
          arguments, 52
          checklists, 217–218, 218–220
          conclusions, 58–59
          convergent thinking, 50–51
          divergent thinking, 50–51
          fact pattern analysis, 46–47
          fallacy types, 53–58
          false dilemma, 56, 58
          high-quality reasoning, 46
          legal inferences, 51–52
          logic, 32–34
          logical reasoning, 51–52
          material fallacies of insufficient
                    evidence, 55, 57
          material fallacies of relevance, 55, 56–57
          overview, 51–52
          reasoning, 49–50
          recapitulation, 58–59
          summaries, 58–59
          weak analogy, 56, 58
letters and correspondence analysis, 162

liabilities, 178
Lieberman, David, 99–101
likelihood of truth, 31
linguistic signals, 154, 155–156
linguistic statement analysis (LSAT),
    153–154, 163, 239
Link Network Analysis, 173
links (nexus), 32
liveliness, 93
Lloyd, Eddie Joe, 43
location, crime scene indicators, 111
logic
    burdens of proof, 32–34
    circumstantial evidence, 34–35
    cognitive skills, 23
    deductive arguments, 26–28
    deductive reasoning, 28–29, 30
    deductive validity, 29–30
    defined, 25
    formal logic, 28
    historical developments, 25
    inductive analogy, 32
    inductive arguments, 26–28
    inductive evidence, 34–35
    inductive logic, 30–32
    inferences, 34–35
    legal inferences, 32–34
    objective, 28
    overview, 25–26
    psychology of proof, 28
    science and hypothesis, 30–32
    structure of science, 28
logical consequences, 11
logical presentation methods
    checklists, 247–249
    court testimony, 213–214
    cross-examination, 202–203
    digital imagery, 213
    discrediting testimony, 202–203
    graphics and reconstruction software,
        208–213
    impeachment, 202–203
    Microsoft PowerPoint software, 204–208
    Microsoft Visio Standard software,
        208–213
    opening statements, 202
    overview, 199
    preparation, 199–200
    presentation software, 204–208
    theory and themes, 200–201
    video technology and software, 213

logical reasoning
    argument analysis diagram, 53
    arguments, 52
    checklists, 218
    conclusions, 58–59
    convergent thinking, 50–51
    divergent thinking, 50–51
    fact pattern analysis, 46–47
    fallacy types, 53–58
    false dilemma, 56, 58
    high-quality reasoning, 46
    legal inferences, 51–52
    material fallacies of insufficient
        evidence, 55, 57
    material fallacies of relevance, 55, 56–57
    reasoning, 49–50
    recapitulation, 58–59
    summaries, 58–59
    weak analogy, 56, 58
LSAT, see Linguistic statement analysis
L-shaped gesture, 147
L-squared mode, 142
lying gestures, 140–141, 237

M

management-by-exception systems, 167
manager-confident/predictable type, 226
Manager type
    communication type and actions, 89
    interaction tips, 101–104
    performance type and actions, 87
    traits, 99
mandatory electronic recordings,
    interrogations, 43
map, 98, 225–228, see also Personality
    profiling
marker words, 156
Marston, William, 83
Mason, see Perry Mason
material fallacies of insufficient evidence
    checklist, 219–220
    overview, 54–55, 57–58
material fallacies of relevance
    checklist, 218–219
    overview, 54–55, 56–58
maxims, 37
MBTI, see Myers-Briggs Type Indicator
mean length of utterance (MLU), 160–161
medical reports, evidence, 113
memory
    cognitive skills, 18–20

cross-examination, 202
deception, 145
reanimation gestures, 147–148, 238
working memory, 29
metaphors, 32, 200
method of operation, *see Modus operandi*
Microsoft PowerPoint software, 204–208
Microsoft Visio Standard software, 175,
208–213
milestone approach, 166
Minnesota Multiphasic Personality
Inventory (MMPI), 94
Miranda v. Arizona, 51, 131
missing items, 112
MLU, *see* Mean length of utterance
modifiers, 195–196, 246–247
modifying terms, 157
modus operandi (M.O.)
checklist, 230
crimes against property, 76
crime scene analysis, 110
organized/disorganized crimes, 117
perpetrator behavior, 119
profiling, criminal mind, 119–120
mouth, hiding, 146
mouth cover gesture, 140
Myers-Briggs Type Indicator (MBTI), 94
mystery to be solved, 200

N

narcotics, 70, 77–78
narrative amplification, 162, 242
narratives
overview, 181–182, 243
statement semantic analysis, 159–162, 242
statement structure analysis, 158–159, 242
summary, 182–183, 244
neck scratch gesture, 141
negation terms, 157
nested modifiers, 195, 246
network-based project management
methodology, 167–168
network logic techniques, 166
networks, PERT element, 169
neurolinguistic eye movement, 148,
238–239
nexus (link), 32
nominalizations, 185
non-answer statements, 144
non-sequential statements, 159
nonspecific denial, 143

nonverbal communications, 137, 139, *see
also* Kinesic interviewing
nose touch gesture, 140–141
nouns, 154, 161, 185
number of crime scenes, 111

O

objectives, 28
objects, 192–193, 245
observation, 10, 139
OIR, *see* Other Intelligence Requirements
on-the-spot profiling, 92–95
opening statements, 202, 249
open source intelligence (OSINT), 170
opinion, critique checklist, 196–197
organization (order), 183–184
organized/disorganized crimes
checklist, 229
crime scene indicators, 111
disorganized asocial typology, 118–119
organized nonsocial typology, 117–118
overview, 115–117
organized/disorganized physical evidence
crime scene indicators, 111
organized nonsocial typology, 117–118
OSINT, *see* Open source intelligence
Other Intelligence Requirements (OIR), 170

P

paper, VIA, 174
parentheses, 189
parts of speech, 154–155, 239–240, *see also*
Language
passive *vs.* active voice, 191–192, 245
PATC, *see* Public Agency Training Council
Paul Coverdell Forensic Science
Improvement Grant Program, 41
pause, behavior, 146
Pease, Allen, 138
pencils, VIA, 174
pens, VIA, 174
perceivers
combination types, 82–83
communication with, 98, 226
dimensional components, 80
perception qualifiers, 145
perceptions and thought processes
cognition and reasoning, 23
cognitive neuroscience and psychology,
16–17

cognitive skills, 17–18, 23
cross-examination, 202
explicit *vs.* implicit memory, 20–21
eyewitness testimony, 20–21
learner types, 14–16
logic, 23
memory, 18–20
overview, 13
perceptions, 17–18, 23
tachistoscopic training, 21–22
thought processes, 17–18
trained observer, 21–22
perfectionism, 94
performance types, 91–92, 224–225
periods, 190
permissible inferences, 50
perpetrators
number of, 111
vs. suspects, 38, 73
Perry Mason, 33
personality profiling
Accountant types, 103–104
Artist types, 104–105
California Psychological Inventory, 94
checklists, 220–225
Combination types, 105
communication types, 85–90
communication with, 97–98
compass, 83–87
conformist type, 92
dimensional components, 79–80
Dynamic Factors Survey, 95
Edwards Personality Profile Scale, 95
four rules, systematic accuracy, 106
Guilford-Zimmerman Temperament
Survey, 95
Korem Profiling System, 83–85
map, 98
Minnesota Multiphasic Personality
Inventory, 94
Myers-Briggs Type Indicator, 94
on-the-spot profiling, 92–95
overview, 79
performance types, 91–92
personality type combinations, 82–83
reading others, 106–107
Salesman types, 102–103
self-assessment tests, 92–95
Sergeant types, 101–102
sixteen combinations, 100–105
Sixteen Personality Factor
Questionnaire, 93–94
successful reads, 106–107
systematic accuracy, 105–106
three levels, systematic accuracy,
105–106
traits by associated types, 99–100
personality type combinations, 82–83, 221
personal zone distances, 137
personation
checklist, 229
crime scene analysis, 110
overview, 119
signature, 120, 230
perspective, persuasive elements, 201
persuasive story, 201, 248–249
PERT, *see* Program Evaluation and Review
Technique
Peterson, Larry, 45
petitio principii fallacy, 56, 219
photo arrays, 75
photography, crime scene, 111
phrase defined, 186
physical evidence, 111
physical surveillance, 68
pins, VIA, 174
place, crime scene indicators, 111
planning, intelligence cycle, 170
plot, persuasive elements, 201
Polaris Missile Program, 165
politeness, 144
polygraph tests
checklist, 239
deception detection, 151
interrogation, uncertain guilt, 130
possibility, 27
post-closing trial balance, accounting cycle,
178
posting, accounting cycle, 178
postulate, 37
potential informants, 124, *see also* Informants
PowerPoint software, 204–208, 250
pre-crime stage, 116
predicate defined, 186
predictable-unpredictable type, 85, 91–92
prediction
masquerading as conclusions, 117
scientific method, 11
premeditation, crime scene indicators, 111
premises, *see also* Statements
arguments, 52
deductive and inductive arguments, 26
general to specific conclusion, 29
inductive arguments, 30

legal inferences, 32
logic, 25
psychology of proof, 28
preparation
    checklist, 247–248
    interrogation of suspects, 125
    logical presentation methods, 199–200
preponderance of evidence, 33, 51
prepositions, 155, 162, 186
prescriptive interviewing, 111
presentation software, 204–208
primary sources, evidence, 113
privateness, 93
probability
    calculus of, 32
    deductive and inductive arguments, 27
    degree of, 28, 33
    inductive logic, 31
    legal inferences, 32–33
    logical structure of science, 28
    reasonable degree of, 32–33
probability of success, PERT element, 169
Probable Cause Affidavit, 69
problems, fact pattern analysis, 38–46
processing, intelligence cycle, 170
processing data
    accounting cycle, 178
    analysis, 171
    checklists, 242–243
    collection, 170
    CPM-PERT network diagrams, 165–167
    direction, 170
    dissemination, 171
    feedback, 171
    financial information, 178
    intelligence analysis, 171
    intelligence cycle, 169–171
    network-based project management
        methodology, 167–168
    network logic techniques, 166
    overview, 165, 171–173
    PERT elements, 168–169
    planning, 170
    processing, 170
    visual investigative analysis, 173–177
procrastination gestures, 142, 237
professional close, 125
profiling criminal minds
    additional indicators, 112
    assessment, 119
    body disposition, 112
    crime classification, 110, 113–115

crime scenes, 110–113
deductive reasoning, 109–110
disorganized asocial typology, 118–119
environment, 111
forensic evidence, 113
indicators, crime scenes, 111–113
inductive reasoning, 109–110
left items, 112
missing items, 112
modus operandi, 119–120
number of crime scenes, 111
organized/disorganized crimes, 115–119
organized/disorganized physical
    evidence, 111
organized nonsocial typology, 117–118
overview, 121
perpetrators, number of, 111
personation, 119, 120
physical evidence, 111
place, 111
signature, 120
staging, 119, 120–121
time, 111
victimology, 119–120
weapons, 112
Program Evaluation and Review Technique
    (PERT)
    analytical investigative methods, 172
    elements, 168–169
    network diagrams, 165–167
    visual investigative analysis, 173
prologue, 159, 161
pronouns
    analyzing content of discourse, 156
    overview, 152
    parts of speech, 154, 185
    semantic analysis, 161
proofreading, 196–197
proper nouns, 185
proprietorship accounts, 178
props, persuasive elements, 201
proxemics, 137
PSE, see Psychological stress examination
psychological autopsy, 120
psychological stress, 120
psychological stress examination (PSE),
    151, 162
psychology of proof, 28
psychopathy, 100, 117
Public Agency Training Council (PATC), 153
punctuation rules
    apostrophes, 190

capitalization, 187
colons, 188
commas, 187–188
dashes, 189
ellipses, 190
exclamation points, 190
hyphens, 190
overview, 187
parentheses, 189
periods, 190
question marks, 190
quotation marks, 189
quotations, 190
semicolons, 188–189

Q

qualifiers, using, 145
question marks, 190
questions
    checklist, 235
    CLOSeDSS, 203
    cross-examination, 202
    inappropriate, 144
    interviewing and interrogation, 134–135
    posing, 152
    repeating, 143–144
    scientific method, 10–11
    True-False, 10
quotation marks, 189
quotations, 190

R

Rabon, Dan, 153
racketeer influenced corrupt organizations
    (RICO), 78
random actor-fearful/unpredictable, 227
Random Actor type
    communication type and actions, 90
    interaction tips, 102–105
    performance type and actions, 87
    traits, 100
rational credibility
    inductive logic, 32
    legal inferences, 33
rational reasoning, 50
READ acronym, 197
reading others
    cold read, 138
    fine-tuned read, 105

personality profiling, 106–107
    snapshot read, 105
real activities, networks, 168
reanimation gestures, 147–148, 238
reasonable degree of probability, 32–33
reasoning
    and cognition, 23
    fact pattern analysis, 37
    logical reasoning, 49–50
    Sixteen Personality Factor
        Questionnaire, 93
    strategies, 49
recall, *see* Memory
recapitulation, 58–59, 215, *see also*
        Checklists
reconstruction software, 208–213
recordings, 180
referral statements, 145
religion, 145
repetition, 145, 162
report copies, VIA, 174
report elements
    checklist, 277
    critical documentation, 183–184
    critique checklist, 196–197
representative nature, 28
repression, 156
residential burglaries, 76
resistance reduction, 125
Ressler, Robert, 115, 117
RICO, *see* Racketeer influenced corrupt
        organizations
right eye movement, 149–150, 239
ritualistic behavior, 120
robbery investigations, 72
rule-consciousness, 93
Rule (IRAC acronym), 51
run-on sentences, 193, 246

S

Sagan, Carl, 1, 25
Salesman types
    checklist, 227
    communication type and actions, 86, 87
    overview, 102–103
Samenow, Stanton, 106, 107
Sapir, Avinoam, 120
SCAN, *see* Scientific content analysis
Schaeken, Walter, 50
science, structure of, 28, 216
science and hypothesis, 30–32

scientific content analysis (SCAN), 151–153,
    163, 239
scientific method, 9–12, 215, *see also* Fact
    finding
Scotland Yard, 25
secondary sources, evidence, 113
second-person referencing, 157
security, 70, 78
selective memory, 145
self-assessment tests, 92–95
self-reference, 160
self-reliance, 94
semantics analysis, 159–162, 242
semicolons, 188–189
semiotics, 155
sensitivity, 93
sensors
    combination types, 82
    communication with, 97, 225
    dimensional components, 79
sensory channels, 148–150, 238–239
sentence fragments, 193, 246
Sergeant types
    checklist, 227
    communication type and actions, 86, 87
    interaction tips, 101–102
sex crimes, 72–73, 75, 113
Sherlock Holmes
    deductive reasoning, 30
    inductions and deductions, 25
    uncanny abilities, 4
shopping list, 181
SIGINT, *see* Signals Intelligence
signal, linguistic, 155–156
signals, linguistic, 154
Signals Intelligence (SIGINT), 170
signature
    crime scene analysis, 110
    personation, 120, 230
Silence of the Lambs, 4
similes, 32
single-entry bookkeeping, 178
sixteen combinations, 100–105, 227–228
Sixteen Personality Factor Questionnaire
    (16PF), 93–94
slack, PERT element, 169
smiling, 138
snapshot read, 105
social boldness, 93
sophistication, 111
sounds of deception, 143–145, 237–238
space distances, 137

special pleading, fallacy of, 57, 219
speech pattern and discourse content
    analysis
    checklist, 240–241
    deception detection, 152, 155–158
Spell Check, 179, 184
Spock (*Star Trek* series), 1–2
spontaneity, 111
spread, PERT element, 169
staging
    checklist, 230
    crime scene analysis, 110
    crime scene indicators, 112
    profiling, criminal mind, 119, 120–121
stalling mechanisms, 157
standard of proof, 32–34
Star Trek series, 1–2
state-complete approach, 166
statement preparation, accounting cycle,
    178
statements, *see also* Premises
    inductive arguments, 30–32
    opening, 202
statements analysis
    deception, 144, 145
    generalized, 160
    linguistic, 153–154
    non-sequential statements, 159
    semantic analysis, 159–162
    structure analysis, 158–159
steps of interrogation, 133–134
stereotyped fillers, 181
storytelling, *see* Conveying information
straw man fallacy, 57, 219
stress responses, 140
structure analysis, 158–159, 242
structure of science, 28, 216
subject defined, 186
subnets, 177
subordinating words, 193
successful reads, 106–107
suicides, 8–9
summaries, 58–59
supplemental reports, 182–183, 244
supplication gesture, 148
surplus words, 193–194
surveillance, 68
suspects
    checklist, 231
    checklists, 230–233
    interviewing and interrogation, 125–130
    vs. perpetrator, 38, 73

suspension of disbelief, 202
sympathetic technique, 126
syntactical ambiguity, fallacy of, 57, 219
systematic accuracy, 105–106
system of inductive logic, 31–32
system variables, 40

T

tachistoscopic training, 21–22
tape, VIA, 174
tape recordings, 180
Tatsuoka, Maurice, 93
Taylor, Frederick W., 165
technical surveillance, 68
Tellegen, Auke, 94
templates, VIA, 174
temporal lacuna, 156
temporary proprietorship accounts, 178
ten commandments, 139, 236
tenses
    changes, 152
    semantic analysis, 161
    semantic indicators, 160
tension, 94
testimony, discrediting, 202–203, 249
testing, 11, 107
The Cosmic Connection, 1
theorems, 37–38
theory and themes, 200–201, 248–249
The Untouchables, 1
thinkers
    combination types, 82–83
    communication with, 97, 226
    dimensional components, 79
thought processes, 17–18, *see also*
        Perceptions and thought
        processes
three levels, systematic accuracy, 105–106
three sensory channels, 148–150, 238–239
time
    crime scene indicators, 111
    PERT element, 169
Time Flow Analysis, 173
titles describing people, 182, 244
trained observers, 21–22
traits by associated types
    checklist, 226–227
    personality profiling, 99–100
    under pressure, 107
transcript analysis, 162
trash value, 63

trauma, 113
trial balance, accounting cycle, 178
True-False questions, 10
truthfulness, cross-examination, 202
tu quoque fallacy, 56, 218
Turvey, Brent, 117
Twain, Mark, 3

U

uncertain guilt of suspects, 129–130, 231–233
undercover operations, 66–68
undoing, 120
Unforgiven, 6
United States v. Ron Pair Enterprises, 179
U.S. Army Criminal Investigations
        Command (USACIDC), 6–7, 62

V

valid arguments
    deductive and inductive arguments, 27
    logical structure of science, 28
    overview, 52
validation, 25, 32
vehicle descriptions, 182, 244
verbs
    correspondence/letters, 162
    parts of speech, 154
    semantic analysis, 161
VIA, *see* Visual investigative analysis
vice, 70, 77–78
victimology, 119–120, 230
victims
    crime classification, 113–115
    crime scene indicators, 111
video technology and software, 213
"view from the other side," 6
vigilance, 93
Visio Standard software
    checklist, 250
    logical presentation methods, 208–213
    visual investigative analysis, 175
visual construction, 150
visual investigative analysis (VIA), 165,
        173–177
voice stress analysis (VSA), 151, 162, 239

W

Walters, Stan, 137
warmth, 93

weak analogy, 56, 58, 220
weakened assertions, 157, 159
weapons, 112
White Chapel murders, 25
who and whom, 192, 245
Willis, Calvin, 40
witnesses, 124, *see also* Eyewitnesses
word choices
    checklist, 240–241
    deception detection, 153, 155–158
word classes
    checklist, 239–240
    deception detection, 154–155
word usage
    active *vs.* passive voice, 191–192
    actor, action, object, 192–193
    checklist, 245
    compound constructions, 193–194
    conditions, 195
    critical documentation, 191–196

exceptions, 195
first person, 192
incomplete sentences, 193
modifiers, 195–196
nested modifiers, 195
overview, 191
run-on sentences, 193
sentence fragments, 193
surplus words, 193–194
who and whom, 192
word-wasting idioms, 194
word-wasting idioms, 194
working memory, 29, *see also* Memory
work sheet construction, accounting cycle,
    178
written confessions, 131–133, 233–235

Z

zone distances, 137